MOON JAE-IN'S

DESTINY

MOON JAE-IN'S

DESTINY

Autor Moon Jae-in

THEHUMAN

Like Rivers Merging

Time flies by like a shooting arrow. It had already been two years since we said our goodbyes to President Roh Moo-hyun, and everyone's feelings of sorrow were different.

"The day he departed" left some shocked and grief-stricken; for others, "Roh Moo-hyun" still conjures up sorrow and pain. And for some, just longing memories of the 'times spent together with him.'

Whatever it may be, it was a reality that we had to accept. Now, we must consider the responsibilities of those still living. We have to worry about the task that he had left behind, look beyond Roh Moo-hyun's era, and prepare for the future.

We can't linger in the past forever. We must put our shock, grief, anger, sorrow, sympathy, and memories aside and objectively begin what we must do.

The most beautiful farewell is for us to willingly shoulder the burdens that he had carried. That is how we relieve him from the 'burdens of the times.'

With the 2nd anniversary of his death quickly approaching, many proposed that I write a book, and it was a justifiable suggestion. It was because President Roh did not leave an autobiography or his memoirs. He once said that when documenting, one needed to be straightforward and honest, but he was apprehensive concerning his ability to accomplish such a feat. He was not ready, and it was too overwhelming to do alone. So, he requested that his staff and co-workers embark on a collaborative effort to author "a memoir" of their journey or experiences together while in office. He asked us to recollect and document the times we worked together, and he would finish it.

However, we suddenly had to bid farewell before we could consummate his request. It was clear to me that his most important assignment was entrusting us to document the era spent with him. Since President Roh and I spent so much time together, and I am currently the chairman of the Roh Moo-hyun Foundation, though unworthy, many believed I should be the first to begin.

However, I didn't have the courage. All this time, I had been so busy working with what was in front of me that I wasn't diligent in recording things. We experienced so many things together that if I did not review old data, I would have had difficulty remembering everything.

There were also many hesitations, like the president's apprehension. I wasn't confident in myself that I could be 100% honest. Many lived in the same era, and if one was not careful of what or how it was written, it could be burdensome for some and controversial for others.

However, the reason I was compelled to write this book was because another regime is coming to an end. The people of Korea are yearning for assurance, and I hope the previous despairs will not be repeated. Suppose President Lee Myung-bak and his administration personified examples of cautionary tales in which historical lessons can be learned. In that case, it is important for us to preserve a variety of testimonies so that President Roh Moo-hyun and the Participatory Government can also serve as helpful learning experiences of history.

For those who lived in the same era as President Roh and those who were with him and the Participatory Government, it is their first obligation to testify about what they had seen and experienced. When one does, it can be a historical lesson that can be learned from and recorded to guide the future.

It is now time for people to cope with the loss of President Roh, and it's acceptable to move beyond the Participatory Government. Success should be surpassed, and frustration must be overcome as frustration. With these desires, I started to write.

While recollecting my thoughts, I realized I spent much time with him. He was the warmest and the most intense person I had ever met in my life. We both had difficult lives growing up. We tried to look at the world with caring hearts and promised to be kind and warm-hearted to others. We wanted to change the world together and made an effort to create hope.

With that desire, we established the Participatory Government. Many things were accomplished, and some still needed to be achieved. We tried our best, but there were things that we regretted as well. Some people drifted apart due to differences of opinion. It seemed as if the progressive and reformist camps had estranged themselves from their past friends. It wasn't just us. Many wounds and disappointments were left in the progressive and reformist camps. But with the passing of President Roh, new opportunities were made for us. We need to get together to prepare for the next era. If we gather our minds, we can combine our strengths.

I hope President Roh and the Participatory Government are no longer the objects of love and hate. He has departed, and the Participatory Government is in the past, both being part of history. I hope that our successes and failures are left as objective lessons, that the things well done are left that way, and that we've done wrong are reflected upon and overcome. I am sure he would have wanted it that way, too.

President Roh and I met at a small stream and traveled far into the dangerous waters. There were many rapids along the way, but we were always together. Though we may now be physically separated, our minds and values will always run together like the water. The closer one gets to the ocean, eventually all the waters will meet. There will also be times when the waters meet to form the ocean. Whichever way it turns out, it is fine.

There is a poem written by my favorite poet, Doh Jong-hwan, that expresses my feelings so accurately.

Far Flowing Water

Rivulets, at first, spring forth with pure minds
lightly tread upon the mountainside
towards where the people stay.

However, as it passes through the world,
it will flow by with muddy hands to meet the water standing by.
Meeting with water that is already polluted
or merging with water rotten to the core.
Once encountering the various waters in the world
how many become stagnant bodies of water?
Mislaying their body, their mind rotting
how many waters have lost their way?
But notice the water returning to its original form,
and the murkiness becomes clear again,not carrying it along as it flows.
Observe the water as they find themselves again
going a long way.
Though flowing with many burdens and stains,
if it does not lose its original self
nor lose face or heart
wouldn't the water go far.

I wish the same for the people, ultimately becoming rivers that meet again, forming the great currents of history and flowing together. Though rivers may bump to the left and fold to the right, they eventually reach the ocean. It's called cháng jiāng hòu lóng tuī qián lóng, a Chinese idiom which means "the backwash of the Yangtze River pushes forward the forewash." (*This idiom is often used to describe the natural process of generation change.*) The backwash of the Yangtze River must forcefully push forward the waves of Roh Moo-hyun and the Participatory Government. The flowing stream of history is the natural order. Though I feel that this work may be insufficient, if it was a bit of help, there's nothing more I would wish for.

Many people sacrificed a lot for this book to be published. First, many persuaded me to write the book, and I warmly accepted their encouragement. I would especially like to show my gratitude to former Secretary Yang Jung-chul, who worked hard to organize massive amounts of recordings and testimonies. Without his hard work, I wouldn't have been able to write or start the book. Thank you for taking care of the manuscript as if it were your own, and I am grateful to those who provided their invaluable feedback. I hope that the efforts of all those who helped were not in vain.

It was not easy to dedicate this book by publishing it on the memorial of the 2nd anniversary of President Roh's passing. Though I tried my best, sections might be lacking or not precise. Let this book be the beginning of the memoir written together like he wanted.

I am looking forward to other books that will be written by others who have accompanied him.

June, 2011

문재인

Table of Contents

2 My Life

3 My Accompaniment

1 My Encounter

2 My Life

3 My Accompaniment

4 My Destiny

That Morning

The phone was ringing quite uproariously, and I was quickly awakened from my sleep. *Who can it be at this hour*... For some reason, whenever the phone rings in the early hours of the morning, it's accompanied by uneasiness.

"Chief, this is Kyung-soo speaking."

"Yes. What is it? Did something happen?"

"We ask that you arrive quickly. The president fell from the mountain while he was hiking. It looks like he fell from Bueongi Rock. We don't know the exact reason why. His bodyguard is transferring him to a hospital, and they say it's quite severe."

"Severe...do you mean he's in critical condition?"

"We're not sure. That's what the bodyguard has told us. I think we'll know more once we arrive at the hospital."

There was an uneasy feeling lingering inside me. If Secretary Kim Kyung-soo, who was at Bongha, called at this hour, one can assume that there was an emergency regarding the president. He fell from Bueongi

Rock...?

"You're saying the president went out for a walk at dawn? Did he go out for walks frequently?"

"No, not since the start of the investigation. He didn't until today."

That was my understanding too. Once the investigation was underway, he confined himself at home, not going outside. He was always conscious of the press cameras. However, he went on a hike up Bonghwa Mountain, fell off Bueongi Rock, and his condition is severe...

I tried my best to suppress this haunting feeling.

Secretary Kim Kyung-soo was in the middle of assisting the president to Seyoung Hospital, which was in town, and promised to call once it was confirmed that he needed to be transferred to a bigger hospital and hung up. I hastily prepared myself to leave and waited for the phone call, but it didn't ring. I couldn't wait any longer and called Secretary Kim. He said he also had not received any follow-ups of the situation from Secretary Moon Young-wook was with the president and informed that he will notify me right away as soon as he calls.

I was anxious. How much time has passed?

After a long time, Secretary Moon Young-wook called.

"His conditions critical. I think it's extremely severe. Seyoung Hospital said that it'll be too difficult for them to do anything. So, we thought it'd be better to bring him to a bigger hospital and am currently transferring him to Busan National University Hospital located in Yangsan. Please meet us there. And...from what his bodyguard has said, the president jumped off Bueongi Rock. Secretary Kim Kyoung-soo and Park Eun-ha confirmed that they had found a will on the president's personal computer."

He jumped off Bueongi Rock?? How could this be? ... so many questions started to fill my head. I had doubt, yet I couldn't suppress the ominous thoughts.

I left my wife, whose face was filled with worry, and headed towards the hospital. My hands were shaking tremendously on the steering wheel, and I had to take deep breaths to control my breathing while I drove.

That's how that day started. May 23rd, 2009, was "the day." The most painful and difficult day that I had to ever endure.

I had never been to Busan National University Hospital in Yangsan. Mist the frenzied state of my mind, I relied on the road signs to lead me to where I needed to go. To be honest, I don't even remember how I got there... Secretary Moon Young-wook was there to meet me and his face was filled with distress, looking spiritless.

The entrance of the president's VIP room was heavily guarded. I had to check with my own eyes how bad his condition was. I went in his room, and I ended up closing my eyes... There were no words that could describe his horrible state.

He was on life support. I could see that a signal was being monitored and thought *there was still hope*. But I was wrong.

The medical team was able to tell me the truth. The reason there was a signal was because his life was being prolonged with an artificial cardiac pacemaker. If the equipment was to be taken off, the signal will be lost. Maybe the doctor read *there might be a possibility*... written all over my face, because he started to be more straightforward regarding the president's condition. He was medically proclaimed dead when he arrived at the hospital, and that was the same opinion Seyoung Hospital made as well. By the look of his condition, one was able to make the judgment that he had passed right at the site of the incident. The reason to have him connected to the artificial cardiac pacemaker was because that was all they could do for his family and wanted them to make the ultimate decision on what needed to be done, which was the rationalization behind placing him on life support.

It felt like the sky was crumbling.

Secretary Moon Young-wook explained in detail what the bodyguard had told him and a few moments later Secretary Kim Kyung-soo came with the printed will. It was evident that it wasn't an accident, but something that he chose to do. No words came out, and my mind was becoming distant.

The doctor in charge spoke.

"When the First Lady comes, she needs to know that there's no hope for his condition and need to get her permission to take him off life support. This is extremely difficult for us to do, so we're asking you, the chief, to speak to her first."

When I heard his words, I came to my senses. *I can't lose focus. I must think about what needs to be done. I need to think clearly and make decisions on what needs to be done right away. Focus! Be calm.*

When I got my head back into the situation, the first thing I worried about was the arrival of the First Lady and how she would react to the president's current state. I verbalized my worries and the medical team sympathized with me. When she arrived, the medical team made her wait while the doctors quickly stitched up his wounds and cleaned up his blood.

She was unable to steady herself and needed help getting to the president's room. As if it was all a lie, he was completely cleaned up and there were no scars on his face. Even his facial expression was gentle. Yet, when she saw him, she fainted. Clearly, she was unable to accept his condition... the husband that was by her side just two to three hours earlier.

What was more agonizing was the task of candidly explaining what had happened. The only thing she knew was that 'he had fallen from the mountain and was in a critical condition.' She had a feeling that his condition was extremely serious when she was notified that Seyoung Hospital couldn't do anything and he needed to be transferred to Busan National University Hospital. The secretaries didn't have the heart to tell her the truth.

After the truth was revealed, that he in fact jumped off Bueongi Rock and viewing the will, she collapsed.

Yet, there remained something even more devastating to tell her. "He's completely reliant on life support sustaining his physical bodily function. He's already considered medically dead, and they say there is no hope. You need to decide whether to keep him on life support... or let him go...." His physician supported me as I discussed things with the First Lady.

It was difficult for me to keep my composure as she stood weeping and wailing. She fainted and went in and out of consciousness. This continued until she was able to collect herself and agreed with the decision to take him off life support.

It was May 23rd, 2009, 9:30 a.m. when we said our goodbyes.

The truth had to be told to the public. With the assistance of medical consultation, it was agreed that I would announce President Roh's passing and the details surrounding his death. Afterwards, the medical team will provide additional medical information regarding the incident. A short outline of what was needed to be said was written and I stood in front of the reporters. Though hundreds of cameras flashed as I was about to speak, I couldn't feel or notice anything. The sounds of reporters speaking rowdily in the press conference room just sounded like heavy silence. It felt like the whole scene was on pause.

"It has been an extremely shocking and tragic accident. President Roh Moo-hyun has passed away today at 9:30 this morning at Busan National University Hospital. At around 5:45, the president left his private residence and went hiking at Bonghwa Mountain. At approximately 6:40 a.m., it was reported that he leaped from Bueongi Rock to his death. Only one bodyguard accompanied him at the time. When the president

The truth had to be told to the public.
With the assistance of medical consultation,
it was agreed that I would announce the former President
Roh's passing and the details surrounding his death.

was found, he was immediately transferred to the nearest hospital but due to the severity of his injuries, he was moved to Busan National University Hospital where he was pronounced dead at 9:30 a.m. The president left a short will forwarded to his family."

It only took a few minutes to explain the extremely complicated situation. Consequently, there was nothing else to explain and the reporters didn't ask any questions either.

I had to concentrate on what was needed to be done immediately afterwards. *Where are we supposed to hold the funeral? Should we hold a temporary memorial here, or should we take him to Bongha?* I directed and urged everyone to quickly go to Bongha and prepare the funeral service and incense altar there.

The hospital was crowded. There were many familiar faces with tears streaming down their cheeks. Like me, I wondered, how long it would take for them to accept the reality of his passing. Soon, the influx of politicians from the ruling and opposition parties started to arrive. Even the Chief of Presidential Secretary under President Lee Myung-bak, who had no inauguration ceremony, attended. There was a mix of people I wanted to embrace and cry with, as well as the customary condolence visits.

I needed to be alone for a couple of minutes. Someone offered me a cup of tea. Looking at it, I suddenly remembered when we first met and when we were both handsomely young. We talked over a cup of tea the day we met for the first time.

Our First Encounter

In August 1982, I graduated from the Judicial Research and Training Institute *and wanted to become a judge. As a result of ranking second in my class, I received the Ministry of Justice award. At that time, it was customary that since many didn't pass the bar exam, all graduates were appointed as either judges or prosecuting attorneys once they completed their studies at the institution.

So, I never doubted I wouldn't be appointed as a judge. I had an arrest in my undergraduate years for leading a demonstration at the university. It was a protest against the Revitalizing Reform (Yushin) *, and I believed that there was no reason for the Revitalizing Reform demonstration to receive any criticism. I didn't expect it to cause me any trouble, but it was deemed as a cause for disqualification.

Finally, at the last minute, I was told that I wouldn't be appointed as a judge. Even to this day, I cannot forget the interview I had. All candidates for judges had to follow the procedure of having an interview with the deputy head of the Office of Court Administration *. Interviews usually took one to two minutes, a simple procedure. However, I was the only one with an interview that lasted thirty minutes. Many questions weren't asked. The interviewer only asked, "When did you protest and why?" That was all. Unfortunately, the interviewer didn't understand the situation.

It was the year 1982, and I was imprisoned seven years earlier, in 1975. Nothing further needed to be said once I explained that I was part of the April 1975 protest against the Revitalizing Reform. However, when I answered, I was cross-questioned and asked, "Was it the Garrison Decree then?" I explained to the interviewer that the Garrison Decree was done a couple years earlier, in 1971 . Then he asked, "Was that when the Revitalizing Reform's constitution was made?" I had no other choice but to explain the history of the Garrison Decree*, the Revitalizing Reformation proclamation, the establishment of the Revitalizing Reformation constitution, emergency measures*, and other things that happened in the 1970s. This interviewer had a well-known reputation among court officials for his sentencing skills. He also served for the justice of the Supreme Court. But I couldn't believe that he, a high-ranking official of the Court, didn't know the history that took place a couple of years' prior concerning the many civilians who protested even though they were tormented. As a result, many were incarcerated as political prisoners. It was as if I was watching the judge living "out of touch with reality." It wasn't very pleasant, and at the end, I was not appointed.

At the time, the Minister of the National Court Administration was my instructor, who taught the Civil Procedure Code when I was in school. When he heard that the prosecution might consider me, he suggested I first accept the appointment as a prosecuting attorney. He explained that once I became a prosecuting attorney for two to three years, the judgment could be rescinded, and I could be granted a judicial position. But I didn't want to go that route.

Inevitably, I changed my focus towards opening a law practice. Since it was a period when many who graduated from the Institute were appointed as judges or prosecuting attorneys, it was very rare for one to open a law practice. Since I had good grades, rumors started circulating. Even though there weren't many law firms at that time, I received a lot of recruitment offers from the practice of Kim & Jung, as well as others. I even met with some of them and listened to their proposals. The offers were quite appealing.

The salary offered was avant-garde and promised to include the incentive of a vehicle. If I worked for them for three years, they would also send me abroad to study in Los Angeles. It was tempting at first, but it was very different from the legal image that I had in mind. Maybe it was because I was a part of the student movement when I was in school. The jurist image I conceptualized, though they didn't have to be attorneys for human rights, listened ordinary people's cases and helped those who were treated unfairly. So, that role wasn't suitable for me. If I had accepted their recruitment offers, I would probably be living a different life now. Perhaps, I'd be an international or corporate attorney. It looked luxurious, but I wasn't attracted to that lifestyle.

I decided to take the path of an ordinary attorney. If I was going to go this way, I decided to take care of my mother and thought it would be best to go to Busan. I wasn't hesitant about the idea, but I felt sorry for my wife for a minute. She graduated from the College of Music and, at that time, was working in Seoul as a member of the Seoul Metropolitan Choir. During our university years, she supported me throughout my imprisonment and came to visit. She wasn't a woman who dreamed of wealth. She was just grateful that I passed my bar exam. I felt errible that I had to ask her, a woman from Seoul who loved working here, to leave everything behind and go to Busan with me. Fortunately, she agreed.

That was when I had the opportunity to meet Attorney Roh Moo-hyun. Park Jung-kyu, my bar exam cohort and my Senior Civil Affairs official replacement, was the one who introduced Attorney Roh to me. The way it all folded out was a bit odd.

Park Jung-kyu passed the bar exam after me. He was one of the oldest amongst the cohorts, so I remember him saying that he would graduate from the Institute and become an attorney. He studied for the exam with Attorney Roh at Gimhae Jangyuam long ago, which is how their friendship began. Attorney Roh finished his exam first, completed his justice term, and came to Busan. He was actively practicing as an attorney when he reached out to Park saying, "Let's work together." Attorney Roh prepared an office, provided a desk for Park, and waited for Park Jung-kyu to join him once he finished at the Institute.

Back then, it was common for lawyers to open individual offices because there was a common belief that lawyers who started a practice together wouldn't succeed. There were only a few law firms in Seoul, but everyone was their own boss in the provinces. However, Attorney Roh was different from others and had foresight. He thought that lawyers should specialize and work together in a law practice.

Attorney Roh opened his solo practice in 1978 and worked for almost two years. He then gained experience practicing with two other lawyers and operated a joint law and notary public office called Kaya Joint Law and Notary Public Office. This was probably Busan's first joint law office; however, it didn't go as planned.

It was because the public was unfamiliar with attorneys' legal specialization. Though they tried to assist clients in terms of specialty, the clients didn't like it. They didn't understand the idea of specialization and wanted the lawyer they consulted to take their cases. His dreams were high, but reality didn't coincide with them. So, after he tasted failure, he opened his own office and asked Park Jung-kyu to join him so that they could establish a legal practice specializing in the division of labor.

Unfortunately, there was a problem. Park Jung-kyu, who promised to come, was then appointed a judge. Attorney Roh's plans were interrupted again, and he couldn't start. Park Jung-kyu was so apologetic that when he heard I wanted to become an attorney, he introduced me to Attorney Roh instead. He told me to meet him immediately. I didn't know who Attorney Roh was. He was a total stranger to me; that was our first meeting.

* **The Judicial Research and Training Institute** An educational and training institution under the Supreme Court that applicants who passed the bar exam must undergo before becoming judges, prosecutors and attorneys. The probation period is two years.
* **Revitalizing Reform (Yushin)** The Emergency Decree that President Park Chung-hee carried out on October 17, 1972, to establish a long-term regime, transcends the constitution, stopping all existing democracy systems. It became the basis on which the long-term dictatorship was established under the banner of "Korean democracy."
* **The Office of Court Administration** The institution that oversees all administrative matters relating to the Court, such as budget accounting. It includes a Director and Deputy Director, and the director is led by the Chief Justice of the Supreme Court.
* **The Garrison Decree** An emergency decree that maintains the policing, defense, and public order of an area through stationed military forces. It was activated during the Park Chung-hee dictatorship when the anti-government demonstrations in the universities intensified. A stage higher than the Garrison Decree is the martial law. Under martial law, all powers are transferred to the military.
* **Emergency Measure** Special decree that could be taken by presidential powers under the Yushin Constitution. Through the activation of this decree, President Park Chung-hee had the enormous power to temporarily suspend the freedom and rights of the people as decreed by the Constitution. It was mainly exploited to suppress the demands for democracy and oppress students and opposition politicians. Park Chung-hee promulgated this decree nine times in total. It was abolished in the 1980 Constitutional Revision.

Partner

Attorney Roh's office was located in Bumin-dong, where the previous Court & Public Prosecutors' Office was. It was pleasantly plain, but the building was a bit shabby. Though the courtroom faced the rear, the inside of the office was quite spacious. That was where I first met him. I never dreamed that that meeting would lead to our lifelong destiny. The first time I met him, he was young. When he started in 1978, up until the time I came to work with him, he was the youngest attorney. He was quite impressive; above all, he had a different aura.

Of course, I hadn't met a lot of judicial officers. Still, he was different from the professors (who were judges and prosecuting attorneys) I met at the institution, the seniors I met in high school and the university judicial officer alumni (the judicial officer I met at the judge prosecuting attorney probationary *). Like Attorney Roh, many started as judges or prosecuting attorneys and later opened their private law practices during that time. But, though they called themselves attorneys, they held a sense of authoritativeness and carried themselves proudly. Maybe it's because

Attorney Roh's judicial career wasn't that long or his temperament was like that, but whatever it was, the way he carried himself was different. He was very accessible, honest, and friendly.

Immediately, a sense of kinship was felt. It seemed as if we were from the same time period.

I remember talking about so many things over just a cup of tea in front of us. We talked about me attending the protest during my undergrad years and getting expelled and imprisoned, which caused me not to become a judge...

Attorney Roh talked about his experience defending the *Burim Case** and why that was the reason why I was not appointed as a judge. He wholeheartedly resented my situation. Then he talked about his dreams-not about wanting to be an attorney of human rights but about wanting to be a "clean," incorrupt attorney.

He especially confessed that being a "clean attorney" wasn't as easy as one's heart desired and asked if I would become an incorrupt practitioner working with him. His warm heart inspired me.

He also elaborated on his intention to establish a specialized practice and how he wanted it to grow. No law firm in Seoul had made a proposal like his. I was intrigued, and my sentiment was inspired.

That day, I decided to work with him. I inspected the office. Everything was already prepared and all I had to do was bring myself. And so, my life as an attorney started in the law firm of Attorney Roh Moo-hyun & Moon Jae-In, Law and Notary Public Office.

This was the moment that our destinies began the encounter and long journey together.

* **Probationary** Engaging in and learning a job before being officially appointed to a position.

* ***The Burim Case*** The largest pro-communist fabrication case in the Busan area, created by Chun Doo-hwan's military authoritarian regime to secure the government's foundation in the regime's early days by suppressing the democratization movement. In September 1981, innocent students, teachers and office workers, in a social science reading club through the Good Book House in the Busan area were arrested without a warrant. They were illegally detained from twenty to sixty-three days, were severely beaten, and were subject to fatal torture, including the "roast chicken torture" and the "water torture." In July of the same year, students from the Seoul area were similarly arrested in the Haklim incident, so the case was named *Burim*, short for the *Haklim incident in Busan*.

Like a *Sunbae*, Like a Friend

Attorney Roh treated me well. Though he identified himself as "my friend," it wasn't true. There's a story behind that expression. During the 2002 Presidential Election, I was the chief director of the election planning committee located in Busan. He used that expression during his candidate speech at Busan's election planning headquarters inauguration ceremony. He would start by saying, "There's a saying; you know what a person is like by looking at his friends. What I mean is, it's not to be said 'Roh Moon-hyun's friend Moon Jae-in' but 'Moon Jae-in's friend Roh Moo-hyun.'" That was his way of expressing gratitude to his subordinate, his chief director, a position I thought I was unworthy of. We were six years apart in age and five years apart in terms of passing the bar exam, making him my superior. Because of this speech, even to this day, I am undeservingly called "Roh Moo-hyun's friend."

From the start, Attorney Roh showed me a lot of respect. He would always use formal, honorific language while talking to me. He started to speak a little more casually once I entered the Blue House. Until then, he treated me with extreme formality regarding the Korean honorific language style. With my personality, it was easy for me to call my *sunbaes* * "elder brother" once I got to know them, but with him, nothing but "*sunbae*" would my mouth permit me to say.

Attorney Roh's attitude had towards me wasn't customary and somewhat awkward. First, he was a judge and was an attorney many years before me. Even in the legal industry, he was known for his experience and knowledge. On the other hand, I was an amateur who had just graduated from the Judicial Research and Training Institute. One can be sure that it wouldn't have been easy for him to decide to form a partnership, considering my experience and comparable qualifications.

Though it's challenging partner with another attorney due to different styles, it is necessary to have faith in the other's capability. For example, there needs to be trust between each other regarding case workload, progression, and distribution without concern for who accepted the delegation *. If there's no integrity or reliability between colleagues, you cannot partner with someone. Since he was my sunbae, one can automatically assume he would do a better job than me. Although I was a rookie in the field, and he could have been uneasy with my work, he never showed it and always trusted my judgment.

While we worked together, there were many state of affairs cases or other important ones that we would work on. Depending on the amount of work load we had, the first chair (head attorney) was determined. There were times when Attorney Roh was the first chair and many times when

I was as well. Whenever I was the first chair, he always supported and agreed with the direction in which I wanted to lead the case. There was never a time when he voiced opposition regarding how I wanted to execute the lawsuit. He showed me truly implausible respect and trust.

Looking back, I realize that because of him, I was able to embark on my life's journey as an attorney with confidence and stability. When I first decided to become an attorney, I worried a lot about how I was going to obtain the startup money, but I was able to cast my worries away.

Attorney Roh and I lived in the same apartment complex. Since he was there before me, he lived in a bigger apartment than I. Though our apartment sizes were different, we communicated with each other quite comfortably and shared many conversations. I went over to his house often and visited his hometown, Bongha, with him. Once or twice a year, he would hold an outing for the entire staff and their families, which was very accommodating of him. Though Attorney Roh did not drink frequently, he often did enjoy attending social events.

The firm was operating well. It was a period when the number of attorneys and those with practices were few. Though they weren't experienced and had just graduated from the Judicial Research and Training Institution, they received a lot of cases. The following year, the number of applicants for the bar exam increased in addition to the number of attorneys. There was a time when a doctor's wife cut out our firm's advertisement and came to us. She thought we would do our best since we had just started and were young. We accepted our first civil case from this client.

Once or twice a year, he would hold an outing for the entire staff and their families, which was accommodataing of him.

Once we started working together, the number of cases presented to Attorney Roh decreased. Before, he was known as the youngest, most hard-working attorney and had the highest success rate in Busan. He was a fine attorney, but after we partnered up, all his commissions from routine cases halted.

Nowadays, the Attorneys-at-Law Act clearly documents that accepting commissions from clients is forbidden, but back then, it was a common occurrence. It was normal for the court, the prosecuting officer, the prison officer, the police officer, and others to receive a 20% commission when they brought a case to an attorney. This practice escalated so much that even banks and corporate judicial affairs teams would send cases and receive commissions. It was difficult to make an exception for Attorney Roh and his practice.

However, when we started our partnership, the commissions abruptly stopped. The things we said when we first met were being fulfilled. It was the same for entertaining judges and prosecutors. Back then, it was customary for attorneys with criminal cases to entertain the judges in charge of their cases with food and wine. On the day of a trial, it was also customary for the last attorney in the final trial of the day to entertain the previous judicial bench that was prosecuted. The areas surrounding the courts used to consist of high-class restaurants called Bangseokjip. Attorney Roh also visited these restaurants often, becoming a regular, but those entertaining services ended as well.

It must have been extremely difficult to have ended customs that everyone was practicing, but he did. He was the "clean attorney." Perhaps he knew I was an attorney who used to be affiliated with an activist group, which was. my aim. I can assume that he wanted to try it before but used our partnership to go forward with it. I think he also felt that it was his sense of duty as a senior attorney not to be ashamed of his behavior in front of his junior. He really was a conscientious and strong-willed individual.

Immediately, the decline of cases coming our way decreased drastically, which was quite noticeable. We were also advising attorneys at several banks, but that stopped, too. Because of all that, he made less income than when he worked alone, but he didn't seem to mind. When we decided to become civil rights attorneys, our income decreased even more. During his legal career, the period of his economic affluence was not long, but we were content. There were no problems in managing our firm.

Back then, Busan was the second-largest city in Korea, and there weren't many attorneys. There weren't even a hundred certified attorneys registered. Among the registered, if you removed the few that weren't practicing, you only met half of the attorneys you would or were competing against in court. By working diligently, we were able to build a reputation for ourselves as sincere and decent attorneys.

Since the judicial society is very conservative, it's difficult to change one's reputation positively or negatively once it has been formed. Fortunately, during the beginning of our legal services, I was able to leave a good impression amongst the legal groups in the Busan area, which helped me often during my life as an attorney.

In the Busan attorney community, we were quite the center of interest. We were both young, and our backgrounds were unique to the community. We became the object of attention because we were two different people who ran the only joint law office in Busan. Consequently, we had to be extra careful and work harder.

We didn't just work diligently on our cases but were active in the Busan attorney's community. Attorney Roh was the finance director for the Busan attorney's community three times and worked diligently to serve others. No matter how young or old, the attorneys all adored him. Those were good times.

* **Acceptance of Delegation** Taking legal action or administrative affairs of another party by contract of appointment.

* ***Sunbae* (Senior)** Someone who is not only older than you but also regarded in a higher position or status.

Becoming a Human Rights Attorney

Before I started working with Attorney Roh, he had already been litigating two state of affairs cases. He groundwork for the *Burim Case* and the *American Cultural Center Arson Case** in Busan. The logic behind him being assigned to the Burim Case as his first state of affairs case was due to his compassion. His senior colleague, human rights Attorney Kim Kwang-il, was being indicted for financing the case. Since he was going to be imprisoned, he asked and pleaded with younger attorneys to defend him. Due to the large number of defendants, several young attorneys were needed to distribute and share the caseload.

However, Attorney Roh was more invested and led the defense when he took the case. It was also he who vividly exposed the torture and long-term illegal detention that the defendants experienced. Though it was his first state of affairs case, he fiercely pleaded more than anyone from the defense team. Because of that, he was requested again to participate in the joint defense team for the *American Cultural Center Arson Case*. This time, he was accompanied by attorneys Lee Dong-myung, Yoo Hyun-suk, Hwang In-chul, Hong Sung-woo, and other prominent human rights attorneys in Seoul. The defense proceedings for these two cases changed his life.

Due to the two incidents, the Busan Activity Group was almost arrested in one big raid. In other words, it was chaotic. It was the beginning of the brutal Fifth Republic Age, and from that point until 1983 there weren't any state of affairs cases that were available in Busan.

But then, in late 1983 or the beginning of 1984, the Academic Liberalization Reformation was presented, and there was a period of relief in society. Due to enormous fabrications and inconsistencies in the case from the beginning, the defendants involved in the *Burim Case* were released from prison at the end of 1983. They were able to resume their status as pro-democracy activists in Busan.

University student movement cases and labor cases started to gain momentum. Some cases involved laborers who were severely oppressed and forced to obey the Labor Standards Act or be threatened with group layoffs for moving forward with the labor union organization. These people started coming to us.

We never intended to pursue the path of human rights from the beginning. But we didn't avoid the cases that came to us. We sympathized with them and diligently defended them. Gradually, we took on the central role of defending Labor and Human Rights in the Busan area. We also started to take on cases in neighboring areas like Ulsan, Changwon, and Geojae, which did not have human rights attorneys. There were many labor cases in these surrounding regions.

As resistance against the Fifth Republic Age got stronger, organizational cases connected to *Sammintu, Minmintu, and Jamintu** were formed in respective universities. Student movements and ideological conflicts became distinct. We also litigated cases like the Busan Chamber of Commerce & Industry sit-in strikes and the Busan and Seoul student movement organizations organized at the American Cultural Center in Busan.

Before long, our services for legal representation concerning labor and human rights causes in the Busan area became well-known. Since Busan was centrally located relative to the neighboring areas, our law firm was sought after for representing labor rights cases in Ulsan, Changwon, Geoje, and other nearby areas.

* **American Cultural Center Arson Case in Busan** In March 1982, university students in Busan committed arson at the Busan American Cultural Center, holding the U.S. responsible for the bloody suppression of the Gwangju Democratization Movement and protecting the dictatorship. One student lost his life in the process. This began the era of the anti-American movement in the 1980s. At that time, however, under the military dictatorship, Chun Doo-hwan manipulated and fabricated the incident as arson by spies from North Korea.

* **Sammintu, Minmintu, and Jamintu** *Samminitu* is an abbreviation of the *Sammin Minjok* Struggle Council. An organized resistance council was established in April 1985 under the National Student Union, with the participation of thirty-four universities nationwide. The Anti-Americanism-Independence and Anti-Fascist-Democratization Resistance Committee *(Jammintu)* was formed in June 1986 as a student movement organized by the Seoul National University Department of Humanities. In March 1986, the Democratic Resistance Committee (*Minmintu*) led the student movement with *Minmintu*.

Comrade

Managing various state of affairs cases, we forged a relationship with the area's political personnel. The leaders of the political outsider group in Busan at the time were Father Song Ki-in and Pastor Cho Sung-mook of the Busan Central Church, who is no longer with us. Novelist Josan Kim Jung-han was elderly, but he was a source of emotional support who encouraged and gave us direct guidance in critical situations. With these key figures as the center in 1984, the out-of-office democratization restoration and the human rights movement groups began. Formerly incarcerated participants filled the main management and practical administrative roles.

The first out-of-office democratic movement group restored in 1984 was the Busan branch of the Pollution Research Institute. Father Chung Ho-kyung chaired the Institute, and Choi Yeol managed the administrative work.

Only the name was borrowed to form the Busan branch, but there was no actual connection. It was a dangerous time to directly advocate for a democratization movement, so we decided to advocate for the anti-communism movement. Naturally, it was a group that gathered almost all of the notable out-of-office figures in Busan. Father Song Ki-in adopted the role of chairman.

At first, I participated as the initiator, and then Attorney Roh joined at the official launch. We were both on the board of directors.

The following year, in 1985, the Busan Democratic Citizens Council (abbreviated as the Citizens' Coalition) was established. It had similar characterizations to the Democratic Unification Movement of the People in Seoul. It was an organization covering all the out-of-office departments in Busan. The centripetal body of the Busan democratization movement had been prepared. Later, the Citizens' Coalition became the core of the National Movement Headquarters, which led to the 1987 June Struggle*. Father Song Ki-in was also the chairman of the Citizens' Coalition.

Because it was the time needed to prepare for a repression, like the March 1st Movement style, Thirty-three people were designated representative initiators because it was the time needed to prepare for repression, like the March 1st Movement* style. Attorney Roh and I joined as charter members from the start. Later, he also served as an honorary member of the committee. He served as chairman of the labor division, and I was the chairman of the public welfare division.

Through this, both of us became interested in the Out-of-Office Movement. Although neither of us were Protestant Christians, we joined the NCC Human Rights Commission in Busan as human rights commissioners. Since there were only a few people to fill these positions, we couldn't help but spread ourselves among various democratization movement groups and human rights organizations. I thought of it as my duty or mission as an attorney.

The same was true for the state of affairs cases. I couldn't turn away those who needed a helping hand. I had never set my goal to "become a human rights attorney" when I first came down to Busan. I told Attorney Roh this when I first met him. "I don't desire to become a human rights attorney or intend to become one. But I won't avoid these types of cases when they're presented to me." And that's what I did. No attorneys would take these cases, so once I started one, they all flooded in. It couldn't be helped.

We took some cases separately and worked on other important cases together. If there were several defendants in a state of affairs case, we would divide the defendants. Many times, we stood together in court, side by side. As attorneys, Roh and I worked well because of the attitude we approached cases with rather than our personal temperaments or personalities.

Most of the out-of-office organizations participated in the group, and they also delegated and shared roles within the association. There was only one field that I participated in alone. It was the Catholic movement group – Catholic Social Movement Council, Catholic Justice Implementation National Union, Catholic Human Rights Committee, Catholic Justice and Peace Committee – because I was Catholic. It had been a long time since I became a believer, but it was a bit embarrassing to take office in a Catholic group because I wasn't very devoted to attending mass.

But I couldn't turn away the request that the role of an attorney was essential. With such a relationship, I served as a communication liaison for the Catholic Church while I was in the Blue House, even though I wasn't a devout believer. I was able to visit Cardinal Kim Soo-hwan a few times. During the Participatory Government, the number of cardinals increased to two, and he acted as a bridge to send President Roh's correspondence to the Vatican.

Continuing as a labor and human rights attorney, I couldn't become a wealthy one. I was prepared from the beginning and didn't increase the quality of my lifestyle from the start. My wife was also cooperative and was grateful to me for passing the bar exam and becoming an attorney. However, it probably wasn't easy for Attorney Roh, who previously had a good income. He would've had to reduce the cost of living as much as his income had decreased, so his wife, Mrs. Kwon Yang-sook, probably had a more difficult time. But this was nothing compared to what was to come. As a result of litigating only labor cases, Attorney Roh later received a monthly salary of two million won (US $1,600.00).

While working on the state of affairs and the out-of-office democratization movement cases, Attorney Roh and I paid particular attention to two things.

First, we had to be spotless and incorruptible ourselves. We were familiar with the techniques commonly used by the dictatorship—

to secretly find people's weaknesses, like scandals or tax evasion, and to threaten, intimidate, embarrass, and impair them. It could ruin your reputation and affect the entire democratization movement if things went wrong. We stuck to abstinence and were careful not to behave contrary to our cause and conscience.

From trivial things like taking away commission, we paid taxes very accurately and were disciplined in our private lives.

Attorney Roh, in particular, was passionate and devoted, like a college student who dove into the movement for the first time. He believed he should change his entire life to be like the people's lives he served. Expensive meals were avoided, and so was luxurious liquor. He even gave up his favorite sport, yachting. He disliked hypocrisy, only passionately shouting his mantra, "The People! The People!" He was thorough and pure. He tried to change his entire life to reflect deep morality.

Because of such thoughts, I have yet to start playing golf. I thought it was unacceptable to play golf while agreeing with environmental activists strongly opposing the construction of golf courses. Since then, golf has become more accessible and popular, and my negative thoughts about golf have disappeared. I just didn't have any time after that.

The same is true for alcohol. I feel more comfortable with *soju** and *makgeolli** than liquor or wine. I only attend the first rounds of drinks and don't drink mixed drinks if I can. I set this principle for myself because I believed that people who speak for "the people" should not behave in opposition to what they promote.

There were other reasons behind my avoidance of mixed drinks. At the end of the year, when the Coalition was established, I had the opportunity to have drinks with the Coalition staff and people from the ANSP* Busan Chamber. They had asked to meet us. We had people like priests, pastors and myself on our side, and they had lieutenants, field officials, religious officials, and legal officials on their side.

We were laughing throughout our conversation, but I couldn't relax. After drinking enough soju for the day, I tried to end the drinks, but the head of the Chamber, who was from the 14th class of the Military Academy, proposed that we drink a mixed "bomb" drink. It was before mixed drinks became known to the public, so it was our first-time hearing of this new drink. The head of the Chamber explained the procedure, showed us a demonstration, and passed around the liquor. After several cups had been passed around, everyone except the head of Chamber and myself passed out. I was quite drunk, but I forced myself to stay up because I didn't want to lose to him.

When I had about ten glasses, I followed the head of Chamber into the bathroom and saw something ridiculously funny. He didn't go to the bathroom to urinate but stood in front of the mirror and slapped his cheeks loudly to keep himself awake. He was trying hard not to lose, too. And that's how that drinking event ended. However, it felt like an extreme form of a uniform military-style drinking culture to force everyone to drink without exception.

Second, regarding political state of affairs cases, I tried not only to defend but also to investigate and proceed under the provisions of the Criminal Procedure Act. I believed the criminal procedure had to be strictly followed even more in state affairs court cases. More so, especially with the state of affairs trial of the university students. If they didn't follow the legal processes in the trial, what rebukes could the older generation say to them?

When I first opened my practice as an attorney, there were many trials in court that did not obey the criminal law procedure. It was normal to have the defendant stand during the trial, and it was common practice to tie them with ropes and handcuff them. I asked the judge to correct each one by citing relevant provisions: "Please untie the handcuffs," "Please untie the ropes," and "Please prepare a chair and let them sit down."

The appropriate practices of criminal trials were corrected one by one. When tying and handcuffing the state of affairs case, defendants were no longer possible; guards were placed on either side of the defendants to restrict their physical movement. This was also a form of physical restraint, and I argued until they let the defendant go. The defendant wasn't tied with a rope or handcuffed once, but their movement looked unnatural. I asked them what was wrong. They tied the upper part of the defendant's elbow with a rope and then had him dressed so that it would look like they had no physical restraints. Even the judge who witnessed this rebuked the guards.

To prevent people from attending the trial of political state of affairs cases, they filled the courtroom with non-uniformed police officers, who blocked the public from entering. So, I asked the judge to dismiss the police who were present in the audience. The judge, who received the request, confirmed the identity of the officers in the audience and was shocked to discover that the majority of the occupants actually were police officers.

I argued with the judge several times over the defendant's opening procedures. The criminal procedure provisions were insufficient. The legal interpretations from commentaries that I presented regarding court practice acknowledged the defendant's opening proceeding rights.

We didn't allow the prosecutor to speak condescendingly to the defendants during interrogation. I asked the judge to give warnings. In particular, Attorney Roh did not allow the prosecutor to speak contemptuously or unethically bully the defendant. "Why are you talking in such a demeaning tone?" against the wrongdoing of the prosecutor, but it was also intended to help the defendant not to feel inferior and discouraged.

The same was true in terms of the investigation. We decided to visit the defendant as early as possible to prohibit a coercive investigation of the political state of affairs cases. However, the police often refused the early morning interview meetings because the investigation was ongoing. In the case of an inquiry at the Anti-Communist Chamber, the Chamber told us to go to the police station where the defendant was detained, and when we went to the police station, they would tell us to return to the Chamber for entry. It was a common practice intended to interfere with and discourage such interviews. No one argued with it in the past, but we strongly protested. If our protest alone couldn't resolve the problem, we raised the issue with the attorneys' association. I also received a reply from the Busan City Police through the attorneys' meeting that they would make "corrections." Attorney Roh once sued a chief investigator who repeatedly refused to let us in for an interview.

Through our insistence, many illegal trial and investigation practices were corrected. The result of this endeavor changed trial procedures regarding political cases, which quickly impacted general cases, too. Now, those practices have almost disappeared. It hasn't been that long ago, but younger attorneys nowadays cannot believe that that time ever existed.

* **Struggle of June 1987** The National Democratic Movement arose nationwide in June 1987. It is also called the June 10th Democratic Movement. Amid the military dictatorship of Chun Doo-whan that suppressed the nation's desire for democracy and strategized a long-term regime, the death of a Seoul National University student, Park Jong-chul, caused by torture, lit the fuse of the movement. In addition, the election of Roh Tae-woo, the leading figure of the same military coup as Chun, as the next presidential candidate caused the anger of the people to escalate. More than 500,000 people participated in the movement nationwide for nearly a month.
* **March 1st Movement** Independence Movement Day. Today, March 1st, is a national holiday in Korea, commemorating the day Koreans publicly resisted the Japanese occupation.
* ***Soju*** is a clear, colorless, distilled alcoholic beverage of Korean origin. Alcohol content varies from 16.8% to 53%.
* ***Makgeolli*** is a slightly sweet alcoholic beverage native to Korea made from rice or wheat. It has a milky color and has an alcohol volume of 6 to 8%.
* **ANSP** The former name of the National Intelligence Service. The official name at the time was the Agency for National Security Planning.

Passion and Principles

As I recall, Attorney Roh's mood seemed very intense during that time. It was as if someone had found religion for the first time, professing more passion and faith than the members who attended church longer than they had. Since I'm an attorney and should have self-imposed restrictions, I set up certain boundaries for my actions. But I wasn't the only one; everyone else did as well. It was common to think that there were certain methods that attorneys followed, but Attorney Roh wasn't like that. He didn't have any boundaries, doing what he thought was the right thing to do. Roh Moo-hyun was like that even when he became a politician.

When the Busan branch of the Pollution Research Center was launched, the Intelligence Agency monitored those who worked there. The agencies and detectives were stationed in front of the office, monitoring the movements of the office staff and visitors. They even entered the office as freely as they pleased. Attorney Roh offered them a room in the law firm for the research center. By providing office space, he protected the employees and their financial support. Though the agency continued to reside in front of the building, they did not try to enter the offices.

As an additional step, he even set up a labor law office in the law firm. Before this event, if labor incidents occurred, we helped with the trial and defense. It was the method that attorneys used. However, Attorney Roh was not satisfied with this. He wanted to establish a labor union and help them organize the union's daily activities.

It was the day Busan's Democratic Party's inaugural meeting was to be held. The event was organized into two sections: a lecture was supposed to be held in the first section of the agenda, and an inaugural meeting was scheduled to be held during the second section. The lecturer was Cho Gab-je*, who was known as the discharged journalist for the International Newspaper and was highly recognized for his position. However, the police blocked the auditorium where the venue was taking place, blocking all entrances starting from the program's first section. Everyone denounced the unlawful activity of the police blockade. The police force did not budge, so Attorney Roh laid down on the floor before them, shouting the chants himself.

This single act immediately spread rumors that he was an aggressive attorney. There was even word about it being a problem, a matter of the dignity of attorneys. Nonetheless, he maintained his well-mannered protest behavior against the unlawful police blockade because he knew that he wouldn't be able to cross it. Regarding the matter, we initiated a criminal complaint with the commissioner of the Metropolitan Police in

Busan (now the commissioner of the National Police Agency in Busan). However, though Attorney Roh became the representative accuser, a proper investigation was never conducted, causing everything to pass quietly.

Even though this event happened later, it was the same in 1987 during the Park Jong-cheol* Memorial Assembly. I was taken in and investigated. While I was under investigation, I confronted them by insisting on justification. I later discovered that Attorney Roh refused to make a statement and sign. He stood his ground because he knew being brought in and investigated was illegal and unjustified. As an attorney, it was his first time experiencing this, and it wouldn't have been easy to refuse an investigation. Nevertheless, he stood firm on what he thought was correct.

I believe that this was the future politician Roh Moo-hyun's principle belief. He would choose paths that would disadvantage him for the general cause. Many people knew that this was his principle. Also, he was thorough in not having limitations concerning his actions for the cause. This was his other principle. One might believe that there could be considerable efforts to break down the cause of regionalism while continuing to work as a member of the National Assembly at Jongro (located in Seoul). If he was asserting the eradication of regionalism, he was the type of person who would bump heads and throw himself into regionalism. In this respect, I wasn't able to follow him.

When the resistance of the Fifth Republic gradually escalated, the demonstrations became more frequent. When major demonstrations were being held, police forces would come to the office and block us to prevent us from participating. This was called office probation. It was a time when these kinds of activities were committed against attorneys. So, whenever opportunities for these types of demonstrations occurred, we had to consider ways in which we could ditch the police officers. Either we didn't go into the office, or we would find ways to distract them and attend the demonstrations. There were also times when the information division investigator would assist and accompany us to the venues where the demonstrations were being held.

There was a time when my home was searched and possessions confiscated. It was when I lived in an apartment complex, and investigators conducted surveillance for two to three days in the security office before issuing a formal search warrant. The investigation was because there was suspicion that a participant involved in the May 3rd Incheon Situation* was hiding in our house. When I checked, the only explanatory source of information that police had was that "there was an anonymous civilian that called it in." I couldn't believe it. It was ridiculous. It was a dark period when that type of warrant was issued for legal practitioners, where if the prosecuting attorneys demanded a warrant, the judge would issue it.

There was a breakout of labor cases once the laborers came to their senses. Attorney Roh and I enjoyed dealing with labor cases rather than cases involving students. It was because the lives of the laborers were filled with pain and sorrow, unlike in student cases, where their opinions and perspectives were always similar to each other.

During that time, the treatment of female workers at shoe factories, a major industry in Busan, was terrible. Salaries, including overtime work, of six to seventy thousand won (US $53.00- $63.00) were usually delayed. The presence of personal insults and sexual harassment were also common in the workplace. Many female workers demanded the Labor Standards Act based on the right to live, and soon afterward tried to organize a labor union, but many female workers were fired. Many were also arrested for obstruction of business due to a verbal group demonstration. Every time I met them; my heart ached. We defended free of charge and pleaded for them, but there were still many who we couldn't aid.

After Attorney Roh experienced these types of cases, he was determined to become a labor attorney. That was one of the reasons why the Busan Labor Legislation Counseling Center was associated with the law firm. The purpose of this merger was so that we would be able to build our professionalism.

Most labor law books at the time were largely conservative. They weren't very helpful in dealing with the labor cases that continuously emerged during that period. A thesis written by Professor Shin In-ryong, who presented the most progressive and theoretical theory in accordance with the reality of labor, was a great help. However, because I faced a lot of problems that this thesis series did not cover, I had a lot of independent studies to carry out. The judges and prosecutors also dealt with cases with paradigms regarding civil law, not understanding the difference in terms of labor law.

On the other hand, we realized that our assistance regarding events that had already occurred was limited. I believed we should help with the establishment of unions and workers' daily activities. The Labor Law Counseling Office was established for this purpose.

In the case of Attorney Roh, his fervor became a challenge for his junior lawyers later on. Many years later, there were labor attorneys in the Changwon area, but some left it because it became too burdensome. There must have been enormous pressure to be compared with Attorney Roh all the time. Clients would say, "Attorney Roh gave us free defense and even fought alongside us in court, but why don't you do that?" I realized it might not be so good to be dedicated and devoted.

From the second half of 1986, Attorney Roh solely focused on human rights work. He didn't take general cases at all. He said he would only accept political and state affair cases, but they ended up being mostly labor cases anyway. He not only defended the clients in cases but also held lectures for labor unions and workers. By doing this, he only received a monthly salary of two million won (US $1,900.00) from the office.

In the Great Labor Struggle after the 1987 * June Struggle, Ulsan, Changwon, and Geoje, the areas surrounding Busan, became the center of the Korean labor movement. Under the principles of positive law, they were all illegal strikes, and we defended almost, if not all, of the large, often violent, strike cases. It was a great reward for us to have been in the midst of the historical scene of the fierce labor movement of this country.

It was a great reward for us to be a part of this country's historical scene of the fierce labor movement.

* **Cho Gab-Je** An extreme far-right conservative commentator and former editor and director of the magazine Monthly Chosun.
* **Park Jong-Cheol** A former Seoul National University student who died from torture and assault when he was investigated at the Namyong-dong Anti-Communist Chamber in January 1987. Police initially concealed the lethal torture and announced the death was a result of mere shock. It was the doctor's testimony who performed the autopsy, which consolidated that the cause of death was due to torture. Five days after January 19th, the police publicly admitted what they had done. The offending officers were arrested. However, in June of 1987, it triggered the uprising.
* **May 3rd Incheon Situation** On May 3rd, 1986, a large-scale demonstration was held with more than 10,000 students and out-of-office activists, demanding the establishment of a national constitution. 319 people were taken to the police station, and 129 people were arrested, and this event became the starting point of Chun Doo-hwan's dictatorship's major suppression of the movement.
* **87 Labors' Great Struggle** The heat of the democratization that started in the June '87 movement began to spread to the labor unions, which was ignited by the workers' struggle with more than two million workers in 8,990 unions across the country. Workers from all over the country who suffered from low wages, long working hours, and poor working conditions joined. This is an important event that marked the history of the Korean labor movement.

The 1987 June Struggle

When the night gets deeper, one knows that dawn is right around the corner, and that was what was happening with the dictatorial regime's tyranny. It was calling for the break of democratization, and we could even feel the omen, one by one, in Busan. First, the pro-democracy movement organizations began to spread throughout the country.

The so-called Burim and the *American Cultural Center Arson Case*, which occurred in the early 1980s, had already cut off the buds of the already weak democracy movement in Busan. However, the people who were imprisoned at that time began to take root and work in various organizations as they were released. The foundation expanded, and vitality also returned.

In January 1987, a Seoul National University student named Park Jong-Cheol was killed as a result of torture. The police reported that "When the police investigator pounded the desk with a 'bang' during questioning, he suddenly collapsed and died." The entire nation was enraged. Busan was even more so since the victim was from there. His parents were living in Busan, and the 49 *Jae* (a Buddhist ritual for the deceased) was held there. The anger against the dictatorial government's oppression was the fieriest in Busan.

On February 7th, the "Preparatory Committee for the National Memorial Service for Park Jong-cheol" observed the Park Jong-Cheol National Memorial Service all over the country simultaneously. Attorney Roh and I also worked on the preparatory committee. The Busan Democratic Citizens Council (also called the Citizens' Council) prepared and organized the memorial service in the Busan area.

We had planned for the memorial service to be held at the Daegaksa Buddhist temple in the center of Busan City. The police, however, blocked the temple altogether and prevented access. Police troops were placed all around the temple in several layers, and shot tear gas into the crowd of citizens attempting to enter. University students who flocked around the temple confronted the police, shouting the slogan "Save Jong-cheol," but it was impossible to enter the Daegaksa temple.

We couldn't simply give up and retreat. Members of the Citizen's Council held an emergency meeting on the streets and decided to have an informal memorial service on the road in front of Busan Theater in Nampo-dong. We secretly gathered people there.

At 2 p.m., according to the scheduled time, an informal memorial service was held with more than 300 citizens and students. We sang the national anthem and democratic movement rally songs, made denunciation speeches, and Attorney Roh gave an impromptu eulogy. It was the first street rally held since the 1979 Buma Democratic Movement. Citizens quickly merged to fill the streets.

When the police realized what was happening, they besieged the surrounding area and approached with the White Bone Unit*. To protect the citizens and students who were shaken with fear, the standing commissioners of the Citizen's Council intervened between them and the police in a sit-in rally. Attorney Roh and I also sat down.

The police then indiscriminately shot tear gas into the protest; since there was no way to avoid or run, we were drenched in it.

Police ran in and forcibly loaded people into the chicken coop car*. Due to the tear gas, I was unable to open my eyes for a long time, even after I got in. We were taken directly to the Anti-communist Chamber* of the Busan City Police. Even after we were arrested, the success of the brief memorial service on that day continued as approximately 10,000 people gathered in the streets later that evening. It became the catalyst for the June Struggle.

Police categorized the people arrested for protesting and rallying that day and applied for arrest warrants for a representative from each group: lawyers, religious people, out-of-office organization leaders, youth, and students. As for attorneys, Attorney Kim Gwang-il who also participated in the sit-in, Attorney Roh Moo-hyun and I were taken to the police station, and out of the three of us, Attorney Roh was charged with an arrest warrant.

Attorney Roh had already been the most troublesome human rights attorney in Busan at the time. It probably didn't help that he consistently refused to give statements after being brought into the police station. Under the law at the time, whether it was an emergency arrest or arrest of a crime in action if the warrant wasn't issued within 48 hours, you had to be released. However, the police continued to detain us all after 48 hours, including Attorney Kim and me, even though we weren't charged with an arrest warrant.

We kept track of the exact time, and when it got to 48 hours, we demanded, "We're going home!" The combat police blocked the corridors so that we couldn't leave. We stood face to face, chanted, and unavoidably returned to our cell. We went out again an hour later and repeated the confrontation and chants, repeating the same process every hour. We were detained around 2:30 p.m. on February 7th, but Attorney Kim and I were released at around 6:00 p.m. on February 9th, beyond 48 hours.

As soon as I was released, I went to the office because I was worried about Attorney Roh. I checked the situation and found out that his arrest warrant had already been dismissed, but the prosecution reapplied for the warrant.

He should have been released if the arrest warrant had been dismissed, but they hid the fact that it had been dismissed and reapplied without releasing him. I was filled with anger and couldn't stay still.

First, I went to the office of the senior judge on duty who oversaw the reapplication warrant. The chief of the Public Security Department in the Busan District Public Prosecutor's Office, who reapplied for the warrant, was in the room. It was preposterous, and I began to protest loudly.

"Why is the Chief of Public Security here? Is he trying to persuade the judge to issue another warrant? Why didn't you release the man when the warrant was dismissed? I'm appealing this!" I shouted loud enough for everyone to hear, and the chief of the public security department turned red and walked out of the room, embarrassed.

At the same time, Attorney Yoo Taek-hyeong, the chairman of the Korean Bar Association Human Rights Commission, and Attorney Ha Kyung-chul, the human rights commissioner, visited to find out what had happened and came down to the judge's room. They emphasized the facts regarding the investigation at the level of the Korean Bar Association. They stressed that if he re-initiated the arrest warrant that had already been dismissed, the Association would not tolerate it.

Attorney Yoo was a veteran attorney and subtly intimidated the judge. "The Korean Bar Association had already proposed a revised regulation to the board of directors. It dealt with denying an attorney's registration by any judge or public prosecutor that ignored human rights in political and state-related cases." There was such a discussion within the Human Rights Committee of the Korea Bar Association, but the amendment proposal has not yet been brought to the board.

The judge on duty, who oversaw the warrant, gave up and just left. He said he was going out to eat and never returned, which was a wise choice. The prosecution didn't officially apply for the warrant, but the chief of public security had unofficially taken the warrant to ask the senior judge on duty for the issuance. Therefore, even if the senior judge didn't take any action, the prosecution had nothing to say. These demands were rampant in the political or state affairs cases, but it was as if they were knocked out.

It was chaotic within the prosecution. The request for an arrest warrant for the currently practicing attorney was based on the Public Security Department of the Supreme Prosecutor's Office (SPO) guidelines. It was reported and approved by the Minister of Justice (MoJ). Therefore, if the warrant was not issued, the Busan District Public Prosecutor's Office would be held responsible for the incompetence.

Attorney Roh was detained all night, so the chief of the Public Security Department took the warrant around to the house of the senior judges, but no judge would take responsibility. "Why are you bringing something meant for the judge on duty to me?" all of them declined. He ran to the chief senior judge, but he, too, declined. He even went to the chief judge, but it was useless.

Finally, Attorney Roh was released in the late evening hours of the next day. The police couldn't detain him any longer, so they followed him home and remained outside his home all night, leaving the house early in the morning when there was no sign of a possible warrant approval.

The case made Attorney Roh famous nationwide overnight. The news media reported the case headlined "The dismissal of four warrants overnight." It was a demonstration of Korea's current democratic legalism and a symbolic demonstration of the fierce resistance of the Busan area to the political situation.

The illegal detention of three lawyers by the police was not tolerated. The Busan District Attorney's Association decided to file criminal charges, but it fizzled out. Though the warrant had been dismissed, the prosecution could still prosecute Attorney Roh without detention. A tacit agreement was reached that the Attorney's Association would not appeal further if no prosecution was executed without detention. Later, however, when Attorney Roh was arrested in the case of Daewoo Shipbuilding, the prosecution added this case and filed an additional indictment.

The country was on its way to the great June Struggle. There was a wind of democratization throughout the country. Busan was uniquely special. The fervent passion for democratization started in early 1987 and was particularly hot in Busan. The April 13th Constitution Protection Decree* was announced, and violent resistance began. At first, various societies of intellectuals started to mobilize. There were declarations concerning the state of affairs, starting with university professors influencing other intellectual groups. I remember the declarations by attorneys, dentists, and pharmacists that started first in Busan. Attorney Roh and I announced the Busan Attorneys State Declaration with a petition from twenty-four attorneys in Busan, demanding the abolition of the constitutional amendment for a direct election system and the April 13th Constitution Protection Decree. It was something that had never been accomplished before in the history of the Busan legal community.

Street protests frequently occurred in many parts of the city. Citizens'reactions were very favorable. When the protestors marched on shouting slogans, the citizens of the roadside encouraged them with applause. Merchants hid the protestors when needed, even though the demonstrations were hampering their businesses. Passing pedestrians and merchants went out to stop the police from trying to arrest the protestors. Many people distributed bread and drinks and gave money to cover the expenses when protestors distributed printed materials.

In May that year, the Busan People's Movement Headquarters for the Democratic Constitution (Busan People's HQ) was formed based on the Busan Democratic Citizens Council. The People's Movement Headquarters for the Democratic Constitution (People's HQ or Gookbon) was the largest democratization movement since the nation's founding, and all opposition parties and democratic movement groups joined. Busan was the same.

The Busan People's HQ was the first to be established in the country before the People's HQ of Seoul. Attorney Roh served as the permanent executive chairman of the Busan People's HQ. The role of the standing executive chairman was advancing beyond the conventional tasks required of a human rights attorney, which was to serve as a fence and provide financial support for the organization. It also involved leading meetings and public demonstrations. It wasn't a role that was originally expected of attorneys, but Attorney Roh practically volunteered for the position. Consequently, I adopted the role of a permanent executive committee member.

In June of 1987, Busan had street protests daily under the leadership of the Busan People's HQ. More people were participating in the rallies than anywhere in the country, and they were fierce. Daily, city rallies continued late into the night. We followed the demonstrators until they finished, observed and examined the protests, gathered in the Central Church to review the whole situation of the day, and finally returned home after planning for the next day. By seeing the increasingly bigger, relentless protests and the response of the citizens, I was able to sense the collapse of the military dictatorship regime.

But news came from Seoul that the uprising had entered a lull after disbanding the Myeongdong Cathedral* sit-in. The number of protesters in Seoul and everywhere else suddenly decreased. If we left things the way they were, the situation would have passed over like it did before.

However, the atmosphere in Busan was different. It was getting more intense. Attorney Roh and leaders of the Busan HQ decided that Busan would continue to play a central role in the Myeongdong Cathedral's struggle in Seoul. Immediately, we started the Busan Catholic Center sit-in with the help of priests of the Catholic Priests Association for Justice (CPAJ). Until the end of the June Struggle, the Busan Catholic Center played a pivotal role in the Myeongdong Cathedral sit-in.

Busan citizens participated even more. When the demonstrations occurred, demonstrators would line the main road from Seomyeon to Busanjin Station, which leads to Busan City Hall and KBS Broadcasting Station. The atmosphere of other areas, including Seoul, where the protests were fading out, was also revived as Busan pushed forward. Every-

By seeing the increasingly bigger and fiercer protests and the response of the citizens, I was able to feel the collapse of the military dictatorship regime.

one was proud when they witnessed this.

It was about June 20th. There was a rumor that the Garrison Decree had been invoked and the military would be put into operation in Busan. However, the rumor gave us more strength. The dictator regime had been pushed into a corner, which gave Busan the confidence that it was now holding onto its fate. Attorney Roh and I would encourage each other by saying, "If we don't give up and push forward, we will win." We found out later that the Garrison Decree and the reaction from the military were really discussed. The troops were ready to be dispatched but were blocked by internal opposition.

So came the June 29th Declaration*. It was a declaration of surrender of the military dictatorship. Of course, there were people arguing, "We shouldn't end with the June 29th Declaration! It's a deceptive policy! We must finish the job!" However, it was difficult to continue the struggle when we gained the constitutional amendment for direct election. In any case, the democratic camp failed to win the presidential election straight after the direct election amendment due to the "division of the two 'Kims*'", but it wasn't the people's responsibility.

The June Struggle was a tremendous civil democratic uprising that broke down the military dictatorship with the power of the people.

I believe the June Struggle should be one of the most highly appreciated and respected movements in Korea's democratization movement. While the April 19th or the Gwangju uprising had been quite accidental or spontaneous, the June Struggle saw the formation of the solidarity struggle organization called the People's HQ, which set clear goals and consisted of a planned and systematic campaign to achieve the goal of a constitutional amendment for direct election. I think, perhaps, it was the only case concerning our democratization movement.

Although the June Struggle was a nationwide democratization movement, I think Busan should be recognized as the center of the movement, not Seoul. Busan was first to form the People's HQ, and throughout the entire period was the area that most fiercely protested initiating demonstrations more than other areas. More importantly, when the Myeongdong Cathedral sit-in deteriorated and the demonstrations in other regions such as Seoul suddenly decreased, more Busan civilians fiercely protested along with the Catholic Center in Busan, becoming a driving force for the success of the struggle.

In that regard, I'm saddened to see that Busan's role was not adequately acknowledged in the history of the June Struggle and to see Seoul described as the focal point. It can't be denied that there was a movement in Seoul, but Busan citizens were also responsible. Since the three-party merger, the citizens of Busan have become more conservative, and Busan citizens have neglected to acknowledge the June Struggle.

Before the three-party merger, the citizens of Busan were filled with pride. They believed they could change history if they wanted to, as it ended the Yushin dictatorship with the Buma Democratization Movement and the Fifth Republic dictatorship with the June Struggle. It is a pity that Busan, which was a traditional "opposition city" with such a high civil consciousness, overnight became a "Ruling party city" and has not been able to escape from the Grand National Party even to this day.

Meanwhile, it was never an accident that bolder protests were taking place in Busan when the passion of other areas fell suddenly after the disbanding of the Myeongdong Cathedral sit-in. The leadership of the Busan People's HQ kept an eye on the protests and the situation around the country and felt a sense of crisis and urgency. To reverse the trend from Busan, the Catholic Center conducted a protest to increase the demonstration's intensity systematically.

Our intentions were spot-on, and I still remember the pride and catharsis we felt in watching the nation's uprising and knowing that we played a significant role.

At that time, there was a reason why the leadership of Busan People's HQ raised the intensity of demonstrations among the citizens. Unlike other regions, it was due to the attorneys, pastors, and priests who led the rallies in the streets. If they had not, would the intensity of the demonstrations have intensified the way we wanted to? At that center was Attorney Roh Moo-hyun. It was a great reward for me to be there alongside him.

However, when he later became a politician, Roh was treated as a minor figure of the movement from the people who took part in the democratization movement in Seoul. In addition to the Seoul-centered paradigm, I think it was also a result of the academic elitism that was widespread in the democratic movement. As far as I could see, there was no one who fought as hard as Attorney Roh Moo-hyun during the Fifth Republic period.

* White Bone Unit A nickname for a police unit carrying out multiple crime suppression missions consisting of an un-uniformed police officer in the 1980s and 90s. They were called the "white bone unit" because of the distinguishable white helmets they wore when suppressing the protesting citizens. These helmets symbolized the violent brutality of the dictatorship at the time and symbolized the public power that created fear in the citizens.
* Chicken coop car The name of a police bus with a windshield covered with wire mesh resembling a chicken coop.
* Anti-communist Chamber It was a department dedicated to investigating police spy cases. However, it became an organization that acted as the pawn of those in power, taking charge of investigations related to political prisoners, using torture and fabrication. The chamber refers to a separate building that handled those tasks.
* April 13th Constitution Protection Decree The decree of April 13th, 1987, when the dictator of the Fifth Republic, Chun Doo-whan refused to answer to the people's demand for democratization and stopped discussing any amendments to the Constitution. However, contrary to the expectations of the dictatorship regime, it had the adverse effect of adding fuel to the "fire" of democratization. With the announcement of the decree, protests held in various parts of the country began to criticize the long-term ruling conspiracy and demand amendments. In the midst of this, the torture, death, and concealment of Park Jong-cheol were revealed, stimulating the June Struggle of 1987.
* Myeongdong Cathedral Sit-in On June 10th, 1987, protesters chased by police in a large-scale city protest were pushed to the Myeongdong Cathedral and isolated for five nights and six days. These protesters continued their uprising in Seoul in June but voluntarily dissolved in six days.
* June 29th Declaration The Special Declaration announced by the ruling party leader Roh Tae-woo on June 29th, when the Chun Doo-hwan dictatorship gave into the June Struggle of 1987 and accepted the demands of democratization, Constitutional amendment for direct election, a peaceful transfer of military dictatorship, the release of Kim Dae-jung, and other political criminals.
* Division of the Two 'Kims' The two "Kims" refer to the two leaders of the opposition party, Kim Dae-jung and Kim Young-sam. They were eager to see the democratic forces win in the presidential election, but they ran separately and eventually gave the regime to Roh Tae-Woo.

The Great Workers' Struggle and the Imprisonment of Attorney Roh

Before we could enjoy the victory of the June Struggle, the Great Labor Struggle began from July to August. There wasn't any time for a breather. The outcome of the struggle led to the arrests and dismissals of many laborers. From then on, everything was up to me. Attorney Roh and I were still the only labor attorneys in the Busan and Gyeongnam area, where all the workplaces were concentrated.

On top of that, after the June Struggle, Attorney Roh took his hands off the office legal work and swept the streets and workplaces, meeting people face-to-face in the field. He was then eventually arrested. It had to do with the *Daewoo Shipbuilding & Marine Engineering (DSME) Case.*

It was a tragic accident where a tear gas shell killed Mr. Lee Seok-gyu during the DSME laborers' street protest. Attorney Lee Sang-soo from Seoul and Attorney Roh from Busan went to the site to help the protestors and were arrested on the charges of third-party intervention* and "obstruction of funeral services." The third-party intervention was an unjust law that was often abused then, but even then, obstruction of funeral services was an absurd legal trap.

One of the relatives close to the deceased was planning to close the case after receiving settlement money from the company and quietly proceeding with a family funeral. While arguing with the special committee and union, the two attorneys assisting were charged with interfering with the funeral services. The background was obvious. It was probably the first time in the history of the Republic of Korea that "obstruction of funeral services" became an official name of a crime. A long time afterward, Democratic Party assembly official Baek Won-woo was indicted on the same charge at the funeral of President Roh. As far as I know, there were only two cases of "obstruction of funeral services" in history, and I happened to be the defending attorney for one and a witness for the other. This was also an uncanny connection.

Upon receiving the shocking news of "the arrest of Attorney Roh," the Busan Bar Association began a fact-finding investigation. I chaired the committee. We went to the Geoje site to check on the situation and met many people, including labor union officials and special committee officials. I collected details of Lee's death, the funeral, and the role of the two attorneys and then put together a team of legal specialists.

Attorney Roh had ninety-nine attorneys on the team. It was the largest team of defense attorneys ever. Of these, ninety-one were attorneys in Busan. At that time, 120 attorneys were registered at the Busan Bar Association. Except for those who were registered but not practicing, virtually all active attorneys took part. I visited them individually to receive the appointment notice*, and all of them were very open and willing. The most grateful thing was that most of them came to the court during the confinement legality review. There were obviously not that many seats in the defending attorney's seat, so the audience was full of attorneys. When the judge checked the attorneys' attendance, there was an endless answer of "Here" with raised hands. Even without spoken defense, it became a silent state of defense in itself. Eventually, Attorney Roh was released under the Habeas Corpus Claim* in twenty-three days.

However, at the end of November 1987, the prosecution indicted Attorney Roh without detention, and Roh was issued a suspension as an attorney. The suspension was lifted only in June 1988, after he was elected to the National Assembly. I took care of Attorney Roh's main trial by myself. There was no need to trouble other co-colleagues, as the trial was conducted in a state of non-detention. The abstract for the defense I submitted to the court is written in *Chronicles of Pleading Cases* by Attorney Han Seung-heon, as he was one of the co-litigators.

In February 1988, the court sentenced Attorney Roh to a fine of 1 million won (US $1,000.00). It was no different from a sentence of acquittal. The sentencing statement is also contained in the *Chronicles of Pleading Cases* by Attorney Han Seung-heon. I didn't have a chance to thank the ninety-nine attorneys that appeared in the sentencing statement. Even the fine of 1 million won was appealed as it was unjust but was withdrawn because it was difficult for Attorney Roh to attend the trials after he became a member of the National Assembly.

* **Third Party Intervention** The "third party intervention clause" was created in the labor law revision by Chun Doo-hwan, who took power through a military coup d'état in 1980, to limit union-management relations to union-management officials of the company. This was to block the assistance and support that third parties could give to restore the rights of workers who can't assert their rights because they do not know the law or are powerless. It was used as an essential ground for suppressing labor unions.
* **Appointment Notice** A document filed with the court to notify that a particular attorney has been appointed as the client's litigator. Unless an appointment notice is submitted, no litigation action can be taken.
* **Habeas Corpus Claim** The Court examines the legality and necessity of the suspect's arrest and suspends the detention if it is deemed invalid.

Sending Attorney Roh to the National Assembly

In April 1988, Attorney Roh was elected a member of the National Assembly during the 13th General Election. Earlier that year, Kim Young-sam, the president of the Democratic Reunification Party, offered a proposal. This was when "the two 'Kims'" lost the presidential campaign and were recruiting someone to argue for the opposition personage.

Another nominee, Attorney Kim Kyung-il, made up his mind earlier on. However, Attorney Roh didn't decide by himself; rather, he had the pro-democracy activists in Busan who were with him during the June Struggle discuss the matter. Many opposed the idea. Traditionally, in the Busan area, there was great reluctance to enter the political community from the democratic and citizen movement.

Many believed that the effort and success of the June Struggle's frustration could be achieved through politics. I agreed. I felt that he wanted to do it and believed that if he ran, he would win. Attorney Roh didn't have personal ambition. He believed that he could help the laborers better if he became a member of the National Assembly. Ultimately, the discussion concluded with the majority agreeing that Attorney Roh should enter politics. He, too, made his decision.

He didn't go because people sent him or for his personal advancements, but many understood and perceived that he was sent to represent the Busan activists of the democratic movement. So, the democratic activist camp positively joined the election campaign, campaigning as if they were doing it for their own cause.

First, the decision was made by the local constituencies. When Attorney Roh was running for office, many thought he was representing Nam-gu, Busan, because he had resided there for a long time. Even the United Democratic Party thought that and left Nam-gu, Busan alone. Since many apartments and residents were living in Busan at that time, it was the best place to hold elections.

On the contrary, Attorney Roh didn't choose that area. Instead, he decided to represent Dong-gu, Busan, a place where he knew no connections, for running his candidacy. At that time, Hu Sam-su, the central figure for The New Military and the Fifth Republic *, was the Democratic Justice Party candidate running, and Roh wanted to take him on and judge the Fifth Republic. Many people tried to dissuade him, but no one was able to break his stubbornness. That was just like him.

I wasn't able to help him with his election. It was because, even though many of the Democratic activist camps agreed to help both attorneys Kim Gwang-il and Roh Moo-hyun's campaigns, most of them wanted to help Attorney Roh Moo-hyun.

It was natural, probably because Attorney Roh played an important central role in the pro-democratic activities of the Fifth Republic until the June Struggle. It was also their human nature to help him because most of them were defended by him. So, with that being agreed upon, the senior activist group, which had prior acquaintances with Attorney Kim, decided to help with his campaign. However, since the team numbers were small, I took the general manager role for Attorney Kim's campaign.

I still remember the election posters that Attorney Roh used during that campaign. It was a black and white picture of Dong-gu's hillside village's shanty town, with Attorney Roh standing in front of it, looking pleasantly simple with fierce eyes. A photographer from the activist group took the photograph, and another printed the posters. His campaign slogan was "Making the world a better place." The poster and the slogan went well together. Before then, there was never a campaign poster that was so intense, and one hasn't been seen since. After becoming a member of the National Assembly, he couldn't use that type of campaign poster again. He continued using the slogan "Making the world a better place" as his signature motto during his presidency and even throughout his retirement. Maybe it was because, during his presidency, he thought "Making the world a better place" was still valid and reflected his desires.

Once Attorney Roh was elected, he became a star in the National Assembly hearings*, and we were very proud. However, though the honor was great, there was a lot of discouragement and distress. Whenever I saw him frustrated and in agony, I regretted having approved his entry

His campaign slogan was "Making the world a better place." The poster and the slogan went well together. Before then, there was never a campaign poster that was so intense, and it wasn't seen after it either.

into politics. He, too, would joke and say, "You guys sent me into politics, so you're responsible!" whenever things got too hard for him.

To be honest, there were a couple of times when I suggested that he return to being an attorney. This was probably when we were outside the Assembly after he lost the election into the National Assembly. I wasn't suggesting that he give up politics altogether. Rather, it would be logical to return to legal practice, to do more groundwork for human rights and regional activities, and then return to elections rather than suffering with assembly work. However, it was difficult for him to leave once he set foot in the political world.

There was a time when he did have an opportunity to give up politics. It was when he left Jongro and was defeated while representing Gangsu, Busan. He said that if he lost the election, then he would quit politics. However, after his loss, an extraordinary event occurred where the people were moved by him, as Roh Moo-hyun, a politician of principle. And with that energy, he made a comeback and finally became the president. However, after experiencing the tragic event, I regret being unable to keep him out of the political world.

* **The New Military and the Fifth Republic** The military force took control of the military through a military coup and seized the regime after the death of President Park Chung-hee. At the center of the power was a private group within the military called "Hanahoe," primarily run by the 11th and 12th class of the Korea Military Academy, including Chun Doo-hwan, Roh Tae-woo, and Chung Ho-yong. They conspired to pull President Choi Gyu-ha out of office and, through indirect elections, made Chun Doo-hwan president, establishing the Fifth Republican government. He was later sentenced for high treason for the military coup and homicidal suppression of the Kwangju Democratic Uprising.
* **National Assembly Hearing** Hearings were held in November 1988 by the National Assembly Audit to investigate corruption in the Fifth Republic. Several hearings were held, including the Ilhae Foundation Hearing to investigate the corruptions of the Fifth Republic and the collusive links between business and politics; the Gwangju Democratization Movement Hearing to investigate the illegality of the 12.12 coup and to determine the commander that ordered open fire at Gwangju Democratization Movement; Hearing on the government's control over the media, including media merger and forced dismissal of journalists. The opportunity made Assemblyman Roh Moo-Hyun, a hearing committee member, a star politician because of his persistent and piercing questions and rebuttals.

Left Alone

After Attorney Roh left, I was alone. All the work we used to do together needed to be tackled on my own. In the past, Attorney Roh took most of the responsibility for the work, and I would assist him. But now I had to do both. It wasn't a problem running the firm. The reason was that it had already been some time since Attorney Roh took his hands off general cases. Later, when there was a suspension concerning services, I learned how to run the place by myself.

Under the Roh Tae-woo administration, many cases still dealt with state of affairs and labor cases. There was no change in public expectations; the firm was still regarded as the "center" for Busan and South Gyeongsang Province. When one is called a human rights attorney, pitiable people come with all types of cases, no matter how irrelevant they may be to the state of affairs cases. There were also times when I needed to take charge of massive civil affairs cases. The number of cases came in large quantities, so it became too difficult to handle alone. I would take a load of work home and prepare for trials or write pleas until the break of dawn. My children thought being an attorney was a 3D (dangerous, difficult, and dirty) job. Still, I accepted that it was something I needed to do and accepted the work. I was always happy to know I could help others with something I did well.

Though there was a lot of work and I was tired, I think that was when I had the most stability in my life. Even though it wasn't the best, it was when I felt that my personal life and sense of duty toward the world were well-adjusted and in balance.

Like the opportunity Attorney Roh had given me, I started to accept attorneys who had just completed the Judicial Research Institution, increasing the number in the firm. Even though our firm did not make a lot of money, many attorneys agreed with what we were doing and wanted to join our firm.

There was also an attorney who sought out our firm because he was aware that we were basically managing the labor cases in the Busan and South Gyeongsang Province. He was determined to become a labor attorney and came looking for us. Then, in 1995, when we had five people, and it was a requirement, we established a law firm together. It is called Busan Law Firm, where I am still the senior attorney. When Attorney Roh returned to Busan, he became an affiliated attorney. And when he became the president, he stopped being an attorney temporarily.

These days, attorneys in Busan are actively serving in "Lawyers for a Democratic Society," and depending on their specialty, they secured positions in either human rights groups, civic groups, or labor groups.

After Attorney Roh entered politics, the pro-democracy movement in the Busan region gradually evolved and divided into civil movements, environmental movements, labor movements, and people's movements. Since many people participated in and liked the conditions of civic and environmental movements, I mainly focused on groups supporting the labor movement or labor union activities.

The organizations included the Busan Labor Research Institute, which was formed in the latter half of 1987 and joined by Attorney Roh until he became a member of the National Assembly; the Busan Council of Societies of Labor, which gathered all the labor counselors in the Busan area in April 1989; and Solidarity for Workers that started in April 1994.

The Solidarity for Workers was created by lawyers, dentists, oriental medical doctors, pharmacists, and medical professionals to support the labor movement and trade unions. Through these groups, I focused on establishing trade unions and supporting their daily activities.

After the June Struggle, the labor movement was undergoing a period of major eruption, and the establishment of trade unions was sought. However, there were few places at the time where workers could receive systematic consultation and support about how to set up trade unions, create regulations, and make collective agreements when unions were established. Busan Labor Research Institute facilitated this role. There were about 200 labor unions that the institute helped to establish, even writing all the necessary documents for establishing the union.

The "Busan Council for Societies of Labor" and "Solidarity for

Workers" were operated by the member union system. When unions became members, the lawyers would become union advisor lawyers, and medical workers provided services with medical benefits along with industrial safety and health counseling.

The "Solidarity for Workers" organization had reached about 130 member unions. It didn't matter whether they belonged to the Federation of Korean Trade Unions (FKTU) or the Korean Confederation of Trade Unions (KCTU). "Solidarity for Workers" was the only labor organization comprising unions from both federations. I regularly gave legal counseling to labor union members and provided training for union officials. Nowadays, there are resident attorneys and legal counsel teams in both labor federations, solving most of the problems themselves without external assistance. That is to say, they now have self-generating power. Seeing the contrast now is quite moving and sad but rewarding at the same time.

The "Solidarity for Workers" was created by lawyers, dentists, oriental medical doctors, pharmacists, and medical professionals to support the labor movement and trade unions. Through these groups, I focused on establishing trade unions and supporting their daily activities.

The Incident at Dong-eui University and Yongsan's Disastrous Accident

I took part in countless cases, among which many remain unforgettable. The 1989 Dong-eui University case is one of them. It was a heartbreaking incident in which several police officers lost their lives.

This case is still in dispute. First, the controversy surrounding its truth continues. The Lee Myung-bak administration has also raised controversy over the fact that the committee for democratization compensation recognized this case as a "democratization movement-related event" and approved compensation. There was even an argument beyond common sense that suggested a special law be established to reverse the decision made by the democratization compensation committee.

Both the students who held the sit-in at the Dong-eui University Library and the police force which was dispatched for strike suppression that day were all young people of this country. They just simply stood in different positions. Some police officers were even students at Dong-eui University who were enlisted to become combat police officers. The students were also at the fire scene and could escape safely because they knew the structure of the library.

As such, the police officers who lost their lives because they were dispatched to suppress the strike and the students who were arrested and imprisoned for what happened that day were all victims of the times. If there was a perpetrator, it was the dictator regime that created such a situation. Currently, attempts are still being made to raise hatred and hostility by highlighting the police officers as victims of students.

The reports by the press and the investigation announcements were very different from the truth. It was reported that the students had poured paint thinner and waited for the combat police, and when the police entered, they threw firebombs on the thinner to create fire in a flash, which burned the police officers to death before they could escape. The controversies that are still circulating today are mainly due to these misunderstandings. However, as confirmed during the court trials, these reports were inaccurate.

There was oil on the floor, not paint thinner. The location where the firebomb was thrown was different from the location where the oil was located. Because the firebomb was self-extinguishing, the police concentrated on searching inside the building. Later, when the flames of the firebombs gradually extinguished and seemed to have gone out completely, explosive combustion suddenly erupted.

It was the oil vapor* that was presumed to be the cause of the explosive combustion during the trial. As the firebomb flame was dying, there was oil vapor from the oil on the nearby ground. When the oil vapor reached combustion concentration, it reached the last flame, dying out, resulting in instant explosive combustion.

The reason for the oil on the floor was not apparent. The question of whether the oil vaporization could occur in such an amount of time, in such an open space with so many police officers conducting a search and with the windows broken by tear gas fired into the building, could not be clarified. In any case, the facts confirmed by the trial proved that the students did not cause the large fire or the death of police officers.

On the other hand, the operational responsibility of the police was clearly identified during the trial. The cause of death of four of the seven police officers was death from a fall, not by fire. The place of the accident was on the seventh floor. A high-rise building operation requires mattresses and safety nets to be placed around the building in preparation for a fall or a death leap. This is especially the case with windows.

On the day of the incident, the police took mattresses and safety nets, but they were piled up at the entrance of the building. The police started the operation without implementing any safety measures. On the seventh floor, where the students were located, there were windows on the north side of the building, but there were no safety devices or boundary troops watching.

When the fire broke out on the seventh floor, police officers hung on the windowsill to avoid the flames. People outside the building weren't aware of this situation for quite some time. The students who were hiding on the roof saw the situation and shouted to the police below, "People are hanging here!"

They screamed, "Mattress! Mattress!" However, the police below didn't know what was going on. They thought the students were cursing at them, so they responded with profanity. Later, they realized and started to bring safety nets and mattresses. On the rooftop, the students encouraged police officers to hang in as the mattresses were installed.

However, police officers who started to lose strength began to fall one by one. The first officer fell to the ground before the safety net and mattress were up. They fell a few minutes apart, and the same happened with the second and third policeman. The fourth officer fell onto the safety net that was installed, but it was useless because there was no mattress under the net. So, while the mattress and the safety net were yet to be installed, four young police officers lost their lives.

The police officers who fell after the safety net and mattress were all set-up, survived. At that time, there was also a student on the window frame. Fortunately for the student, there were fewer flames where he was, so he was able to sit on the windowsill without hanging onto it. He also encouraged the hanging police officers to wait a little longer. He was the last to fall after the safety net and the mattress were installed. He first dropped his glasses to estimate the position and jumped safely onto the safety net and mattress.

Even if the police took only the most basic safety measures, four people didn't have to die. There was another person responsible for neglecting operational safety. The school authorities and the police all knew that the protesters had created firebombs on the seventh floor and also had large amounts of gas and oil. So, it was natural for the police to have prepared for the possibility of a fire there during the operation. The police on that day also considered that and divided the troops' role into three groups.

In other words, when the "opening group" busted the door with a hammer, the "extinguishing group" would first enter and extinguish the fire, followed by the "search team" who would conduct the search. However, on the way to the seventh floor, the extinguishers lagged behind, and the search team went up first, so when entering the seventh floor, the extinguishing team had not arrived yet, and the search team went in first, ill-equipped to extinguish the fire, but left it while they searched. In the meantime, there was the oil vapor. In addition, though one of the extinguishers arrived late, the portable extinguisher was not working.

If the police had extinguished the flames of the firebombs in accordance with the basic safety rules and went into the search, there wouldn't have been a fire or injuries. Apart from the students' responsibility, I believed that the police commanders deserved to be reprimanded for the insufficient operational safety measures. However, there was no such action, even though the combat police officers protested vigorously against the reckless operation. So, after the trial was over, the commanders were charged with professional negligence resulting in death, but this also fizzled out, and they were acquitted.

Such insufficient analysis of safety negligence regarding this incident by the police resulted in the recent Yongsan disaster. The Yongsan disaster was identical to the Dong-eui University case in that even though the police knew that there was a lot of flammable oil in the high-rise watchtower, they rushed to suppress the strike without proper safety preparation, losing many lives, including those of police officers.

Had the police reflected on their responsibility concerning the neglect of safety in the case of Dong-eui University and learned a lesson, the Yongsan accident would not have happened. Police officers I knew at the time of the Dong-eui University incident acknowledged that it was a reckless operation that ignored the basic rules of high-level operations. The police recognized it for themselves. Nevertheless, they went without any form of censure in this case and diluted the apparent responsibilities of the students. I believe the Yongsan disaster is the same. It is indeed a deplorable society.

The Dong-eui University case was the biggest criminal case I worked on in my time as an attorney. It was also the biggest single state of affairs case under the Sixth Republic. There were seventy-seven arrested defendants.

The charge was extensive, and the number of defendants was so large that the prosecutors divided and filed it into eight cases, which the court treated as eight separate cases. I couldn't afford to take care of it alone, so I asked the attorneys of Minbyun to co-defend and share the case with me. Even then, someone needed to oversee the whole case and the entire group of defendants. I couldn't help but take the role.

Though the case was divided into eight, I participated in all eight trials. Even when they were divided, there were so many defendants, and the charges of public prosecution were so enormous that every case was on trial all day. It was challenging to prepare for the trial, but there was also no time to look after other cases on the day of trial. Until the Dong-eui University case was completed, I couldn't even dream of taking on other cases. It was a difficult time.

The prosecution had demanded a death sentence for the student who threw the firebomb that caused the fire. It was also the first death penalty that I received in my tenure as an attorney. The student didn't throw the firebomb, expecting the oil vapor would cause a fire. It was a firebomb that wasn't much different from the countless firebombs thrown by the students of that time, but he was accused of murder because of the unexpected fire and its consequences. Even though I wasn't the one sentenced to the death penalty, I couldn't help but be in tears once I heard the verdict and had to ask for a recess before making the defense.

Fortunately, all the defendants were released in sequence following the suspension of sentencing. In 2002, during the People's Government Administration, forty-six of them were recognized as "democratic activists" at the Democratization Compensation Review Committee.

It's not an insult to the police officers who died on duty to have the students recognized as "democratic activists." The police officers were faithful to their duties and became men of national merit. However, it is regrettable that some people encouraged hatred by claiming that the students' recognition as "democratic activists" was insulting to the officers.

* **Oil Vapor** Gas produced by evaporation or sublimation of oil.

Fabricated Spy Case

Another case that I could not easily forget was the request for re-deliberation concerning *The Shin Family's Spy Ring Case*. The first time I requested a trial was in November 1994. Even then, the pro-democracy movement would not dare present the issues of the fabricated spy case.

This was the period when one could easily be condemned as a communist, so it was hardly thinkable to have someone argue and interfere with the court's decision concerning the case being guilty, declaring that the spy case was fabricated. Even if the case reeked of manipulation, they would pretend not to have seen it.

The one to break that taboo and interference was the Catholic Church. In 1993, the Catholic Human Rights Community founded the "Countermeasures Committee for the Investigation of Espionage." Many priests and a portion of the bishops participated. It was the first time during the military dictatorship era to raise social security issues by presenting the fabricated spy case as a social problem.

The committee's statement was distributed to all Catholic churches and their believers. Special sermons were held, and donations were collected. It was a situation in which our human rights movement received a huge public appraisal.

I was a member of the Catholic Human Rights Commission at the time. The committee conducted basic investigations on cases that were identified as fabricated and made a list. On that list, there were cases associated with the Busan area. They asked that the cases in the Busan region be reviewed.

Amongst them, *The Shin Family's Spy Ring Case* came up, and it was evident by just glancing through the sentencing and the investigation materials that it was manipulated, so I asked for a retrial. Back then, such a case couldn't be appealed for retrial, nor was there any before. That was why I thought it was essential to make a successful retrial case with the most obvious one so that a precedent road would be established for those who were oppressed.

First, I had to interview the defendants who were confined at Jeonju prison, listen to their testimonies, and receive their agreement to file for a retrial. Afterward, I had to go to Japan to meet with the brother, who was instructed to spy on the defendants, record his testimony, receive his notarization, and collect evidential data.

That is how this case became the first to be requested for a retrial amongst the other manipulated cases. I was confident that if the court had the courage, they would accept the request for a retrial.

As I anticipated, the Busan District Court granted the decision on the commencement of a retrial. This was unprecedented and was given prominent coverage. The prosecution appealed but remained in the high court. However, the Supreme Court accepted the re-appeal of the prosecution, and the decisions on the commencement of a retrial were retracted. The first try wasn't successful.

But that didn't mean that we needed to give up. It was decided that the cause for a retrial was to be differently composed and to apply again. In order to secure a new cause for retrial, a lawsuit was filed against the country for indemnification for damage. For this lawsuit, the witnesses who testified regarding espionage in the former spy case trial were summoned. One witness confessed that he couldn't overcome the torture and that what he testified was perjury. With this as the basis, the second attempt for a retrial went through in July 1999. Again, the Busan District Court approved the commencement of a retrial. However, the Busan High Court accepted the prosecution's appeal and canceled the decision to resume the retrial.

We had to wait for the decision to clarify the truth from the "Truth and Reconciliation Committee" (Past Relations Committee) in order to request a retrial for the third time. Eventually, after I retired from the Blue House and returned to my legal practice, the decision for a retrial was received again in February 2009.

Finally, in August 2009, the verdict of not guilty was returned. Afterward, the court pronounced the innocence in a separate written apology, which stated, "No words, written or spoken, can express our sincere apology for the unbearable torture and illegal detention of the defendants, inflicted by the governmental institution coercing a guilty plea. We sincerely apologize for the unspeakable pain that may have been caused."

It had been almost thirty years since being convicted guilty as a spy and nearly fifteen years since the first request for a retrial. During that time, one defendant who filed for a request for a retrial had passed away due to old age, and other defendants who were in their 40s at that time were now in their 70s. Another defendant died in prison due to torture, so the daughter applied for her father's retrial. As the verdict was confirmed, the Shin family received 20 billion won (US $17,520,000.00) in compensation from the country and 3.8 billion won (US $3,327,861.00) in damages. Nevertheless, the question remains: what happened to their lives that were erased due to coerced testimony?

The court quickly straightened the wrongdoings of the past trials and apologized. But the country still did not properly do so to those who were victims of the fabricated spies. The police and the prosecutors still had no remorse or self-reflection on the scandal involving massive torture and illegal detention. The majority of the perpetrators, who were police officers who received special promotions and bounty bonus benefits, continued to strongly argue in court, refusing to take any type of responsibility for torture and improper investigation policies.

I believe that in order for a country to become a proper one, it must be able to financially compensate and sincerely apologize for the past damages derived from the governmental authority's illegitimacy and unjust exercises.

Fight Against Regionalism

As a member of the National Assembly (NA), Roh quickly became an attention-grabbing politician. He not only became a nationwide NA hearing star, but his other parliamentary activities were also unparalleled among the newly elected MNAs. However, it wasn't the election to the National Assembly that evaluated him as a political leader but his career of defeat. Since his opposition to the Three-Party merger*, he repeatedly faced failures and frustrations in the pursuit of his cause, and those experiences put him on the list of presidential candidates.

The people thought of him highly as a politician of principle who tolerated personal disadvantages, but in reality, it was truly a painful journey.

All I could help with was lending him some money when he was running short of operating expenses for his office during his time out of the National Assembly office. He continued to do what he considered worthwhile, and I similarly continued with what I thought was worthwhile.

The first time he told me about his desire to run for president in the 15th Presidential Election was after seeing candidate Lee In-je leave his

He continued to do what
he considered worthwhile,
and I similarly continued with
what I thought was worthwhile.

party to run independently because Lee couldn't submit to the regulations of the ruling party's candidate nominations. Roh said he would run as the opposition candidate because "You shouldn't tolerate such foul play." Everyone opposed it at the time.

I, too, disagreed. I believed that it was too early. It was feasible to keep the goal in mind and try for the next election. Although he had a good image as "The NA Hearing Star" and his principles, there was also a lingering image due to "nameplate throwing" and "resigning from office." A sudden run for the presidency could seem like an overt action. He accepted the objections of the people around him. But from then on, I kept his vision in my heart and prepared steadily for it. We established a planning team and studied hard.

I had the same thoughts when he came down to Busan to run for the 2000 general election. I objected to leaving Jongro and coming down to Busan for that reason. My response to him was, "Looking ahead to the presidential election, coming down to Busan won't help. Rather, it could be a disruption. YS* from Busan just finished his presidential office, so another president getting elected from Busan was unlikely to happen. Even if you were elected, there is the possibility of becoming just a local leader. It is advantageous for the presidential election to leave the area and be elected again in Jongro. Then, you can benefit from the advantages of being from Yeongnam. Park Chan-jong also left Busan to be a member of the National Assembly for Seoul and became a rising candidate for the presidential election." I also didn't want to see him suffer the pain of losing the election again.

But no one could break his stubbornness. His will to break the regionalism was too strong. During the Busan Mayor's Election in 1995, the people around him and even his advisors suggested running as an independent candidate without a political party, but he refused until the end, saying that there would be no advantage in winning the election.

In fact, if he had been elected in Busan in the 2000 general election, I think the presidential campaign would have been delayed a little longer.

But who could understand how this world worked? He lost the election again, but tremendous support and encouragement flooded in. It was different from the previous support. It was a support that looked forward to him as a national leader. It was a collective support to draw him beyond that simple support.

Finally, on September 6, 2001, he officially declared his candidacy for the presidential election in Busan.

* **Three-Party Merger** In January 1990, the Democratic Justice Party, the ruling party in power, led by President Roh Tae-woo, merged with two opposition parties (the United Democratic Party led by Kim Young-sam and the Republican Party led by Kim Jong-pil). To overcome the difficulties caused by the opposition being the majority, the Roh government offered a secret agreement to amend the Constitution to create a cabinet-run parliamentary government. It birthed an enormous ruling party through the three-party merger. Not only did the Democratic camp divide, but it also instigated regionalism, resulting in regional politics and executive politics. There was strong opposition arguing that it was a collusion with the military regime.
* **YS** Former President Kim Young-Sam's English initials and nickname.

2002's Admiration

After that, he started the presidential campaign, but it was different from any other politician we had seen before. The staff around him naturally recommended he grow the organization and prepare funds. Instead, he set up a learning team with experts in each field and worked hard to learn the necessary knowledge and skills for the state's administration.

He listened to and discussed with young experts from various fields, including foreign affairs, security, education, welfare, and economy. More than half of his entire schedule was probably immersed in learning. Quite a few experts who helped study at that time became members of the Participatory Government. Minister Lee Jong-seok was a classic example in foreign affairs and security. Roh's outstanding debate skills during the presidential election and his excellent intellectual ability during the presidency were achieved through this continuous learning process. It was very much like him to prepare in that manner.

During the process of the Public Participatory Election for the Democratic Party Candidates, I helped with the Busan and Ulsan elections.

The electoral roll system at the time was a method of selecting a certain number of electors from a pool of pre-registered electors through a lottery. Therefore, it was important to register as many electors as possible, who were sure to participate directly in the vote. More than having several lists of existing names, it was important to secure a lot of loyal voters. We made every effort to secure real supportive people and people with actual voting commitment.

We pulled out every possible card in the Busan and Gyeongnam areas. We utilized our entire democratization movement network. I was especially confident that Ulsan's labor line was strong. The results of the labor movement and the support for the labor movement that Assemblyman Roh and I had been doing for a long time were plain to see. The entire democratization movement in Busan was on board. In addition, the network of existing democrats, as well as the Busan Commercial High School network (Roh's alma mater), were very favorable. We definitely won the electoral roll registration battle.

The emotional work was done in Gwangju. Later, I found out that countless people at the bottom of the working class worked as hard as we did to bring about the success. At last, he was confirmed as the Democratic presidential candidate. But this was only the beginning.

As each campaign headquarters launched into the respective provinces, I took the role of the campaign leader in Busan. If the favorable ratings from the early days had been maintained, I wouldn't have taken the role. Candidate Roh probably wouldn't have asked me if that was the case. But it was a very difficult situation. I had to take the position.

After becoming a candidate, the most difficult time in the presidential race centered on the local election defeat, the drop in the approval ratings, the shaking of the candidates of the Democrat members of parliament, the drop in the approval rating again, the discussion of candidate substitution in the party, the partial withdrawal and many other things...

There wasn't much we could do in Busan. All we could do was keep the campaign going to defend the candidate against a huge conspiracy to intimidate the candidate to fall off eventually. It was a desperate situation. I asked university professors for assistance and various intellectual groups. Support declarations followed in various areas of Busan. It was the same nationwide. I have frequently traveled to and from Seoul because of this. Candidate Roh fought through well. There was no shaking, no uncertainty. He faced many difficulties head-on with his heart and his gut.

The turning point was the candidate's unification with Chung Mong-joon. I expressed my opinion that it was necessary to unify with Candidate Chung and that it would be better to use polling as the unification method.

The unification of the survey method at that time was a huge adventure. Candidate Roh was quite behind in the polls, so there were concerns from the Democratic Party and Seoul about unifying candidates in terms of polls. However, the bold acceptance of disadvantages resulted in a favorable appeal to people.

However, Candidate Roh's worries were elsewhere. They weren't about decisions on the unification method or the survey. He did not worry about *"Am I going to win if I do that? What do I do if I don't?"*... He pondered whether he would be able to campaign for Candidate Chung with heartfelt enthusiasm when he lost.

Candidate Roh's core identity differed from Candidate Chung Mong-joon's. Deciding to run for him like his own election was not an easy task. However, he accepted that it was his duty to help Chung unite in unification. He believed that he shouldn't consider unification at all if there was no such attitude. If Roh had lost his race, he would have really worked hard for Chung as if it was his own election. Dramatic drama with a twist was redrawn from the candidate unification.

However, the difficulty was waiting again. It was a more difficult challenge than the unification process. Chung Mong-joon asked for a coalition government for "half the power." Not only that, he wanted it to be in writing. He wasn't just asking for half but for certain parts of the cabinet to be shared. If Roh had not accepted it, Chung wouldn't have completed the unification plan.

The majority of the democrats asked Roh to do what Chung was asking for. I persuaded Candidate Roh to deal with the situation later because it was a "political promise" anyway. It was pressure, not persuasion. Since so many people were talking about the same thing, Candidate Roh had a difficult time sorting through it all and asked for my opinion.

I talked about principles. "We've been through it many times, but it's the right thing to go on principle when it's difficult. Looking back, it was always the best choice. Even if it was difficult, it turned out to be right again afterward. I think your idea, Candidate Roh, is correct." He must have been quite lonely, as he was very pleased to hear that I supported him.

The election was coming to an end. Two days before the election, a huge crowd gathered at the Busan Seomyeon intersection. It was the last Busan campaign. Candidate Roh stood proudly on the podium and received applause, which sounded like thunder, supporting him. The speech had captured the people's hearts. It was on a whole new level compared to his former parliament or mayor campaign speeches. It was more than just his speech skills. His insights on the overall management of the country couldn't be compared with that of the past. I could feel how vigorously he had studied after deciding to run for the presidency. It was truly outstanding. It was to the point where I wondered if anyone could speak Korean that well in a political speech. The people who gathered at the Seomyeon interchange seemed to be mesmerized by his speech. Even I went back as an individual citizen and was deeply moved. If it was Election Day, we couldn't possibly have lost.

However, in the 2002 presidential election, the day of fate was not the day of the presidential election but the day before. I wondered if there would be another election like this.

The night before the election, Candidate Chung Mong-joon completely broke the unification agreement and withdrew his support. The whole nation shook. It was as if the election had been completely ruined.

It seemed as if all the key people in the vicinity of Seoul urged Candidate Roh to visit Chung. The persuasion probably didn't go well, as

Candidate Roh stood proudly on the podium and received applause, which sounded like thunder, supporting him. The speech had captured the people's hearts. It was on a whole new level compared to his former parliament or mayor campaign speeches.

I received a phone call. It was the former National Assemblyman, Kim Won-ki. Candidate Roh was apparently sleeping, despite everyone's urges, so I was asked to convince him. He ended up going and was turned back at the door. His lonely return made the supporters even angrier.

The next day, there was only one thing we could do: to encourage voter participation and increase turnout. Busan had dismissed its frontline headquarters telephone team the night before. I hastily called them back. Not only them but also the entire campaign headquarters; everyone, all day, was on their phones, appealing to their friends and family to vote. We thought it was just us, but apparently many people around the country seemed to have done the same thing. The hearts of the people began to move. I could feel it.

The campaign headquarters office continuously analyzed the results of the turnout and exit survey every hour. Usually, in the morning, a lot of elderly people vote first, so it was expected that we would lag behind. By 11:00 a.m., the exit survey was still behind, but the trend was changing. It was clear that the gap was narrowing. It was after 1-2 p.m., and I could see us winning. Lee Gwang-jae of the Seoul situation room told me the same thing.

In the afternoon, the exit survey was reversed. I was convinced. At 6 p.m, I sat down in front of the headquarters office TV. The final exit survey results were announced. It was as expected. It was our victory. Everyone hugged and cheered. Some were crying and celebrating the win. My heart was overflowing. It was one of the happiest days of my life.

*When the results were clear,
people poured out on the streets.
It was a festival in Busan.
The streets were overflowing
with crowds of people rushing
and marching, people hugging,
people singing or shouting
slogans and celebrating.*

When the results were clear, people poured out on the streets. It was a festival in Busan. The streets were overflowing with crowds of people rushing and marching, hugging, singing or shouting slogans, and celebrating. I wanted to be swept into the crowd for that moment.

But I was worried. I was concerned that there would be accidents. I called the Busan police chief and asked for their cooperation. When I still wasn't at ease, I looked around the streets. Citizens enjoyed the night while keeping order and the police understood the people. People who recognized me had gathered and celebrated together. It was a beautiful night.

It was on these same streets I walked with Attorney Roh, shot at with tear gas. We laid down on these same streets shouting democratization. That street was now full of joy. I wanted the moment to last forever. I had no idea what pain or suffering we would face in the time to come.

My Mother and Father

My parents' hometown was located in Heungnam, South Hamgyeoung Province, which is currently North Korean territory. Many generations of our household lived in Heungnam. It has been said that there were enough families and relatives with the surname of "Moon" to have formed a municipal village. Pine forests surrounded the village, so it was called "Solan" village, which was well-known around the vicinity. However, the happiness that my parents and relatives experienced there was a shortcut when the Korean War started.

My parents left their hometown in December 1950 due to the Heungnam Evacuation*. They had to carry my older sister, who was still nursing at that time, to the evacuation site. The South Korean and U.S. military troops went to the Tumen River but were forced to retreat after the unexpected intervention by the Chinese Army. It was believed that if the battle line had been quickly fortified, they would have recovered.

So, the elderly residents remained, and many of the younger people thought that they would be able to avoid hardships and leave their homes. Even within our household, my grandparents remained. My father passed away without knowing if his parents were still dead or alive. Later, we heard the news that they had passed but received no specific information as to exactly when.

The evacuation was made via the U.S. LST* vessels. However, the refugees didn't know where the U.S. military troops were taking them. We lived in the bottom of a boat for the next two nights and three days. During the middle of the evacuation, when U.S. military restrictions loosened, we were able to climb up the ladder to the deck. At that time, the nearby light that seemed to be closely shining from land was called Pohang. It was then that we were able to guess that our destination was the southern coast.

On the way, the U.S. soldiers even distributed candy to us because it was Christmas. The place where they brought refugees was a temporary refugee camp on Geoje Island, South Gyeongsang Province. My mother said it was strange to see all the green fields when they arrived in Geoje because when she left Heungnam, everywhere you looked was white, covered with snow. The green barley fields in the evergreen forest were so very different from the landscape of her hometown. My mother's first impression of Geoje was that *this is a really warm southern country*.

Though it was winter, the refugees who were transported there without provisions were welcomed by the warm weather and the equally generous and warm personalities of the Geoje civilians, who embraced the refugees wholeheartedly. They shared their food and cooking utensils, such as pots and pans, and helped the refugees overcome difficulties. Later, after settling down, many people scattered and moved to various places in the country, but there would be times when they'd gather and reminisce about the evacuation years. They would talk about and express their gratitude for the warm hospitality of the people from Geoje Island. We even talked about and wondered, "If the opposite had happened and the southern people had come to Heungnam for evacuation, would we have treated them so well?" The Heungnam refugees, who passed through Geoje Island, couldn't forget their generosity toward them and started a Gratitude Movement. The Heungnam Citizens' Association, or those who survived, personally sent scholarships to the schools in Geoje.

My parents thought they would just be leaving their hometown for two to three weeks. So, they came without any financial support. Empty-handed and penniless, they started their lives in a strange land in the South without any provisions. It was a weary endeavor.

My father was able to evacuate with his close relatives. Still, no one from my mother's side came because my mother's side lived in the northern section of Heungnam, across the Seongchoen River, and the U.S. military blocked the passageway across the Gunja Bridge. According to something I read about the Heungnam Evacuation, the reason for the roadblock was that they couldn't handle the massive crowds of refugees. It also prevented the enemy from interfering with the refugees' evacuation. So, my mother was all alone in the south, with no friends or relatives. She would jokingly say that there were many times that she wanted to run away because everything was just too difficult to cope with, but there wasn't anywhere on earth that she would be able to return to.

I was born during the evacuation. It was when we lived in a rented one-room country house. However, at the same time, the house owner was pregnant. Consequently, my mother had to deliver me in a different house that they found temporarily. It happened because there was a proverb saying that it isn't right to simultaneously birth children under the same roof. There were no sons in our family household, allowing me to become the first, and I was showered with expressions of blessings and happiness.

Later, around my mother's 60th birthday, I took her to the location where my parents lived during the evacuation, in addition to where I was born. Though thirty years had passed, my mother still remembered the neighborhood and the house she lived in. People similar to my mother's age recognized her and happily greeted her by calling her by my sister's name, "Jae-wuhl!" just like they did in former days.

My father worked at a prison camp doing labor work. My mother bought eggs cheaply in Geoje, balanced them on her head, had me on her back, and sold them in Busan. With that, they saved a little, and when they saved a little bit more, we moved to Youngdo, Busan, shortly before I entered elementary school. They didn't move before then, postponing the idea of relocating until the opportunity for my elementary school entrance was secured. On the day we moved, I remember getting off a big boat and passing fields filled with drooping stacks of yellow millet before arriving at the house. At that time, Youngdo was the administrative district in Busan, situated in a rural area surrounded by many rice fields.

Though I was born in Geoje, I don't remember it since I lived there when I was very young. Many of the other households were similar, causing them to have no recollection as well. Still, it is my birthplace, and where my parents evacuated, so I always think fondly of Geoje. When I was in the Blue House, since I was from Geoje, whenever there were requests for guidance with pending issues from that location, I couldn't help but show interest and consideration.

* **Heungnam Evacuation** The withdrawal of refugees from the Heungnam Port by the U.S. Army 10th Corps and the Korean 1st Army Corps of the East Front for ten days from December 15th to December 24th, 1950.

* **LST** A military trap to land troops or tanks.

Poverty

My father graduated from Hamheung Agricultural High School when Korea was under Japanese imperialism. Many called that "The place of Hamheung Farming Industry." It was a prestigious school in that area. My father heard many people around the area tell him he was one of the elite. My older aunt, who practically raised him, said that no one ever saw him studying for the entrance exams when he was a child. Still, he was the only student in the family and neighborhood who had been accepted into the Hamheung Farming Industry. After he graduated, my father passed the civil service examination and served as chief director of agricultural affairs at Heungnam City Hall under the North Korean regime.

At that time, he was forced into joining the Communist Party, but he endured and didn't enlist. Even during the brief period when U.N. troops were stationed there, he served as the agricultural chief. Afterward, he evacuated. Apparently, there was an opportunity to hire people who had worked in the North as civil servants. However, when he was the agricultural chief, he suffered difficulty being pressured into joining the Communist Party, so he decided he wouldn't work as a civil servant any longer. That's why he went into business after we moved to Busan. In my opinion, he didn't seem like the business type. He was very quiet in nature and didn't drink. I saw him as best suited to be a civil-servant or a teacher.

My father's business involved buying socks at the Busan Sock Factory and supplying them to salesmen near the Junnam area.

Unfortunately, my father piled up debt due to the outstanding amounts of credit accumulated over several years while in business. Many of his creditors called for bankruptcy, causing his debt to accumulate even more. He struggled to pay for the things he purchased from the factory for a long time. He kept all his statements, thinking that he might be able to get his payment back from his clients. However, that day never came, and due to overwhelming debt, he was ruined, never being able to recover again. Since he was away from home, he had no one to lean on. Afterward, my father was economically challenged. We couldn't escape from poverty.

My father originally had a quiet personality, but he hardly spoke after he failed in business. It hurt that our family was poor, but what was more heartbreaking was seeing your father lose his purpose for living because of national division and war. My father passed away during the most difficult time of my life. It was the time when I was expelled from my university, got arrested, was released from prison, enlisted in the army, and existed as a wanderer because I wasn't able to re-enter the university after my military service was completed. I know I can't recover and make up for things I have done in the past, and it will be my lifelong regret that I wasn't able to show him the type of person I've become today.

After my father failed in business, my mother was the breadwinner of our home. My mother also did not have any economic advantages and was barely able to sustain the household. She did her best with different odd jobs, but those jobs did not provide much money. My mother's first job was to sell relief supplies at a market stall. There was even a time when we had a small convenience store in our neighborhood that only comprised a few houses due to poverty. So, it was evident that it wasn't going to be successful. She also delivered briquettes. If we had been supplied by a factory that sold briquettes in large quantities, though we would have been exhausted, we could have made some money. But that wasn't the case. We just made a little in our store and sold to local areas. As a result, this was why we were habitually barely able to prosper and meet our basic needs.

However, my mother never asked my father to help with the briquette deliveries. If she needed help, she always asked me or my younger brother. After classes were over or it was a national holiday, we would help carry the briquettes and deliver them. I was always embarrassed delivering them and getting dirty from the briquette soot. My younger brother helped greatly, while I complained a lot, hurting my mother's feelings.

On one occasion, my mother and I loaded the cart. I pulled it from the front, and my mother pushed it from the back. We were going downhill, and she lost her grip, causing me to fall due to the unexpected weight. Some of the briquettes were broken, and I wasn't injured, but my mother was greatly distressed.

Everyone was poor at that time, not just us. There were North Korean refugees at Youngdo then, too. There were more refugees like us than native people around our mountain roads.

A large fire broke out in the shanty towns of the refugee residences beneath Yongdusan Park in Busan and all the shanty towns were burnt down. Several shelters were created for the victims. The village below was one of them, and it was a devastatingly poor neighborhood.

Often, many said that North Korean defectors had a lot of successful people because of their strong willpower to live. But I didn't think so because the people who hated the North Korean regime before the war happened were usually well-off upper class who liquidated their family fortune, so they had a better lifestyle. However, it was different for those who suddenly had to escape due to the outbreak of war. It was never easy for anyone to be successful and escape penniless. Most of the time, it was difficult to escape from poverty back then.

Since many people were poor, a nearby cathedral distributed emergency relief food. It was usually composed of surplus agricultural products that the United States provided gratuitously. The distribution mainly consisted of corn flour and powdered milk*. It helped to supplement a meal. When I was in first and second grade in elementary school, I would carry a bowl and wait in line during distribution day to receive our family's portion after school. I hated doing it, but it was something that the eldest son had to do.

Sometimes, the nuns gave us candy or fruit in our hands. At that time, the nuns in their attire looked like angels through my young eyes. Because of their hospitality, my mother was the first to become Catholic, and I was baptized into the faith in third grade. In Youngdo, there is a cathedral called Shinsun Cathedral, and I got married there. Even to this day, my mother attends that cathedral. Since she has been attending the cathedral for a long time and is strong in her faith, she served as a vice president of the women's pastoral association and was the director of the cathedral's credit association.

Poverty was also present in schools. The Namhang Elementary School, which I attended, was initially small. However, due to the increased number of refugees, there were more than a thousand students per grade level. Inevitably, the school built a temporary classroom on the playground by putting up boards on the sides and a roof above the area. It was called the "Temporary School Building," and I studied there until I attended third grade.

The classroom flooring was just dirt, forming a lot of water puddles on the ground when it rained a lot. If that happened, the classes were discontinued and students were sent home. During Chuseok* in 1959, when I was in first grade, "Sarah," the biggest typhoon to hit the area of Busan, swooped in. Nothing was left of our classroom when I went to school after the Chuseok holiday. Everything flew away due to the strong

At that time, the nuns in their attire looked like angels through my young eyes. Because of their hospitality, my mother was the first to become Catholic and I was baptized into the faith when I was in third grade.

winds. From that point on, we just sat on the ground in the classroom to learn. There weren't any desks, so we had to hang drawing boards from our necks and put our books on top of them when we needed to study. Since we didn't have a roof, whenever it rained, classes were canceled, and we were sent home. After the sixth graders graduated, the school constructed a temporary school building for the students.

When "Sarah" passed by our house, the roof also flew off, and I remember that day quite vividly. At that time, our house was built of mud bricks, and the roof was made of roofing*. It was the day my father left for his business and couldn't return home.

The wooden kitchen door rattled as the storm thundered in, causing the hinges to fall off. My mother and I tried to keep the door from opening, and my sister helped. But we couldn't overcome the power of the wind and lost grip of the door. Once the door flung wide open, the rest of the hinges were gone. And in an instant, the wind blew into the house, filling it and expanding it to the point where I felt the wind swirling from above and realized that our roof was completely gone. We couldn't even find where the roof had blown away to.

When I was in elementary school, a monthly fee was required to be paid. At first, it was called "Monthly School Fee" and later changed to "Parent-Teacher Association Fee." When I was in sixth grade, it changed again to "School Supporting Association Fee." Due to poverty, many children couldn't pay the money on time. The homeroom teacher would call the names of the students who didn't pay and pressured them to do so. Sometimes, they would call our names, make us stand up, and scold us in front of the class. If the students still didn't bring the money, they would tell them to go home and get it during class.

There was a time when eighty students were sent home, and only twenty were left in the classroom. Though we were poor, my parents were always able to pay the school fees on time. However, there were times when I was late with my payments and was kicked out of school and sent home like the other children.

I realized that when one is poor, one matures more rapidly. When the teacher kicked them out of the class to go home, most didn't because they knew going home wouldn't solve anything and would only cause their parents heartaches. We would go to the back of the school by ourselves and return to class when it was time for it to end for the day. We would lie as if we went home by saying, "No one was home," or "My mom said she will give it to you on so and so day."

When I was in sixth grade, some of us were kicked out of the classroom again, so we went to a manhwabang*. After spending some time there, we literally bumped into my homeroom teacher on our way out of the building. We were all taken to school and were beaten. Some students even dropped out due to the repetitive difficulties of their school life. Later, when I met some of them, they would be working at a shoe store or a tailor shop as an assistant. When graduation was getting closer, I discovered it wasn't necessary for the entire class to pay the school fees. If my memory serves me correctly, only 2/3 of the class needed to pay.

If there was more money collected than necessary, it became part of the homeroom teacher's income. That was why they urged everyone to pay.

The poor children would go to the public bathhouses during the Lunar New Year and Chuseok. The teachers would hold hygienic examinations and have students take off their shirts. They would scrub the students in front of the class and embarrass them in front of the others if their skin exfoliated with dirty, dead skin. I had never experienced such embarrassment, but when I saw other children going through it, I felt mortified and rebellious.

When it was time for lunch to be brought to school, many of the students weren't able to. The school provided lunches for the students who couldn't bring anything. There were many times when the school wasn't constantly supplied with the same amount of lunches, so there were times when we would receive one whole corn rice cake or a half. When there wasn't enough to do that, they made corn porridge with the supplies.

However, there were no bowls to serve the meals in. It wasn't much of a problem when we received the rice cakes, but we didn't know what to do when it was porridge. There were times when we would borrow the lids of the lunch boxes of the children who brought their own lunch. We would take turns if there weren't enough lids to go around. I also received my lunch meals like that, and whenever I had to borrow a lid, it hurt my pride. I also thought *the school should be providing us with bowls, and if they couldn't, why can't they just tell us to bring bowls from home?*

Due to my personal experiences, I'm interested in the free school lunch debates. During the Participatory Government, it started to provide meals for the "underfed children during vacation." When the first vacation ended, I checked the data to find that the delivery rates were unexpectedly low. When I researched the reason for the low delivery rates, many students decided to go hungry rather than have their self-esteem hurt. We had to find a way to deliver the food without hurting their feelings. I confirmed that it was important to keep and protect the children's pride as much as providing them with food.

There were many things I wanted to do but couldn't due to poverty. I couldn't ask my parents for anything that involved money. Even to this day, I can't ride a bike. There never was a bike in our household growing up. There was a bicycle rental shop in front of the junior high school that I attended, and many students borrowed bikes after school, but I couldn't because I didn't have money.

Because I didn't have money, I had to make my favorite toys, such as tops, stick-tossing, and kites, at home. Other children had their fathers or brothers make them. However, since my father was never home and on the road selling things, I had to make them myself. Even if my father were home, he wouldn't have been much help since he had no craftsmanship.

I wanted to make a reel for my kite. I knew how to make a straight reel with my skills, but I needed carpentry skills to make a bottle reel to wind up the string quickly. I remember not being able to make it well and being sad about it every year. I even tried making a hoop many times but always failed to make the hoop stick.

When I was in third or fourth grade, there was a time when I used a kitchen knife to carve a stick-tossing stick and accidentally cut my index finger. I nearly cut almost 1/3 of my nail off. It was excruciating, and there was a lot of blood. I was scared, but no one was home, and I took a cloth and took care of the wound myself.

Until the wound healed, I applied a mercuricum* application called akajingki. I was able to endure the pain, so I ended up not telling the adults and hiding it. If something like this happened these days, I'm sure that I would have been taken to the hospital and gotten stitched up. I believe my self-reliance and independence developed because I tried to resolve and try things myself, no matter how hard it seemed. This is a gift that poverty has given me.

There is an even bigger gift that poverty has given me. Because of being poverty-stricken, my present values of "Money isn't that important" seemed to have been embedded in my mind. Perhaps it was my pride that helped me survive poverty. It was probably the same for my parents. Though they raised us in poverty, they taught us not to think of money as the best value. "Money is important, but it isn't the most important thing." I believe that those values have helped me a lot during my life.

My parents thought education was very important. Though the monthly payments were late, they made sure I had it. But poverty still made me shy. When the teacher asked questions, other students would raise their hands and shout "Me, me!" but I never raised mine. When the teacher directly asked me questions, I would reluctantly answer, but never was there a time that I voluntarily raised my hand. And of course, I provided no reason for my parents to have been called into school.

* **Powdered Milk** Dried milk powder without additives was used as reconstituted milk when water was added, and it had a nutty taste.
* **Roofing** Long roofing material in the shape of a sheet.
* **Chuseok** Korean Thanksgiving.
* **Manhwabang** A cafe like place where you can read comic books.
* **Mercuricum** A disinfectant made from a reddish-brown organic mercury compound.

Problem Child

When I was in elementary school, I was an inconspicuous child. I was small and weak. I was very introverted and never received attention from my teachers. I don't even remember meeting my teachers outside of class. But I'm sure that the teacher wasn't able to give individual attention to every student because there were more than eighty students per grade level in that poor neighborhood.

The teacher would give out report cards at the end of a semester and school year. Up until fifth grade, we were given As, Bs, Cs, and Ds. There weren't many As, but more Bs, Cs, and Ds. Even my behavioral development wasn't that great. I wasn't interested in my grades, and my parents didn't say much when they saw my report card.

Back then, there was an entrance exam for Junior High school. So, when we entered sixth grade, the school made us stay late and study. We took exams every day and frequently took mock examinations as well. After I studied like that, I realized for the first time that I was good at studying.

One day, my homeroom teacher called and praised me for my good grades. He told me that if we had tutoring sessions together, I would be able to get accepted into a prestigious school, and I should go home and tell my parents. I found out that the students who studied well generally started to have study sessions with the homeroom teacher during the second semester of the fifth grade. Students met after school and would study late into the night at the teacher's house. However, the tuition fee was impossible for our household, and I told him I couldn't afford it. I didn't even bring this conversation up to my parents.

I was quite naïve back then and just studied diligently. The entrance examination consisted of all subjects, including music, art, and physical education. Physical education was the only practical course, while art and music were written exams. Throughout elementary school, I had never been taught music with a harmonium. We only memorized the scale's basic notes and syllable names, do rae mi fa so la si do, and were tested.

The physical education exam consisted of running, long jumping, throwing, pull-ups, and more. My arm strength was very weak, so I couldn't do pull-ups. A friend recommended consuming a lot of vinegar to make my bones flexible and do well with pull-ups. It was tempting, so I gulped vinegar when my mother wasn't around. It wasn't the type of vinegar we have these days, which is brewed, but it was glacial acetic acid*. As soon as it entered my mouth, it felt like it was on fire. With sudden reflexes, I spit it out and didn't swallow. If I did, I'm certain it would have been dangerous. Still, my lips, the inside of my mouth, and my esophagus were swollen, and I wasn't able to eat properly for several days. The embarrassment was much greater for me to deal with than the actual pain that I wasn't able to lift my head. Later, the story spread to the lower classmen, providing them an example of what being too tenacious for preparing for entrance exams could be like.

Fortunately, at that time, I was able to get into Gyeongnam Middle School, which was considered a prestigious school in Busan. There weren't many who were accepted from my elementary school. My parents were ecstatic. I think this may have been the greatest accomplishment I was able to give them since my birth. My father took me to a tailor shop to get my school uniform tailored at Gukje Market. And whenever he went there, he made sure to find someone from Heungnam and requested service from them. When the owner asked for the school name, I still remember how proud my father was when he received congratulatory messages from him.

Once I passed the entrance exam for junior high school, the high school exam wasn't that difficult.

Gyeongnam Middle School was located in the downtown neighborhood where the students were generally well off. On the first day of class, I learned that many students learned English at private institutes before enrollment. Many were able to read books before they were taught at the junior high level. Quotes like "Boys, be ambitious!" were posted in the hallways, and the students read them and tried to understand what they meant. For me, all this was new, and I was disheartened. The atmosphere was quite different from the elementary school, where there were many poor students.

The way they hung out and spent their money was quite different, and it was difficult for me to get along with them. There was a time when I went to a friend's house and was amazed at the luxurious house, garden, and furniture that I had never seen before. When I saw the workers in the house call him "young master," I felt even more intimidated than before. There were many houses that had housemaids as well, and for the first time, I experienced what true inequity in the world felt like.

Gradually, I started spending much of my time at the library. I was the happiest when I read books. The habit of reading books was a great virtue inspired by my father. Whenever my father left for business, he usually returned home in a month. When he did, he would bring back fairy tale books, children's literature, and biographies home, such as *The Fairy Tales of Hans Christian Andersen*, Kang So-chun's children's literature, and the children's version of Plutarch's biography. He would also bring novels authored by foreign writers like *A Homeless Child*. It was fascinating to read such books that weren't school textbooks, and until my father brought me new ones, I would read them repeatedly a couple of times.

Once I realized the joy of reading, I thirsted for them. When my father quit work, the books stopped coming as well. So, when a new school year started, I would read all my books as well as my sister's, who was three years older than me. I read the stories in the Korean language and Social Life textbooks. Then, I entered junior high school and discovered the library. There were endless numbers of books, and I read them. I fell in love with reading so much that when I was a sophomore, for three months, I stayed until they were about to close, helped them organize the chairs, and then headed home.

Every chance I got, I would go to the school library or borrow books until I graduated from high school. First, I started reading Korean novels, then foreign novels, and gradually expanded my reading scope. Because I read randomly, I read *the Sasangye Journal** relatively early, waking my consciousness and senses. I even read sexual novels as well. I read everything without systematic plans or goals. For the next six years, I read a lot of books throughout junior and high school. I became aware of and learned about the world and life through them, and a sense of society was formed.

Reading books like Kim Chan-sam's *Travelogue of Traveling around the World Penniless*, which I read during junior high school, gave me the dream to travel around the world. Of course, the dreaming never stopped. Still, going to Nepal, trekking in India, and visiting the Silk Road were the results of that dream.

I still enjoy reading books. It actually goes far beyond enjoyment, but sometimes I feel like I have a reading addiction. Whenever I go on a trip, my luggage is always heavier than it needs to be because of the books I bring. Even when resting, I need a book at arm's length or feel emptiness.

Naturally, my school studies were pushed back. I didn't think studying for the college entrance exam was important. I was just satisfied with maintaining my high rank. Even when my parents saw me reading other books during the test period, they didn't scold me. Since I was maintaining my high rank in school, they just believed that I was doing my job.

My parents didn't nag or interfere with me studying for the six years I was in junior and high school. They just believed in me. With the freedom they gave me, I didn't use it for my studies but in other areas of interest. Eventually, I paid the price for not studying hard at school for my college entrance exam. Through reading, I developed my inner thoughts and social consciousness, which I believe was the reward for the price I paid.

I was able to raise social consciousness relatively early because I started reading newspapers quite early. For the same reason that I thirsted for books, I began reading the newspaper that my father read when I was young.

It was because I needed to read. There were quite a lot of Chinese characters in the newspaper at the time. At first, I only chose parts like serial novels that did not contain any Chinese characters. Gradually, I started to read articles that were mixed with them. As I continued to read, I understood the Chinese characters by understanding the context of what was in the front and back of the articles. The ones that were used often became easy for me to understand. My father was a regular subscriber to the *Dong-A Ilbo*, and I was able to analyze and develop criticism of the reality of society.

As I entered high school and as my knowledge grew, I started to develop rebellion against society. When I became a senior, I began to drink

My parents didn't nag or interfere with my studies for the six years I was in junior and high school. They just believed in me. With the freedom they gave me, I didn't use it in my studies but in other places.
Eventually, I paid the price for not studying hard at school for my college entrance exam. But through reading I was able to development my inner thoughts and social consciousness and believe that it was the reward for the price I paid.

and smoke. The Gyeongnam High School that I attended was very proud of its prestigious school and would boastfully say it was "The best, south of the Han River." They emphasized on college entrance exams, but it was different from nowadays. Students studied on their own. It was also because the entrance examination courses differed from university to university. Seoul National University tested on all subject areas, while Yeonsi University and Koryo University tested on core subjects. Students didn't only study as students do these days, but they also participated in club activities and traveled or went camping during vacation. There were also a lot of students who smoked and drank when they were seniors in high school, and the administration pretended not to notice. Once I started to drink, I began to hang out with others who also drank and some who only "hung around." Since I liked soccer and enjoyed kicking the ball around, I became friends with athletic students as well. Studying was pushed even further, but I was able to make a lot of diverse friends.

Then, there was a time when I was punished at school. It was during my senior spring picnic. Because of college entrance exams, our autumn picnic was canceled, making this our last school outing. During our free time, a couple of my friends and I went to a nearby village, bought drinks and drank. One drank too much that he could not take care of himself. We were worried that we would get caught, and we did. During assembly time, he lost consciousness and collapsed in front of the homeroom teacher. We had no choice but to admit the truth, and some of us had to take our friend to the hospital. He woke up after getting his stomach pumped. The school debated whether or not we should be punished but agreed that we learned our lesson by admitting the truth, and only the student who passed out was suspended.

Afterward, towards the end of summer vacation, I played a game of soccer with my friends. We went to the back of the school and drank and smoked there. We were singing loudly when we got caught by the teacher who was on duty. All of us were suspended. During my junior and high school years, my nickname was *"moonjae-ah."** I thought it was a nickname that derived from my name, but with the two incidents under my belt, I really became a problem child.

My parents weren't aware that those incidents happened. They were aware that I was drinking and smoking but didn't think that I would stray too much... or maybe they just pretended not to know.

During the period when I was attending high school, there weren't many college students like there are today. It was believed that if you were a high school student, you belonged with people that learned a lot. Back then, society didn't treat high school students as children like they do these days; instead, it treated them as adults. The April 19th Revolution was still ongoing, and when important circumstances of the state of affairs were presented, high school students also participated in the demonstration. When I was a junior in high school, the entire student body took part in the demonstration movement against the Three Term Constitutional Amendment* for the presidential election and tried to leave the school. However, due to the newly introduced pepper fog car* blocking the school's front gates, we couldn't leave. Because of that incident, the school closed for a while. Drills were also conducted in high schools from the beginning of the school year. For the long-term seizure of power, the school was militarized and tried to dominate the students, causing many complaints. Sometimes, we declined to answer the high school drill test, handing in blank answer sheets. Due to these things, our social and political consciousness grew.

Anyway, we lived in good and naïve times. There were a lot of classmates from Gyeongnam High School who had done well for themselves. Ulsan Mayor Park Myeong-woo, Grand National Party chairman Seo Byung-soo, former assemblyman Park Jong-woo, and Choi Chul-gook, Mayor of Seocho City Jin Ik-chul, etc were my classmates who are in politics now. There were also friends and associates in arts and culture, such as architect Seung Hyo-sang and director Lee Yoon-taek. Some passed the Public Administration Examination and are high-ranking officials, and some are in the field of law. There are some who are teaching students at universities and some who are serving as university presidents. It has already been forty years since we graduated from high school, and recently, we celebrated the 40th anniversary with a homecoming ceremony.

* **Glacial Acetic Acid** Acetic acid is the substance that gives vinegar its sour taste. Glacial acetic acid is 99% or more acetic acid. If undiluted, liquid glacial acetic acid touches the skin, the skin's protein will melt, and if it reaches the main organs, it can cause damage and even death.
* **The Sasangye Journal** An independent magazine created in the 1950s. Since then, it has become a magazine for the conscious forces to fight against Rhee Seung-man's and Park Jung-hee's dynastic regime. It was very popular amongst the intellectuals and students at the time.
* ***Moonjae-ah*** In Korean, *moonjae* means "problem," and *ah* means "child." So, Moon Jae-in thought that he was given that name because the first two syllables are similar to his.
* **Three Term Constitution Amendment** The Sixth Constitutional amendment in 1969 by President Park Chung-hee for the third consecutive term. Park Chung-hee has provided legal grounds for running for the seventh presidential election in April 1971, and since his election in 1972, he has been in power for a long time.
* **Pepper Fog Car** A special police vehicle equipped with a gas-fired device so that tear gas fumes can be blown out to dissipate the protesters.

University and the Resistance

I originally wanted to major in history in college. Throughout school, historical subjects were the most interesting, and I achieved the best grades. Even now, I love to read history books. When I first became an attorney, I thought I would become an amateur historian if I was liberated from earning money. So, when I was choosing my university degree in high school, I wanted to go to the History Department, but my teacher and my parents objected because I had enough grades to study law or commerce. I couldn't help but change my course, but I paid the price of neglecting my entrance exam. I failed the college entrance examination. After retaking it, I entered Kyunghee University Law School and resided near it.

The era was becoming increasingly gloomy. In my first year of university, the Park Chung-hee regime declared the October Revitalizing Reform (Yushin). It wasn't enough for him to prolong the regime via the Three-Term Constitution Amendment, but he intended to permanently take over power. The night before, tanks rumbled throughout the city.

The next morning, each university had tanks surrounding the campuses in residential areas, and an indefinite number of school closures occurred at the same time as the Yushin declaration. College students gathered at the bar or boarding houses instead of lecture rooms, lamenting and sharing their anger over the then-current state.

The October Yushin was even more absurd for law students. When the Yushin Constitution was created, the existing Constitution and textbooks became useless. "Nevertheless, can law truly be regarded as an academic discipline?" "Is law, indeed, an academic study?" These questions oppressed law stu dents, and they did not want to go to class.

I still remember the first lecture after the school reopened during the new semester. Our professor of Constitutional Studies was a well-known constitutional scholar at the time, and he used his own constitutional book as the lecture text. He wrote a new Yushin Constitutional Law book during the university closure period and lectured with it.

He wasn't able to look at the students during the entire 100-minute lecture but lectured looking at the classroom ceiling. It was his expression of shame before his students that he had to write a new book and lecture on the Yushin Constitution.

My university boarding experience raised my awareness of society back then. Since there was freedom and no one to control their daily lives, university students gathered together and often debated about the country's state well into the dark hours of the night. I boarded with my high school sunbaes. Students from various universities were there, so I was able to hear news of other campus resistance movements concerning the social science clubs' criticism on reality and from the rural movements, the underground press, news on campus protests, and declarations made during protests. Following my friends and colleagues, I went to see the Seoul University Liberal Arts and Sciences and Korea University protests, as they had the strongest student movements.

Professor Lee Young-hee* was one of the greatest trend setters on criticism and social consciousness during my university days along with some fellow students.

I first read Professor Lee's Vietnam War thesis in *Creation & Criticism** magazine before the Logic of the Transition Period was published. I remember the first and second articles were first published in a series in magazines when I was a freshman and sophomore at university, and the book was published when I was a junior. I was shocked when I first read Professor Lee's paper, dealing with the nature of the Vietnam War, the nature of the imperialist war, and the anti-war movements in the United States. The conclusion said it was a war that the United States, recognized as the stronger country, could never win.

It wasn't the first time I had heard this. It was a story that we shared privately in our boarding house. However, no one could deny the evidence presented, and it was clear that we needed to strip the false awareness that our society had of America's unconditional justice, deeming that all that they claimed was true and defeating opponents as if treating evil. I encountered the brutality of the intellectual through the thesis and the book that needed to be emulated. It was to face the fearful truth, not to avoid it. Pursuing the truth to the end and confronting the world with grounds that no one can deny. It was to expose the truth to the world even though a knife was put to your throat and to expose false consciousness that suppressed the truth.

After the collapse of Vietnam *, Professor Lee published three papers in the *Creation & Criticism* magazine to conclude the Vietnam War. Therefore, this three-part paper was written between the world's historical events and the collapse of Vietnam. The development and flow of the logic couldn't be any more consistent. Parts 1 and 2 predicted America's defeat and Vietnam's collapse at a time when no one doubted America's victory. The third part was to confirm the realization of the prediction as it was and to settle it. At least in writing, I was able to read about the truth of the triumph and vividly remember a feeling of great ecstasy.

Attorney Rho was also influenced a lot by Professor Lee. The *Burim Case* became the momentum for Attorney Roh to become a human rights attorney, and it started because young people and students studied dozens of basic social science or criticism literature books. The indictment included "reading the books that were praising and encouraging the activities of the North Koreans or other overseas communist activities." Attorney Roh read dozens of books in preparation for the defense. Among them there was Professor Lee's book *The Logic of the Transition Period* and *Idol and Reason*. He was influenced by the books he read for his work as an attorney. Since then, Attorney Roh has read a more comprehensive range of social science books and has become more conscientious through them. Professor Lee's book was the beginning of it all.

After that, we invited Professor Lee as a guest lecturer a few times when we were active in the Busan Lawyers Association. I asked Professor Lee at a dinner afterward, "Wasn't it an error to highly promote China's Cultural Revolution*?" He answered clearly without any hesitation. "It was. Every time I write, I try very hard to secure objectivity, but it was difficult to access data back then, so I think it had its limits. I think I was also excessively devoted to idealism at that time." His honesty was truly admirable.

At that time, Kyunghee University's student movement was weak. Conscious students were scattered individually. There was no such thing as study groups. There was no proper social science club. In the latter half of my second year in 1973, the nationwide struggle against the anti-Yushin movement began. The protests of university students began to spread to universities nationwide, beginning with Seoul National University's Liberal Arts and Science Department. The one million petitioners' signature campaign for the Constitutional Amendment Petition, Emergency Decree 1, Emergency Decree 4, National Federation of Democratic Young Student Incident, and People's Revolutionary Party Incident followed. Even then, Kyunghee University didn't have anything to protest for. There was an intermittent attempt to protest, but there was no central power to lead it.

In the fall of my third year, there was a sit-in protest for the resignation of the school foundation. Taking this as an opportunity, I planned a protest against Yushin with my friends, who shared the same thoughts. Our team prepared and distributed the declaration and gathered students at the front of the campus "school tower." After that, the vice presidency team of the student council decided to lead the demonstration. Our team planned to prepare everything in secret for the protest and avoid punishment by disappearing, while the vice presidency team had to inevitably lead on that day because of their position.

I wrote the declaration. It was my first written statement. There was no other reason. I was the only one who knew how declarations were written since I frequently encountered many of the declarations of other universities.

We prepared 4,000 copies of the handout overnight at my friend's house through a Mimeo graphic copying press (the usual way to make handouts at that time), and the next morning, we secretly left them in all the lecture rooms.

At the appointed time, 500 to 600 students gathered in front of the school tower. It was the vice presidency's team's turn to lead, but no one showed up. The staff of the student council tried to disperse the students. At that time, the police weren't allowed to enter the school grounds. Some students who couldn't wait tried to go up on the podium and read the declaration, but the student council staff pulled them down. If left alone, I felt the demonstration would be a failure.

Without any choice, I went up to the podium and read the declaration.

In the fall of my third year, there was a sit-in protest for the resignation of the school foundation. Taking this as an opportunity, I planned a protest against Yushin with my friends, who shared the same thoughts. Our team prepared and distributed the declaration and collected students at the front of the campus "school tower."

The student council staff rushed to stop me, but the students blocked them. It was raining, and the declaration got wet, but I was able to read it since I had written it. Then, I led students to the school gate. Suddenly, there were more than 2,000 students.

The battle of tear gas and stone-throwing began with the police outside the gate. This was my first proper demonstration after entering Kyunghee University.

After confirming that the demonstration was on track, we left the school and stayed under the radar for a few days. The police arrested some of the leaders at the demonstration, but when they couldn't find connections with the team that prepared the demonstration, they closed the case with a suspended sentence. One of the students who was arrested at that time was Jung Bum-koo, a member of the Democratic Party. He was a fourth-year Political Science and Diplomacy student at the front of the protest. Criminal punishment ended with detention, but because he was suspended indefinitely from school, causing him to graduate later, which caused him difficulty in finding work. Looking back, it seems that this ordeal trained him to be a better person.

Once the police case processing settled down, my friend and I were led by the head of student affairs to appear at the police station voluntarily and eventually ended up in confinement. When the head of student affairs saw that I was reading the wet declaration, he realized I was the author. No punishment was received from the school, making us a central figure in the student movement. After that, we formed an organization that covered the whole school by rallying people who could lead students in each department. Furthermore, I created a social science club and broadened the base. The political tension was rising, and we prepared for the following year.

* **Professor Lee Young-hee** He was a professor at Hanyang University and a former journalist. He was a symbol of a progressive intellectual and practical intelligence who broke all taboos through numerous books that conveyed the truth of the era. During the military regime, he was fired four times and arrested five times. He died in 2010 of chronic disease. The funeral was held for a democratic social leader, and he was buried at the 5.18 National Cemetery in Gwangju.
* ***Creation & Criticism*** The cradle of national literature is a quarterly literary magazine founded in January 1966. In the 1970s and 1980s, it acted as a channel for the intellectual society eager for democratization at the time.
* **Collapse of Vietnam** North and South Vietnam went through the Vietnam War, and the South collapsed after the defeat and was unified into the current Vietnam.
* **China's Cultural Revolution** A socialist movement led by Mao Zedong, China's top leader for 10 years, from 1966 to 1976. It was a mass movement that emphasized the struggle for socialist class, but China eventually became a rigid society. All opposition to Mao Zedong was turned down or killed. After Mao Zedong's death, the Chinese Communist Party officially evaluated the Cultural Revolution as a "paranormal error."

Imprisonment and My Mother

At the beginning of the new semester in 1975, the universities were flooded with the idea of having an all-out war against the Yushin regime. Since the second half of 1973, the anti-Yushin struggle with protestors outside the government and Christians interlocked with the press defending freedom of speech was at its peak. In Vietnam, news of the monks burning themselves to death for the resistance against the dictatorship continued. It had been said that to overthrow the Yushin administration, it needed to go through such struggles. So, in April 1975, Kim Sang-jin, a patriotic martyr from Seoul National University's College of Agriculture, committed hara-kiri*, making that struggle a reality.

At the beginning of April 1975, Kyunghee University held its first voter-based election for its student body council president. Until then, it was an indirect election based on representative count. We took control of the student body council and decided to hold an anti-Yushin protest with the supervision of the student body council. We decided to send forth our own candidate and mobilize the student body council's organization capacity so he could be elected. We succeeded. Kang Sam-jae, the student who was elected to become the president of the student body council, later became secretary general for the Democratic and New Korea Party as well as vice chairman of the Grand National Party. I was responsible for being head of the general affairs department of the student body council, and my friends were also executives in the organization. Once the student body council was established, we held an emergency meeting for the students.

We decided that our team would prepare for the demonstration while the student council president held an emergency meeting and lead the demonstration later that day. We made handouts with the student council's mimeograph throughout the night. It was the declaration under the student council. The next day, an announcement was posted by the student body council for an emergency student meeting in front of the school. The student body council executives distributed the handouts to students going to school in front of the school gates. We were also prepared for the consequences that came as a result of this action. With the elected student body council leading the anti-Yushin demonstration, an enormous number of students gathered. Kyunghee University's student count was between 7,000 to 8,000, and around 5,000 students participated. All the students gathered, but the student body council president didn't. While he was on the way to school, he was temporarily detained by the police. So, since I was the head of general affairs, I took the lead in holding the emergency meeting. After discussing the current situation and holding a burning ceremony against the Yushin dictatorship, I led the massive group toward the school's front gate. I held the Korean flag and led the march. The police had the school passage blocked and waited for us with their pepper fog cars.

When we approached the front gates, we tried to push it, but suddenly, the police fired pepper fog gas on us. They even spewed tear gas on us, too. Since I was in front of the line, I was hit directly in the face with the gas that spurted from the pepper fog, and I lost consciousness. When my classmates retreated and saw that I was on the ground, they brought me into the school. I was wiped down with a wet towel and was taken care of. I wasn't able to wake up for a long time. The mood of the protest rose even greater, and it continued vehemently late into the afternoon.

Later that afternoon, the president of the student body council escaped from the police and came back to school barefooted. From then on, he was able to finish the demonstration. At that time, it was common to arrest three leaders from the school when on-campus demonstrations were held. Three of us, including myself, were chosen to be imprisoned, and we met to get our facts straight. Back then, police officers weren't allowed to enter school campuses, so they waited around the school, ready to arrest the leaders. Once the demonstration finished, we walked out and got arrested. They arrested and imprisoned us at Cheongyangyi police station, something that we were prepared for from the start.

At the same time we were imprisoned, we were expelled from school. Sixteen students were expelled at once, including those who had been detained. It wasn't until 1980 that we were able to return to school. Everyone is living well now, but I was sorry for a very long time.

I wasn't allowed any visitation from my family until I was moved into the detention center. I thought it was natural and didn't think it was unfair because I didn't want to notify my family anyway. I knew they would find out sooner or later, but I hoped it would be later.

The police interrogated me for ten days before they sent me to the prosecutors. The day I was being transferred to the prosecutor's office, the sun blinded my eyes while I was leaving the detention center. I got in the prison van. Holes the size of quarters were throughout the convoy's steel plates. I was curious about the outside scenery since I wasn't allowed to be outside for so long, so I looked out through one of the holes in the back of the van.

When the car was about to leave, my mother was chasing the vehicle. I couldn't hear anything, but I was able to see that she was swinging her arms and calling my name... "Jae-in! Jae-in!" As the car continued to move forward, my mother soon disappeared. She continued to look at the van until it was out of sight. It seems like she heard the news and rushed up from Busan. Since they weren't allowing visitations, she thought her coming was useless until she heard that I was being transferred. She waited, hoping to get a glimpse of me, and once she saw me getting in the convoy from afar, she came running.

I didn't know about this and wasn't even able to make eye contact with her. It was like a scene from a movie, and even to this day, it lingers in my mind. Whenever I think about my mother, that scene always comes back.

Once I was confined at Seodaemun detention center, my heart was more at ease. The only thing that I was agonizing over was the pain I was inflicting on my parents. They tried their best and sent me to college despite difficult times, and I let them down. I couldn't erase the image of my mother running after the convoy. When my mother came for visitations, I was always sorry because it felt as if she was asking, "Though it was the right thing to do, did you have to do it?". I had nothing to say, and my father never came up for visitations.

* **Hara-kiri** is a ritual suicide by disembowelment with a sword that Japanese samurais have formally practiced as an honorable alternative to disgrace or execution

Meeting My Wife

When I was at the detention center, my wife unexpectedly came for visitation. My wife, at that time, was a music major student at the same university and was two years younger than me. I met her for the first time when I was a junior, and she was a freshman. She was my partner at our law school's Law Festival, which was held annually in early May to coincide with Law Day. Though it was the first time we met, we really enjoyed the festival together, and I was attracted to her. But afterward, we weren't able to meet again. My heart didn't have the time or freedom. So, whenever we passed each other on campus, we just greeted each other with our eyes.

During the demonstration in April 1975, our roads crossed again. It was necessary to secure a few speakers to help the mood of the demonstration if the volunteer statements were suddenly discontinued during the emergency student meeting about the current state affairs. We thought having a female speaker close the discussion would be good. While students were waiting for the general assembly, I was looking for female speakers when I saw my wife at the open square. She was with her department student president. I was told they were close friends. I walked up and asked if any one of them would like to do the final speech, and her friend decided to do it. She ended her speech by screaming, "Let's go!" and concluded the emergency student meeting by joining the march. As a result, she wasn't detained but was suspended from school.

After the emergency meeting ended and the students started to march towards the front gates, I was hit with the pepper fog and lost consciousness. After a while, I felt someone wiping my face with a wet towel. I came to my senses and opened my eyes to see my wife. She was marching when she saw that I got hurt. She was worried and was taking care of me.

During my incarceration, I had visitation rights, resulting in visits from her. It was unexpected. When she heard that I was detained, she seemed concerned. But during her visit, she was holding onto a folded newspaper. She wanted to show me the paper because it headlined sports news about my alma mater, Gyeongnam High School, winning the national baseball tournament. High school baseball was at its peak of popularity then. I was from a school that regarded baseball as the representative of all sports, and I really loved baseball at that time. During the same year, my wife was my partner for the Law Festival; I was the captain of the school's baseball team and won. So, my wife remembered how much I enjoyed it and brought me news that would cheer me up. But, no matter how much I enjoyed baseball, why would I be interested in it while detained? Still, she was adorable for thinking such thoughts, and

I met her for the first time when I was a junior and she was a freshman. She was my partner at our law school's Law Festival, which was held at the beginning of May every year to coincide with Law Day. Though it was the first time we met, we really enjoyed the festival together, and I was attracted to her.

whenever I thought about it in my cell, I would laugh.

After that, we became closer once I was released, but soon after, I had to enlist in the army. This time, my wife came to visit me at the military base. After I completed my services and studied for my bar exam, she visited me where I was studying. My wife would say sometimes that we have a history of visitations in our love story, and I would tell her that I thought the main reason I was accepted into Kyunghee University was to meet her. I said this truthfully and whole-heartedly.

At the Detention Center

The prison life in the Seoul detention center was bearable. I had a reasonably good stay. Originally, a political prisoner was on the blacklist and detained in solitary confinement, but there were too many at the time, so we were confined in general detainment. There were around eight people in one cell. Some said they preferred the solitary cell, but I liked the communal atmosphere because I was able to learn about life.

Attorney Han Seung-hun, who was imprisoned for violating anti-communist laws, was in the next cell. He was indicted for his literary work *A Eulogy*, which was published in a magazine. When I was imprisoned in the next cell, he gave me an undershirt and underwear through the prison guards. It was a great help since I came in without any preparation. He presumed that was my situation and helped me out.

I met him professionally later on, when he started to work as a human rights attorney again. We were co-attorneys in the DSME case when Attorney Roh Moo-hyun and Attorney Lee Sang-soo were arrested. He remembered when I talked to him previously at the Seoul detention center. There were a lot of outstanding opposition supporters in the detention center at the time, including Pastor Park Hyung-gyu, Pastor Kim Kwan-suk, and poet Kim Ji-ha. Some reporters had been dismissed from the *Dong-A Ilbo* for partaking in the free speech movement. About three weeks after I was arrested, Emergency Decree 9 was issued at the end of April. People detained for related violations were pouring in. When someone came to visit, it was a joy to meet and greet them during the detainment before and after the visits.

In the cells, they divide the prisoners into the wealthy "tiger fur"* and "dog fur"* without money. The "tiger fur" and "dog fur" have different lives in jail. There is no place in the world like prison where money is considered frank and powerful. Our room was in good condition, with about half "tigers" and half "dogs." The "tiger fur room" and "dog fur room" also had different bathroom schedules in the morning.

Everyone in my cell called me "student" and treated me well. Since I was in my fourth year of law school and passed the first round of the bar exam, I helped inmates write petitions. Then, people in other cells started asking for help.

There was an event that couldn't be forgotten during my stay. There were many pigeons around the detention center. The pigeons would sit down in the front yard of the confined complex. When I was bored, I would often look down. Some people threw leftover rice at them. Our room had enough money, and many people bought private meals. They also bought a lot of snacks. The snacks were hard barley biscuits, but if you mixed margarine with egg yolk and made it into a cream, it was a rather good dipping sauce. Naturally, there was a lot of food given at the detention center, so there were leftovers at every meal. I gathered some and threw it to the pigeons.

As this continued, the pigeons would gather around our room and wait for the rice. But every time I threw the rice, the young boys in the opposite cells at the juvenile center would gather at the window and watch the pigeons fight to eat. At first, I thought they were watching the scene for fun. But that was not the case. It wasn't for fun. Someone informed me that it was because they wanted to eat the leftover rice we were giving to the pigeons. I was shocked. I was embarrassed and sorry that I had enjoyed throwing the remaining rice to the pigeons, not knowing their story. The boys were all "dog fur" and had nothing to eat other than the rationed food given at the detention center. Since then, with the help of the inmates, we left one or two meals untouched and sent them to the boys' cell.

I also learned what "necessity is the mother of invention" truly meant. A detention center cell has four walls and timber flooring – nothing more. But there was nothing we couldn't make in that small area. We made wallpaper by gathering the logo stickers on the back of the bread packaging and made a laundry line with the plastic bread bag. We made a knife by grinding the back of the toothbrush. We also made Korean checkerboards, Korean chessboards, and chess pieces. We crushed rice to make go pieces, and when we applied carbon paper ink to them, they became black stones. I was surprised to see how solid and hard the "go stones" were.

As my sentencing approached, my fellow inmates began to make a gift for me, wishing me the best for my release. A couple of people worked hard for a few days. I watched them twist a vinyl bread bag like a straw and apply frictional heat made by hand to make a vinyl string. According to the pattern of the bread bag, it became a red string and a yellowish-green string. The thickness of the strap was adjusted according to how hard they pulled. They made a pretty flowerpot, weaving together thick and thin strings of different colors. They told me not to forget when I became a judge or a prosecutor, that there were a lot of people in the world who were being treated unfairly, and to keep it on my desk and always think about these difficult times.

At the trial, I was sentenced to two years. Just as Attorney Han Seung-heon ridiculed humorously, the sentencing at that time was serialized and called a "fixed system." It was also a time when almost all sentences were jail sentences, but the judge gave me ten months of jail time and probation. Among the other universities, we were the only ones sentenced to probation. The judge acted on his convictions. Not long afterward, he failed to get a reappointment. We guessed that it was because of his conviction-led judgments regarding political cases.

Later, after I passed the bar exam, I was a probationary prosecutor at the Northern Seoul Prosecutors Office, where I was investigated, and was a probationary judge at the Northern Seoul Court, where I was tried. This also was an uncanny connection.

* **Tiger fur and Dog fur** is Korean slang for a wealthy person and a poor person.

Compulsory Conscription

Soon after being released, I was issued a warrant for enlistment in the army. Since my physical examination had not been completed, both the enlistment warrant and a medical note were delivered. I was scheduled to receive a physical the day before I enlisted. Basically, this was a forced draft.

There was another unjust incident. The prosecutor appealed our probation. I enlisted without even knowing about it. My friend living in Seoul, who was also my accomplice, said the enlistment was delayed due to the prosecutors' appeal. I didn't know that that had even happened. Later, when I applied for the "Honorary Recovery and Compensation Review Committee for Democratization Movement Related People," I saw the file, and the appeal against me was rejected. When I was in the army, an appeal trial was held in my absence, and I wasn't even notified about it. Since I was in the army, if it was really necessary to have the trial, the case should have been transferred for a military trial, or the prosecutor should have withdrawn the appeal, but they just dismissed it. As a result, no damage was done, but that was how the courts and prosecutors worked then.

I went to the Busan Korean Armed Forces hospital for my physical, and just like it is done nowadays, I had to go to different places to get checked up. When I was getting my vision tested, I wanted to see their reaction if I couldn't see well. So, I pretended to do horribly on the test. But the examiner laughed and continued carrying out the complete medical examination, saying, "Still, you're a grade A level*!" and stamped "Grade A" on my physical check-up paper. Then he gave me a warrant for enlistment again. It was a warrant postponing my enrollment a week later than the original date I received.

Since I had already said my goodbyes to my parents, I went to Gyeongnam, Hadong Galsari, where my *sunbae* was running his night school. At that time, it was in a very remote area, and the night school tutored students who weren't able to enter junior high school. At night, he would borrow an empty elementary school classroom and hold his classes there. A variety of students, all different ages, filled the classroom.

What was really impressive was when I saw the students bring cement bags whenever they came to school. Galsari was originally an island at the mouth of the Seomjin River, situated on an embankment connecting it to land. Because of the embankment, water started to pool, stagnating it and causing it to be the breeding ground for mosquitoes. I have never seen so many mosquitoes in my life. It was as if there were a hundred mosquitoes per cubic meter. When standing on the school playground, mosquitoes would be everywhere within seconds. So, the students covered their lower bodies with cement while studying because the mosquitoes were ripping through their clothes and biting them mercilessly.

My heart became solemn when I saw the students studying like that deep into the night. Compared to those children, I was pretty well off. The students couldn't enter junior high school due to poverty and because the school was too far away from where they were. At that time, there was only one junior high school in the Geumnam area where Galsari belonged. It was frustrating to think about what would happen to those children if my *sunbae* could no longer run the night school or until when the students could attend school.

The reason why I went there was because a couple of my friends who were a part of the student body council talked about making a night school classroom where they could also do rural activities. I was only able to stay there for a couple of days, so I did rural activities during the day, helped with the children's studies in the evening, and played with them until I had to leave for enlistment. My wife also went there with me and left there with me to walk with me up to the training center.

Galsari was originally famous for cultivating *gim**. The infamous "*Hadong gim*" was produced in that area. When the Gwangyang Bay was landfilled for the Gwangyang Iron Company, the *gim* farms were ruined due to the gravel that flowed in. It was a matter for the fishermen to file a claim for damages. So later, when I became an attorney, they consulted with me. Though I wasn't able to personally help with the claim due to the distance, I heard that they won the case. Afterwards, I heard that the construction of a shipbuilding complex was being promoted, and I wondered how that area had changed.

It was the beginning of August 1975, and the enlisted training camp was the 39th Division of Changwon, the Homeland Reserve Division (HRD). The men who enlisted were strong young men from the Hadong area. Like me, four other people were compelled to enlist.

I thought that attending the military service was something that must be done. Besides, I didn't know when I would be able to return to school, so I thought it was better than nothing. Since I never experienced something like this, I was a bit nervous but adapted. When I was in the training center, I became the chief squad commander. At the Nonsan training center, we were called fuglemen. Maybe it was given to me because I spent some time in college and was older than the rest. My enlistment was pushed back until I was a senior in college, so I was two years older than the rest of the men at the training center. Since respect for elders was still practiced, the platoon members treated me like their older brother.

Minus the heat and sweat, there wasn't much difficulty in the life of the training camp. During the CBR *training, we were to enter a marquee that was heavily filled with tear gas with our masks on and had to endure for a certain amount of time. I don't know if it was a normal part of the training or if the training assistant wanted to give us a hard time, but towards the end, we were commanded to take off our gas masks and sing a military song. Everyone was throwing up and was in agonizing pain, but to my amazement, I was able to endure it. I think it may have had to do with all the tear gas that I experienced while protesting.

The most memorable part of my six-week training was the "Wish List*" that was done before the completion of training. I heard from my son, who also went to the army, that the system still existed. It was something that the trainees were supposed to do before they finished their training, asking them to write down the problems and difficulties they had experienced so that they may use the information to improve the training camps. So, the main subjects that the trainees usually wrote about were the beatings that were done by the training assistants and the enlisted cadre, the punishments, various types of corruption, etc.

The beating was also a target for extermination back then as well. To expose it, higher-level commanders would unexpectedly check the trainees' buttocks to see if there were imprints of the " *bbatta**" beatings. So, when I was a trainee, the training assistant didn't hit us on our buttocks but on our soles so no imprints could be left behind. If you receive the "*bbatta*" beating on your soles, it's more painful than getting the beating on your buttocks. Since I was the senior squad commander, whenever the squad's platoons made a mistake, I would get the beating on their behalf, so my soles were beaten up quite a few times.

When the time for the "Wish List" was approaching, the training assistants would threaten us by saying "I won't leave you guys alone if you write anything on that list. If you do, I'll investigate your handwriting and hunt you down!" Finally, two to three days before we completed training, the higher commanders distributed the "Wish List." The training assistants and enlisted cadre weren't allowed into the room, and we were told to write down the difficulties and improvements that needed to be done, as well as beatings and other corruption that were experienced. When everyone hesitated to write, they were told seriously, "Though you might have completed your training camp, there are still those who will enlist after you that might suffer just like you. You should write everything down so that they do not experience the type of suffering you did and that we can also prevent it from happening so that we may be able to provide a better camp environment."

When the enlisted squad leader was spotted lurking and snorting at the situation, he was yelled at and told to leave. The high commander said to us that "everything will remain anonymous and there won't be any penalty" and that "though the training assistants may have frightened you, don't worry because they're not allowed to look at the 'Wish List.'" Eventually, most of the trainees started to write. To be honest, if we wrote the truth, we would need a couple of pages, not just one.

As soon as we returned, the training assistants entered our ward with the papers in their hands. They were fake papers, but we didn't know that and were heavily punished for them throughout the remainder of the day. He created an atmosphere of horror, saying that he would track down the trainees who reported serious misconduct or incidents. The next day, the "Wish List" paper was given to us again. The commanders said the same thing, creating the same trustworthy atmosphere. But this time, no one was deceived or wrote anything down. However, it turned out to be the real "Wish List" paper. It was so clever how they ostracized the purpose of the "Wish List" that if I had a talent for writing, I would have used that material and written a short novel on it.

When we completed our training, all the trainees gathered at the military training ground. They had us fix our gear and announced where each was assigned in troops and where each of us was to be stationed. "Moon Jae-in, Special Warfare Command!" No one knew where the SWC was located nor knew what it did.

At that time, one of my junior high school friends was a veteran sergeant at the Division of Personnel. Many friends who trained at the 39th division asked him to pull some strings and position them to somewhat comfortable stations, such as medics. That friend apologized to me, saying, "The identity cards of the five people who were forcefully recruited are under special management, so I wasn't able to send you to a good place." He also said, "In the past, students who were brought in from demonstrations were deployed to places like the security divisions, but they had changed their policies to make them suffer." He didn't say I would go to Special Forces or the airborne troops but spoke vaguely that it was a special force center located in Seoul like the Capital Garrison Command (CGC) or Capital Defense Command (CDC). The other four forced recruits were either sent to the front-line force, the armored force, or something equally as difficult.

I discovered that the Special Forces were the Airborne Division when I was on the military train heading to Yongsan, passing Samrangjin. It was the last time the trainees were to be together, so they allowed us to drink as much as we wanted on the train. For those being deployed to difficult stations, the trainees offered more alcohol to each other. My fellow trainees continued to give me drinks for consolation.

* **Grade A** The highest result one can receive on the fitness grade determined by the AHD draft exams.
* ***Gim*** dried laver or also known as dried seaweed paper
* **CBR** Chemical, biological and radiological
* **Wish List** Asking for feedback concerning soldiers' worries and inconveniences in the training camps or within the troops
* ***Bbatta*** Japanese-style pronunciation of a golf putter or baseball bat. Usually refers to corporal punishment that is applied to the buttocks or other parts of the body

Airborne Division

I was assigned to the 3rd Battalion of the 1st Airborne Brigade in the Special Warfare Command. I didn't go to my assigned unit right away. First, I had to complete four weeks of parachute landing training, six weeks of special airfare training, and two weeks of basic brigade training before being assigned to my unit. We were to memorize official ranks and names like "Brigade Commander Brigadier Chun Doo-hwan" and "Battalion Commander Lieutenant Colonel Jang Se-dong." I never got the opportunity to work with Battalion Commander Jang Se-dong, who was once chief of the presidential security service for President Chun Doo-hwan, when I returned from completing my training because he had already been replaced by someone else. I only heard about him, and his reputation as a soldier was quite good. Ahn Hyun-tae, who served as the chief of the presidential security service after Jang Se-dong during the Fifth Republic, was the battalion commander of the next squadron.

During my military preparation, I trained as an explosives expert. Consequently, I became an airborne soldier as well as an explosive specialist. After I completed the six-week special training, I received an award for excellence in the explosives course from Jung Byung-joo, the Commander of the Unconventional Warfare Task Force (COMUWTF). Commander Jung was later recognized as the image of a true soldier when the rebel army shot him while he was leading the December 12th New Military coup*. Brigade Commander Chun Doo-hwan led the coup successfully and later became the president of Korea. The fates of the two immediate superiors, whose official names and ranks we had to memorize, were dramatically crossed.

Truthfully, the award for excellence for the explosives course training wasn't a big deal. In order to detonate a certain facility, it was necessary to calculate the type, amount of the explosives needed, and strategic location. Eighty percent of our training consisted of that kind of instruction, and we also learned how to make homemade explosives that were mixed with chemicals in case unconventional warfare (UW) occurred. So, it was natural for me to do well amongst the recruits since I studied longer than others. After returning from advanced training, I received an award for excellence in CBR explosives from Brigade Commander Chun Doo-hwan. Because of that, I had already become an A-class soldier before I entered my assigned unit. There was a time when the brigade's headquarters wanted to take me, and the battalion tried to keep me where I was, making it a tug-of-war between them.

I never received any type of award in school except for perfect attendance. Actually, I was suspended from school, expelled, and arrested in college. However, when I went to the army, I was able to perform the skills that the military asked of me quite well. I was amazed at myself at how good I was at shooting, throwing grenades, combat swimming and other things that I did for the first time in my life.

The only difficult thing was the armed march. Airborne units' armed march was different from the infantry units. At that time, the army's FM* was to carry 12kg of military gear and run 10km within 61 minutes. However, the airborne units, who were known to be the elite and powerful of the army, had to carry 20kg of gear and run 10km within 57 minutes. At the starting line, there was a scale so that the gear could be weighed before departure and on arrival. There were armed marches every week when I lived in the barracks. It was really difficult. Once I became a veteran soldier, I started to pick up some tricks. I would put an empty locker in my bag to make it look full and would put rocks in it before departure and refill it with rocks when I arrived at the finish line. I just needed to get through the armed marches, and all the other training was doable.

The aerial drop in the airborne training was difficult but jumping was doable afterward. It was better to go for jump training than to stay inside and be assigned to fatigue duties. The first two parachute jumps were normal, the third was a night jump, and the fourth was an armed parachute jump. The night before the first jump, we were asked to write letters to our parents along with a piece of hair and fingernail clipping in an envelope just in case something happened. Before we got on the transport plane, the chaplain even prayed for us. When I was being trained, the chaplain did not only pray for us but was also the first person to jump before the recruits. He was a great person. During the first jump, one of my fellow trainees just fell to the ground and died because his parachute didn't open.

I witnessed the accident quite vividly because I completed my jump and was already on the ground. We looked up and yelled at him to open the pilot chute, but he couldn't and fell to an accidental death. During the second jump, an officer had a concussion and was evacuated. Because of these accidents, I would always be nervous whenever I went for the parachute jump. I was even scared when I had to jump out of a transport plane or a helicopter. And when I would arrive on the ground safely, I would still be nervous because you can get seriously injured.

However, it was magnificent when the parachute spread out, and you floated in the air. That feeling was so good that I was able to endure the stress and fear. Maybe people who paraglide also experience this feeling, which is why they endure carrying the heavy equipment up with them to the top.

Since this is old military talk, it might be different these days, but there were times when we collaborated with the U.S. troops in "Eagle" and "Team Spirit" training. We also jumped together, but when we looked at the American soldiers jump, it was as if we were watching them do sports, doing it so relaxed.

The parachute was to be put on when they signaled "5 minutes" be-

It was magnificent when the parachute spread out, and you floated in the air.
That feeling was so good that I was able to endure the stress and fear.
Maybe people who paraglide also experience this feeling,
which is why they endure carrying the heavy equipment up with them to the top.

fore the drop zone in the transport plane. We waited comfortably in the plane because we had our parachutes on before we got on the plane and got a safety check as well. Inside the plane, we weren't allowed to talk to each other and had to sit in upright positions. Because of this, there were many accidents because soldiers would jump while they were nervous and tense.

Airborne units spent half the year outside the barracks receiving bivouac training. The highlight of this training was the long-distance march, marching over 400km. After a month of bivouac training in places like Mt. Jiri and Mungyeongsaejae, for the next nine days, we were forced to walk at night to trek through the mountain for 400 km back to our unit. Walking the mountain trails for 40 to 50km every night was very tough while carrying heavy backpacks containing our tents, sleeping bags, food, and other necessities. Many agreed that this was the most difficult part of the training in the Airborne Division. But I enjoyed being outside rather than inside the barracks and liked walking the mountain trails. There was also pleasure in seeing the mountains, rivers, and villages I hadn't visited before.

Every year, we had underwater training in the ocean for two weeks. Depending on one's swimming skills, we were divided into groups and were trained step by step from beginner to scuba training. Since I was from Busan, I knew how to swim. In the first year, I trained to be a lifeguard and was also licensed as a qualified advanced water safety lifeguard from the Korean National Red Cross. The qualification exam was held for two days. On the first day, it was to demonstrate our ability to rescue

제 호

赤十

수 료 증

주 소 부산시 영도구 영선2가 110

성 명 문 재 인

생년월일 1952 년 1 월 24 일생

이 사람은 본사의 고급인명구조원 강습과정을 수료하였음을 증명함

1976 년 7 월 16 일

대 한 적 십 자 사

We had underwater training at the ocean every year for two weeks.
In the first year, I trained to be a lifeguard and was also licensed as
a qualified high-ranking lifeguard from the Korean National Red Cross.

someone who was drowning using different techniques depending on the situation. The second day was long-distance swimming, which was about 2 miles (3.2km). It didn't matter how we swam. It wasn't something anyone could even conceive of doing in the outside world, but it was possible because it was done in the army. After accomplishing the distance and looking back, you realize you couldn't do it alone.

The following year, I received basic scuba training. Before we could carry our air tanks, we were trained to hold onto a 20kg sand bag and swim and also to swim with a 12kg lead belt around our waists. Although I was afraid since it was my first time, I was amazed that I was able to do it, even though I swallowed a lot of water.

There was also something called combat swimming. We were to swim with our full individual gear, such as combat boots on our feet, cartridge belts around our waists, and a rifle on our shoulders. In that state, we were trained to get on the rubber boats and infiltrate, and once the headlight was shown, we were to immediately turn the boat upside down so we could not be seen. Once the headlight passed, the boat needed to be turned right side up, and we had to get in.

My wife visited a couple of times. I'll never forget the first visitation I got after being placed in the 1st Airborne Brigade. During those times, when people came to visit, they brought a lot of food with them. No matter how poor the mother was during visitations, roasted chicken was the basic spread. But my wife didn't bring anything to eat; she just brought a bundle of baby's breath with her. Even though she didn't have a brother, she was really naïve about the military world. Since the meeting room didn't have vending machines or food services, we just placed the flowers in the middle of the table and talked. I thought it was funny, but when I walked back into my quarters with flowers and not food, my colleagues broke out in tears from laughter. My wife might be the only person in the Republic of Korea to have brought flowers instead of food for a military visitation. Still, I divided the flowers and gave some to several quarters; everyone liked them. Since they were baby's breath, they lasted for a long time. I'm sure I must have been one in a million to have flowers in the airborne division quarters.

After many years passed, my wife and I went to visit my son while he was doing his military service. It was when I was the Senior Presidential Secretary for Civil Affairs at the Blue House, so I was careful not to let the unit supervisors know who I was during the visit. Some brought food with them like in the olden days, but now they also deliver pizza and other types of food. Because of that, many people came empty-handed to the visitations. There were many phone numbers of places that delivered food plastered on the door of the visiting quarters. We, too, only brought some fruit and ordered what my son wanted to eat: pizza. I was really astonished at how much things have changed.

When I was a corporal, the Panmunjom Axe Case* occurred. In response to the incident, our unit took on the operation of cutting down cottonwood trees. For the first time since the Korean War, DEFCON (defense condition) was declared. It was a feigned exhibition of prepa-

After many years have passed,
my wife and I went to visit my son
while he was doing his military services.
There were some who had brought food with them
like olden days, but now they also delivered pizza and
other types of food to the meeting place. Because of that,
many people came empty handed to the visitations.
I was really astonished at how much things have changed.

ration. When the trees were cut, depending on whether the North restrained or initiated conflict, there would be an outbreak of war. In preparation for such a situation, the most elite soldiers in our unit were put into the cottonwood tree elimination group. At the same time, the rest of the troops were stationed on the outskirts. The forward division was stationed even further out. Luckily, North Korea did not see the cutting of the cottonwood trees and did not respond. The operation was completed safely. Fragments of the cottonwood trees were made into souvenirs and were given to us as a badge of "overcoming national crisis."

When we didn't have bivouac drills and were in the barracks, we were immersed in riot suppression drills. The 1st Airborne Brigade was under the direct control of the ROK Army headquarters and was Seoul's garrison force. All soldiers were provided with riot batons as part of the basic equipment. During the riot suppression training, there were times we conducted demonstration drills. The scenario was that we would make a mock riot team, allow them to hold protests, and then have the airborne troops come in and wipe out the rioters with riot suppression techniques. In order to distinguish the riot team from the suppression unit, we had them wear their sportswear. "Hey, Moon Jae-in! You participated in a lot of demonstrations, right? You be the head of the riot!" And that's how I sometimes became in charge of the mock riot team. We were to stand in line with bayonets on our rifles and sync our verbal commands, "Attack position, move!" while advancing. It was terrifying to see how the riot suppression drill took place.

However, I only learned what to do while serving, and I never actually went to a riot. After I was discharged, the Buma Democratic Movement* took place; the 3rd Battalion of the 1st Airborne Brigade I once served with was deployed to Busan. During the Gwangju Democratic Movement, other airborne brigades were put on the suppression force. Though it was not a riot, the December 12th New Military coup disobeyed Commander Jung Byung-ju and was put into the rebel force main force unit. Had I delayed serving in the military, I might have been mobilized and ordered to take part, aiming my gun toward the people, recounting history.

Anyway, I was safely discharged. While serving in the airborne unit, there were many incidents where people hurt their back or legs during the parachute jump. There were a few friends who were injured and were transferred to the infantry unit. I was lucky. I was discharged three months earlier than my friends because I benefited from doing high school drills till I was a junior in college. When junior officers brought their riot batons, I would say that I never used a "*bbatta*" and would like to give everyone a *"commemorative bbatta."* My memory of what I did afterward is unclear. I don't remember if I did or just laughed it off.

At my discharge, I was declared Army Sergeant Moon or Staff Sergeant Moon. My colleagues and junior officers lined up and sent me off, and I walked towards the front gates of the unit, leaving them behind. My wife was waiting for me outside the front gates. It was February 1978, thirty-one months exactly. During that long period, my wife never cheated on me and was with me when I was enlisted until the day I was discharged.

I recently saw pictures of my army days on the internet. I think one of my friends gave the picture to his daughter, and she posted it online. I asked around and was able to contact him. We conversed for a really long time. Even now, I sometimes meet with fellow airborne soldiers and juniors and talk about those days. It is said in Korea that women hate when men talk about army stories and also stories about playing soccer in the army. Honestly, I think I could write a book about my military life if I wanted to.

After I was discharged, I dreamed about being enlisted again for a long time. It was a dream about army life, but in the dream, it was clear that I was discharged but had to return because my discharge was canceled. I found out I wasn't the only one to have those dreams. It was a common dream of many people who went to the army. I think it's especially true for Korean men who are obligated to serve in the military for a couple of years. No matter how well you did or had fun in the army, many would refuse if asked to do it again.

I realized that after I was discharged, the military experience had been helpful for my life. There were many things I did for the first time after I enlisted, and I could do them when I tried and persisted. That made me more of an optimistic person. There were many things I did for the first time when I became an attorney or when I was in the Blue House. There were times when it was not only my first time, but there wasn't a precedent to refer to. I had to confront my own challenges, but it helped me tremendously.

Because of such experiences, I hope to greatly ease the criteria for the physical examination if such a conscription system continues to exist. Wouldn't it be better to allow everyone to join the military, except for the physically limited situations? Of course, there is a basis. Many duties do not require physical strength in the military, so appropriate duty assignments can be designated according to physical capabilities. I think, then the military service period can be shortened, and the military service evasion and special favors would be solved. It will remain true to the Universal Conscription System*, and there won't be a need for controversy over military conscription.

* **December 12th New Military Coup** The military forces called "Hanahoe," led by Chun Doo-hwan and Roh Tae-woo, caused a military rebellion on December 12, 1979. Until early 1993, when Chun Doo-hwan and Roh Tae-woo, the leading forces under the new regime, were re-elected president, the December 12th events were justified by the ruling powers, but after Kim Young-sam's government, they were defined as a "coup d'état event by mutiny"
* **FM** A term referring to defined rules or principles.
* **Panmunjom Axe Case** On August 18, 1976, U.S.troops and Korean soldiers were overseeing the work of five Korean laborers pruning the branches of cottonwood trees covering the field of the view. At that time, two officers of the North Korean army and dozens of soldiers appeared and demanded that we stop working. When they refused and continued, dozens of North Korean soldiers ran in trucks, assaulted soldiers with axes and clubs, killed two U.S. officers with axes, and disappeared after applying.
* **Buma Democratic Movement** In October 1979, people against Park Jung-hee's dictatorship gathered to protest in Busan and Masan City. Park Jung-hee decided it wasn't possible to suppress the situation with the police force, so he declared emergency martial law in Busan at midnight on the 18th and
* **Universal Conscription System** The system imposes the obligation of military service for all men who have reached a certain age.

Studying

Upon returning home, I found myself in a stifling situation. It was the most unbearable and hopeless period in my life. I was discharged, but I wasn't able to return to school. I couldn't just stay at home, but since I didn't graduate, I couldn't get a job... I was in a dilemma.

When I thought about my parents, who were suffering hardship, I couldn't just lay around at home and wait for my reinstatement to school since I didn't know when I would be allowed to. My *sunbaes*, who were working at the Busan shipping business, suggested I work with them because even though you didn't have a university diploma, the company still treated you as an employee with a degree. I agreed and got myself ready to leave.

But all of a sudden, my father passed away, not from any type of illness, but from a heart attack. At that time, my father was helping out at one of his relative's companies. He went to work, took a shower after he finished, ate dinner, and had a drink. He lowered his head to the side for a bit, and when he wasn't getting up, we realized he had passed.

My father was only 59 years old at that time, the same age as I am now. My mother and I were devastated.

After the evacuation, he longed for his hometown. He was never able to return nor hear about the news of whether his parents were alive or dead before he closed his eyes. He was a poor man who lost his roots in life, came to a new place and couldn't adjust, and had an impotently exhausting lifetime.

I don't have many memories with my father when I think about it. We didn't have many affectionate conversations since he wasn't a man of words. When he rarely did talk, he was a man who had great social awareness. I remember when he explained to the neighboring college students why they needed to oppose the Korean-Japanese conferences. He told us that our country needed to pursue the growth of physiocracy to save our farmland, but Park Jeong-hee's administration was creating a policy to kill off the farming villages by lowering grain prices instead. He left a great impression on my young mind. My father sometimes read a magazine called *Sasanggae**, published by teacher Jang Joon-ha, which was very rare then. I realized later in life that my father greatly influenced my social awareness and criticism. I thought that I resembled my father. As I get older, I see my father's face in mine whenever I look in the mirror. I was unaware he had left behind many things with me.

My father's life and death were very heartbreaking. When I heard the story of how he passed, I felt as if his life was dimming little by little because he was so weary in his life. And when I think like that, I feel remorse because he expected something of me, but I wasn't able to show him how well I was doing or even give him hope.

For my father, I thought it wasn't enough for me to just get employed. Though it would take some time, I wanted to show him how well I was doing, so I decided to take the bar exam. I told my mother, "Let's endure hardship a little bit longer." After honoring and mourning my father's death for forty-nine days, I left home and went to Daeheung Temple in Haenam, South Jeolla Province.

I couldn't ask my family to help with boarding expenses at that time. But there was someone who helped me stay in Daeheung Temple, so that's why I went there. Inside the temple was a Buddhist hermitage called *Daegwangmyeongjun*. Since it was before Daeheung Temple was designated as a provincial park, it was a quiet and beautiful temple. The precincts of the temple didn't have any cement embracing nature. Even the roads were unpaved. If it had been located in Gyeongsang province, it would have been crowded with 200 monks, but since it wasn't, there were about twenty people, giving it a tranquil and secluded feel.

I studied diligently there. I think it was the first time I studied like that since I was in sixth grade, preparing for my junior high school entrance exam. There was another time when I passed the first round of the bar exam during winter vacation in my junior year in college. Since I was the only successful candidate in my grade, I was known as the "Bar Exam's Rising Star." Even though I passed the exam by memorizing certain subjects, since I hadn't studied legislation procedure previously, it was as if I was studying for the bar exam all over again from the beginning.

Daeheung Temple was inspiring, too; the surrounding Duryun Mountain was also very beautiful. When I was tired of studying, I would go to a valley not visible from the mountain trail and bathe. Sometimes, I stood at the peak of Duryun Mountain and saw the "ends of the earth" visible far below the mountains. Only the sea and the breakwater are visible at the "ends of the earth village" in Haenam. One must climb up Duryun Mountain to truly feel "the ends of the earth." Watching the end of the Korean peninsula touch the sea, and the Aegean Sea beyond the peninsula moved my heart.

I learned about our Korean tea *jakseolcha* there. Iljiam at Daeheung temple is where the Dasan Jung Yak-yong and Chusa Kim Jung-hee exchanged tea and conversation and revived our tea through Dongda-song. We could call it the foundation of our tea culture. Even when I was at Daeheung Temple, tea grown at Iljiam was supplied for the temples nationwide. The chief monk of the hermitage where I was staying often called me for tea. It was my first time drinking *jakseolcha*. I learned how to brew and drink tea then. It was a handmade tea made by drying and roasting wild tea leaves. The fragrance of the tea would linger in your mouth so that if you don't eat other foods or smoke a cigarette, the fragrance would remain there the whole day. I resisted smoking because I didn't want to lose the tea fragrance. After that, I was never able to have tea with that flavor. Captivated by the flavor of tea back then, I still enjoy our tea today.

There were many minnows in the valley. I would put a plastic bag over the washbasin with some miso, make a hole, and leave it in the water. As I took a bath, the basin filled with minnows. A couple of times, the people I stayed with at the hermitage would cook soup with the minnows that were caught. When I returned to the hermitage, the chief monk greeted me, saying, "I see there was quite a lot of killing today, sir." He must have liked me, though, because even though he didn't drink any alcohol, he would give me plum wine that he made with the green plums he picked in the temple courtyard.

Another memorable event was the reservist training. At that time, since I was a part of the mobilization reserve army, I had to change my residence registration to Daehung Temple to avoid missing training. I belonged to the battalion of the reserved forces in that area. There would be many young monks from Daehung who were also training in several battalion squads.

The priests and ministers were practically exempt from training because they helped the local defense council instead, but it was interesting to see the monks train diligently. In addition, seeing the monks wearing military uniforms and army caps on their shaved heads instead of their usual holy monk's robes made me smile. Unlike other reservists, the battalion received proper training. Maybe because it was in the countryside, the local defense council would deliver two mals (approx. 18 liters) of makgeolli on a bicycle on the day of training. It was quite an experience, soaking our feet in the valleys of Duryun Mountain and drinking makgeolli.

It was a good place to study, but I had to leave after a few months. It wasn't that I wanted to leave, but the hermitage stopped taking in boarders. I was told that Monk Go-am Yoon, the monk of the Jogye Order, was ordered to turn Daegwangmyeongjun into a shrine for Sun-won when he came to Daeheung temple.

I moved from place to place and continued to study for the bar exam. If I stayed at one place for a long time, I would get too comfortable and complacent and start hanging out with people. I intentionally relocated every few months to maintain the tension and always looked for affordable places.

In 1979, I passed the first round of the bar exam. The goal was to pass the second round the following year. However, in October of that year, the Buma Democratic Movement broke out. There were rumors that the military tank was crushing the protesters. Then, on October 26th, President Park Chung-hee was assassinated.

"Spring in Seoul"* began. From then on, it was difficult to concentrate on my studies because of the excitement. Then, in January 1980, there were discussions with the university about returning to study. I became a representative for the returning students regardless of my intention. When I returned to school in early March of that year, I was dragged into the whirlpool of the political situation caused by the "Spring in Seoul."

* *Sasanggae* magazine was established in April 1953 by Jang Joon-ha. It is a monthly current affairs magazine.
* Dongdasong A book written by a monk of the late Chosun Dynasty describing the tea ceremony as a poem. The order is called *ho ga cho eui*, usually called the choichunsa. He contributed greatly to reviving the tea culture by matching the performance of kindness with tea, which he referred to as the tea ceremony. The title means "to praise the tea of the east country," where the east country is referring to Korea.
* Spring in Seoul It refers to the period from October 26th 1979 to May 17th 1980, during which many Seoul democratization campaigns took place. This is analogous to the spring of Prague in Czechoslovakia in 1968.

Re-confinement

I returned to school. Spring was upon the campus, along with the "Spring in Seoul," which began with the demise of 18 years of military dictatorship. Returning to university was a matter of fact, and I negotiated with the school regarding the conditions of my return. I met with the school many times. The problem of re-admittance to school was settled at almost the same time in all universities. It took the form of autonomous decisions by respective schools, but there were no differences in the content. Students expelled from the school from the second half of the 1974 school year to 1979 were allowed to return to school in the spring of 1980.

The conditions for returning were unprecedented. They accepted the attendance of those who were expelled from the beginning of April of the first semester in 1975 as a full semester. For a senior like myself, graduating was only a semester away. I did not know how that was possible.

I also waived my tuition for returning to school, so I graduated in August 1980. It was a fall semester that was called "Cosmos Graduation*" at the time, but there were no photos of me because I didn't attend the graduation ceremony. I celebrated my nine-year college life by celebrating and drinking with my friends and lower-classmen.

As soon as the new semester started in 1980, Kyunghee University started the Academy Democratization Struggle against the nepotistic foundation. Private schools such as Hanyang University and Sejong University also followed suit. The school responded by canceling classes for a long time.

Returning after five years, I only took one 100-minute lecture and was done. When there were no lectures, there was a daily sit-in protest requesting the resignation of the nepotistic foundation and democratization of the school. Then, from the end of April, other universities began protests against anti-dictatorship, and Kyunghee University naturally turned in that direction.

It was difficult to continue studying for the bar exam once I started negotiations with the school about my re-admittance. It was even more so after returning to school. I thought the bar exam would have to wait. Still, I was eligible to take the second test immediately because I had passed the first round the previous year. I took the second round of the 22nd bar exam during the school protests in April 1980 since I had studied for it, and it'd be a waste if I didn't. I didn't expect much because I couldn't study for two or three months prior to the exam, which was the most crucial time. I took the test with no greed, as it would be enough to build experience and practice for the following year.

I also waived my tuition for returning to school, so I graduated in August 1980. It was a fall semester that was called "Cosmos Graduation" at the time, but there were no photos of me because I didn't attend the graduation ceremony. I celebrated my nine-year college life by celebrating and drinking with my friends and lower-classmen.

I participated in every protest when Kyunghee University turned to anti-dictatorial democratization protests. The current students had no demonstration protest experiences, so the returning students had to teach them methods and provide tips. The police blocked the front gate for the first few days. Almost all the universities in Seoul started the demonstrations, and after the surprise attacks in the city, such as Gwanghwamun, they didn't block the gates anymore. It turned out they decided to concentrate defense on the city's points, including the Blue House, the Central Building*, and Sejongro. Soon after, the rest of the area became like a liberating area where students didn't receive any restraint even when they marched on in protests. University students gathered at the Seoul Station Square every day.

Kyunghee University had an opening ceremony every day at the school, marched to Seoul Station Square, attended the university student union protest, and marched back to the school for a disbandment ceremony. The number of university students gathering at Seoul Station consistently increased. On the last day of May 15th, there were nearly 200,000 people. It was the moment when the resistance to the new military unit's dictatorship reached its peak.

At that moment, the university student councils of each college, including the Seoul National University Student Union, decided to withdraw all their students. It was to not give any reason for military input. This was called the Seoul Station Grand Withdrawal*. It was indeed a futile moment.

There were talks of military input from a few days before. Trustworthy professors would tell me such information and that there shouldn't be any excuse given for military input. However, regardless of the university, the returning student groups believed we should fight "until death," even if the military was dispatched. It was the last critical moment for democratization. If we failed, the military dictatorship would be extended again. Even if the military was dispatched, it was expected that there'd be a limit to aggressive suppression due to the eyes of the international community.

The returning students tried to convince the presidents of the student councils, but those who had no protest experience were afraid at the news of the military launch. The university students who disbanded didn't regroup. While the university students of Seoul were shrouded in the important crossroads, only the citizens of Gwangju had to confront the martial law forces.

I think the last moment's betrayal of university students in Seoul caused the citizens of Gwangju to make such a big sacrifice at the May 18th Gwangju Democratization Movement*.

The new military government extended an Emergency Martial Law* to the whole country on May 17th at midnight. I visited my father-in-law's farm on Ganghwa Island with my wife that day. My wife and I had been in a relationship for quite some time, and our families knew we were to get married. My father-in-law, mother-in-law, the two of us, and sister-in-law and her boyfriend, all six of us, went to Bomun Temple on Sukmo Island, an island in Ganghwa Island. On the bus back to the farm that night, I heard the radio news that an emergency martial decree would be issued nationwide from midnight on that day. The emergency decree had already been issued except for Jeju Island on October 27th of the previous year. The situation in Seoul was unchanged because the emergency martial order was only extended to Jeju Island. However, there was no reason to extend an emergency martial order to Jeju Island.

I just knew with intuition. Even under the emergency martial order, street demonstrations were allowed, and the army was dispatched, but now things would be different. This was too serious to dispatch military forces and enforce the emergency martial law. I told my wife on the bus, "As soon as we return, we should flee for a while, so if that happens, don't panic." I was naive.

As we were getting off the bus at the entrance to the driveway to the farm, suddenly, five or six robust unidentified men surrounded us at gunpoint. They yelled, "Freeze! Hands up! You are Moon Jae-in, right?" It was the detectives of the Information Department of Cheongnyangri Police Station waiting to arrest me.

I said, "Let me see the warrant," but they yelled back, "What warrant?!" and showed me a martial certificate with "martial law" written in red. Under the Emergency Martial Law, the warrant system was suspended. I was handcuffed and taken into their car in front of my in-laws and detained at the Cheongyangri police station.

In those days, I boarded in a dormitory called *Janghaksa* at Kyunghee

University. I later heard that on the eve of my arrest, the martial army officers came to find me and searched even the girls' rooms. When they found that I wasn't there, the detectives raided my in-laws' house that morning, searched the entire house with their shoes on, harassed my sister-in-law, who was a high school student at the time looking after the house by herself, and found out that we went to Ganghwa Island farm. Then, they waited all day, eating bread at the farm entrance. It was a very embarrassing moment, putting my hands up at gunpoint and handcuffing and arresting me in front of my parents-in-law. They were still in shock when I looked out from the bus.

This wasn't the first time I surprised them. At the end of October 1977, when I was a senior sergeant of the Airborne Forces, my wife's graduation recital was at Kyunghee University concert hall. Although soldiers weren't permitted to go out on weekdays, I decided to go out with a false pass that I received from a friend in the personnel unit. I could've gone to military confinement, but I was determined to go. I wore a black beret in the paratrooper uniform to the graduation recital. I met and greeted my in-laws for the first time there. Later, I heard they knew I was expelled from the university and in the army, but they were shocked to see me in the airborne military uniform at their daughter's graduation recital.

At that time, the reason for the arrest was a violation of the Declaration of Martial Law*. Many people across the country were arrested for the same reason at the same time. All those arrested for violating the Martial Declaration were immediately brought to the military tribunals*. However, Kyunghee students, including myself, were kept in a pending state without going to the military tribunals. It was because of the tragic accident that occurred in Namdaemun on May 15th, when university students last gathered in Seoul Station Square.

On that day, there were approximately 200,000 university students at Seoul Station Square. The police focused all their troops and firepower at Namdaemun, City Hall, Sejong-ro, Gwanghwamun, and the Blue House, preventing students from crossing Namdaemun. The students, who were superior in number, banged and threw the pedestal blocks, but the police guards blocking with shields on either side of Namdaemun were like iron walls. Students took turns by schools alternately, but no school could penetrate the wall. In the meantime, several empty buses stood on the left side of the road near Namdaemun. When the road was blocked because of the demonstration, the buses had been abandoned after the drivers were unable to go there.

At first, the students tried to break the police wall by pushing a bus. But the bus didn't go straight without anyone guiding the steering wheel in the driver's seat. We couldn't push the bus straight to the police base. People naturally started asking, "Does anyone know how to drive?" At that moment, a young man in a tracksuit stood up bravely and took the steering wheel. If he could direct the bus in front of the students, the police force would have to open the way, and then the students who followed the bus would break through the line.

But he drove the bus too fast, maybe because he was nervous or his driving ability was poor. As a result, the bus passed the police line, but the police closed the line again before the students could follow after the bus. It was only the bus and the police. We were worried for the student but there was no way to help. The bus, which I thought would get caught, returned to the other side after a while. It went to the left side of Namdaemun and left from the right side. Apparently, at that time, the driver hit the police line that was standing on the right side of Namdaemun, standing toward the students. We had no idea then, and we were relieved that he returned safely.

I found out about that night through the news. The bus had hit the police officers from behind on the way back. One person died, and four were seriously injured. It was a very shocking incident because there were no cases of police force being killed by protesters until then.

The incident was then used as a symbolic example of the radicalism, violence, and extremity of student protests. The authorities set up a special investigation headquarters and announced that they will identify the criminal. At the time, the press reported that "students stole the bus from the bus driver to drive it" to highlight the violence of the demonstration. It wasn't true at all. There was no need because more than twenty buses were left on the scene at the time.

I was suspected of violating the declaration of martial law and, at the same time, a witness at the Special Investigative Division for the incident. According to the photo taken by the police at a neighboring building at that time, Kyunghee University's banner was at the head of the bus during the "bus rush." As we tried to break through the police barricade by alternating between universities, it was determined that there was a "bus rush" while Kyunghee University tried to break it. In addition, the person driving the bus wore a tracksuit, and Kyunghee University was famous for its sports department. So, the police first investigated the possibility of the bus driver being a Kyunghee University student. Another subject under suspicion by the police was the Korea National Sports University. This was because the Sports University students participated in the protest in tracksuits.

The Special Investigation Division had already confirmed that I wasn't the driver because of the photographs, but under suspicion that the driver was a Kyunghee student, asked "You, at least, must know who he is, since you led the protest as a returning student representative." But I didn't know and Kyunghee University's banner just happened to be there when another school was going through the police line.

Ultimately, I was a useless resource in finding out who the driver was. However, they detained me because the Special Investigation Division had no reportable results. As a result, the case wasn't referred to the military court for more than twenty days and remained pending. But that situation instead saved me.

* **Cosmos Graduation** In Korea, most graduations are held in February because Spring semesters start in March, but if one graduates in August, before the second semester begins, it is called the "cosmos graduation" because the flower, cosmos, would bloom near that time.
* **Central Building** The past central government building was located just behind the current Gwanghwamun. It was used as a government building in the Chosun Dynasty during the Japanese colonial rule and was changed to the central government office after the liberation, then was demolished.
* **Seoul Station Grand Withdrawal** The student protests peaked daily around Seoul Station until May 15, 1980, when the student protest leaders decided to disburse voluntarily, saying they would not provide an excuse for military dispatch.
* **May 18th Gwangju Democratization Movement** A Democratic Movement in Gwangju, South Jeolla Province, from May 18-27, 1980, demanding the removal of martial law and the resignation of Chun Doo-Hwan. Hundreds of civilians died when the new military put the martial law forces into power. The civilian slaughter with the most number of victims since the Korean War.
* **Emergency Martial Law** This refers to the martial state that the president proclaims to maintain the order of public good or to meet military needs in an area where the social order is extremely disturbed by the exhibition, affairs, or a similar national emergency.
* **Declaration of Martial Law** Statute or order to publicize martial law under the name of martial law commander.
* **Military Tribunals** based on military law.

Receiving News in a Holding Cell

It had been approximately twenty-three or twenty-four days since my imprisonment when I received unexpected good news, which my wife delivered.

I passed the judicial examination. I completely forgot about the announcement date of the successful candidates. However, my wife didn't, so she went and got the results. Since I was in such a predicament, she might have waited for the results feverishly.

After a while, the dean of student affairs and the law school's president of alums came to visit to congratulate me. Since the police officers weren't allowed to let me meet them outside the holding cell, they allowed them to come in to congratulate me. They even allowed us to drink soju and snack inside as well. The officers said it was unheard of in police history to have outside personnel come inside the holding cell and drink congratulatory drinks with a prisoner.

A few days later, I was released. If my case had been sent to court-martial, it would've been impossible for me to have been released. My passing would have been canceled, or the third round of exams would have been disqualified. Luckily, since my case was undetermined, I was able to be released. There were only two successful applicants that passed the judicial exam at Kyunghee University. However, since there was a chance of cancelation of one of the candidate's admission, the school authorities endeavored to save at least one.

At that time, Kyunghee University's president was Professor Kim Jum-gon, who was a part of the first batch of graduates from the Korean Military Academy (KMA). It was recorded in the war history that he was the first regimental commander to enter Pyeong-yang during the Korean War. When he was a company commander, it was said that former President Park Jung-hee, who was in the second batch of graduates from KMA, was his platoon commander. I was told that he put a lot of effort into the marital law command. I think that the release was probably why. Thanks to him, the Special Investigation Bureau's "witnesses" ended, and the investigation of the Contravention of Martial Law Act was kept quiet.

Personally, it was a very pleasant event. However, the news of the May 18th Gwangju Democratic Movement I heard about while in the holding cell was grim. About two days after I got arrested, detectives from the information division reported Gwangju's situation daily. They showed the papers and provided information they had heard from their sources. What was a bit unexpected was that their attitudes towards the military were very critical. They were infuriated by the soldiers who were massacring civilians. They proudly insisted that Gwangju's chief of police open an arsenal so that civilians could have access to weapons.

But when I was released from jail, it was strange to see that people didn't know what was happening in Gwangju. The press wasn't releasing as much information to the civilians as the detectives provided for me, even distorting what they were releasing.

There was one more critical moment before passing the final round of the judicial exam. It was the third interview. During the third interview, if there was nothing wrong with your identity, there was a 100% rate of passing back then. But, a couple of days before the interview, personnel from the Agency for National Security Planning (NSP) asked me for an interview.

I went to the designated hotel and agreed to the interview. There was only one key question asked. The main theme was "whether or not my thoughts were the same as when I was demonstrating." It was a sort of verification of one's ideology. It was very perplexing for me to answer. So many thoughts were going through my mind. But I was young, and I would rather die than surrender my pride. I thought whatever and said, "I think what I did back then was the right thing to do, and even today, I don't think of it any differently." Then, I regretted answering like that until the final announcement of the successful candidates was announced.

Fortunately, I passed. I don't know if he reported back accurately or if what he reported didn't affect the outcome. Back then, there wasn't anyone who failed the third interview.

Anyway, I think I had great luck in passing the bar exam. The following year, many demonstration ex-convicts failed the third interview. After many years, some of them found out that the Committee of Truth and Reconciliation unfairly exercised governmental authority, and some entered the Judicial Research and Training Institute at an old age.

I was lucky to pass the second round of the bar exam as well. Two or three months before the exam, I stopped studying, and so it would have been impossible to have passed if typical questions were asked. However, that year, there weren't many typical questions asked, but questions on constitutional law subjects, which I studied for.

I had low scores on most of the subjects but almost received the best score for the subjects on constitutional law, which helped me barely pass.

Being an Attorney

The days at the Judicial Research and Training Institute* went relatively smoothly. Unfamiliar laws and sentence structures of written judgments became familiar. It was a small sum, but I got my first salary and became financially independent for the first time. I married my wife, and she gave birth to our first child. We married after a long relationship, seven years since we first met.

Attorney Park Won-soon, Supreme Court Chief Justice Park Si-hwan, Constitutional Court Judge Song Doo-hwan, Minister of Justice Lee Gui-nam, former candidate for Attorney General Chung Sung-kwan, Supreme Court Chief Justice Park Byung-dae, and former Chief Secretary to the President for Civil Affairs Park Jung-kyu were all in my cohort at the Institute. Many entered the path of politics. Cho Bae-sook, Park Eun-soo, Ko Seung-deok, Lee Han-sung, Members of the National Assembly, and Ham Seung-hee, former members of the National Assembly, were also in my cohort. With only 141 successful candidates, we were the last cohort with such a small number, so we shared a strong bond. Almost everyone was appointed as a judge or public prosecutor, so the professors at the Institute treated us as their junior judges or prosecutors.

The late Attorney Cho Young-rae* was also one of my colleagues in the same cohort. He had passed the bar long before us but was dismissed from the Institute for the Seoul National University Student Conspiracy Case. He was then reinstated when we were at the Institute, so we studied together. He influenced me greatly. When my appointment as a judge was rejected, he arranged for a meeting with several law firms, including 'Kim & Chang.'

In 1984 and 1985, at the Onsan Industrial Complex in Ulsan, a large number of residents were sick with a pollution-related disease called "Onsan Disease.*" He contacted me to go to the Onsan complex together with him to conduct an epidemiological survey. We also took samples of the incubator's hair and asked for a heavy metal test. As a result of his efforts, Onsan Disease became a social issue. The authorities that consistently argued that it was not pollution-related eventually recognized the pollution-related issues and moved the people in masses. It was the first case that highlighted a pollution-related disease of residents under the strict military dictatorship as a social problem.

In the 1987 presidential election, he led the "unification of the candidates*" campaign. The majority of the notable figures out of office were inclined to give "critical support*" to candidate Kim Dae-jung. I joined him in the Busan area. At that time, Attorney Roh focused on fair election surveillance activities without holding a special position or support for anyone. We were greatly disappointed when Roh Tae-woo was elected because the candidate unification did not occur until the end. After a while, I also discussed the founding of Minbyun* (Lawyers for Democratic Society) with him.

When the *"Seoul Minbyun"* was founded, because it was difficult to make a nationwide *Minbyun* from the beginning, I established the "Busan & Gyeongnam *Minbyun*" separately in Busan.

When the reformist monks of the Jogye Order established the Emergency Reform division at the *Beomeo* Temple, I was an advisory lawyer for the temple for three years after his introduction. When the Busan Buddhist Human Rights Commission was founded, I participated as a human rights commissioner, although I wasn't Buddhist myself.

Attorney Cho Young-rae was a heavy chain smoker. Especially when writing, he didn't take the cigarette out of his mouth. His famous column and defense statements were all written in thick tobacco smoke. One day, I came to Busan, and we ate sashimi for lunch together. Even a reasonable chain smoker does not smoke while he's eating, but he would smoke while he talked, even in the middle of a meal. He had a unique smoking habit of smoking a cigarette halfway, stubbing it out, and re-smoking it later. The chain-smoking had become quite serious, but he didn't listen even though I told him about my concerns. It was twenty days later that he heard that he was terminally ill with lung cancer.

When I was training at the institute, I wanted to become a judge. I thought it was fitting for my character. I studied how to write a judgment sentence in a mock trial, and I quite enjoyed it.

I was a probationary judge at the Northern Seoul District Court. It was the place where I was arrested and tried when I was in college, so it felt extraordinary. I also participated in actual trials there. If there was no consensus among judges, they said, "Let's see what the probationary judge thinks," so I took part in the consensus. I was also trained to write a judgment sentence on actual case records. The Chief Justice of the District Court, Yoon Kwan, who later became one of the Chief Justices of the Supreme Court, read and corrected every judgment sentence written by the probationary judges and called them one by one to give feedback. He gave me a lot of compliments, saying, "You'd make a good judge." When I wasn't appointed as one, he encouraged me, "Being a judge is actually not a good job. An attorney has more benefits." Later on, he also served as an arbitrator in the case of the Supreme Court Justice crisis under the Participatory Government.

The probationary prosecutor was also a good experience. I was again placed at the Northern Seoul Branch, where I was arrested and investigated. Under the prosecutor's office law, the probationary prosecutor was appointed to act as a public prosecutor substitute, so we assumed the same roles and performed the same duties as the public prosecutor. At that time, the northern branch also allocated a lot of incidents to probationary prosecutors. Of course, they were relatively lighter cases.

The experience of having been investigated as a suspect many times during my university years helped me handle the case as a probationary prosecutor. When I first investigated the suspect and wrote the report, my supervising prosecutor, who was observing from the side, was very impressed, saying, "You seem to have done it many times." Maybe because of my familiarity with my experience at the receiving end of the investigation, I was ranked first in the Prosecutor's Course at the Institute. But I didn't want to be a public prosecutor. It's not that I thought the duties of the prosecutor were negative.

The work of the judge is rather passive. The prosecutor is able to actively and proactively set up social justice, so it seemed to be better. However, as I was dealing with the case as a probationary prosecutor, I decided that being a prosecutor didn't fit my personality.

One time, I was allocated a fatal traffic accident case. Now, Sang-gye-dong has large-scale apartment complexes, but at the time, there were open fields with several block factories. A young couple with an infant worked together at a block factory. There was no one to take care of the baby, so they left the baby between the block piles, and the mother would sometimes go over to feed and take care of the baby.

But one day, as the truck loaded with blocks was leaving the factory, the baby was hit by the truck tires and killed. No one saw the baby go under the truck. It was assumed that the baby crawled out of the pile of blocks and under the truck while the adults were busy loading blocks onto the vehicle.

The circumstances of the arrested driver, as well as the parents of the dead baby, were heartbreaking. The arrest warrant stated that the driver had violated the obligation to look under the vehicle when starting the vehicle. How do you expect to judge such an accident in an actual situation? In addition, the driver was an orphan, a poor young man driving a truck at the factory with the goodwill of the block factory owner.

As I pondered what to do, the owner of the block factory paid compensation to the parents instead of the driver and settled the accident. I insisted that it should at least be a summary indictment if the driver cannot walk without a charge. The director and the deputy prosecutors said, "Even if the court releases the fatal traffic accident case, by principle, the prosecution has to prosecute with an arrest warrant." I went to the Chief of the branch and told him my opinion. Then the director and the deputy prosecutors said, "We need to give him a large fine if it's going to be a summary indictment." I argued my way until I minimized the amount of the fine, allowing him to pay in installments, and then had him released. This was only possible because there was an atmosphere at the time to encourage the probationary prosecutors.

While handling that case, I felt that punishing people didn't suit my personality. Punishing people has always been burdensome and uncomfortable. Even if it was necessary to punish people for behavior like violations of the Food Sanitation Act, it was often difficult to determine the level of punishment because of the difficult circumstances they faced, such as disabilities and offenses that continued to impact their livelihoods. I realized I was not suited to be a prosecutor because of my soft personality.

Because of my demonstration records, I couldn't be appointed as a judge. At that time, I wasn't the only one. There were only two women in my cohort at the Institute. One of them was ranked third out of the entire Institute and received the Presidential Award from the Korea Bar Association. But her father had a criminal record with violations of the anti-communist law and had been charged with probation. It was after the abolition of guilt by association system* that she wasn't appointed as a judge due to her father's history. For that reason, she went to the office of prosecutors with other female cohorts, and they became the first female public prosecutors in history.

The court even excluded four students in our cohort from appointment because they had polio-related disabilities and faced harsh criticism from the public. After three months, the court appointed them as judges, but that was the court's level of consciousness at that time.

It was not because of external pressure that I wasn't appointed as a judge. The Supreme Court, in particular, had a consciousness and awareness that lagged behind the times and made an outdated decision. And so, I was forced into the legal path. On the way, I met Attorney Roh Moo-hyun.

All the steps and moments that made me become an attorney seemed to be a destined progression that was set in advance for me to meet Attorney Roh Moo-hyun.

I married my wife, and she gave birth to our first child. We married after a long relationship, seven years since we first met.

I married my wife, and she gave birth to our first child.
We married after a long relationship, seven years since we first met.

* **Attorney Cho Young-rae** Cho Young-rae is a representative lawyer for Korean lawyers who wrote *Jeon Tae-il's Biography*. Died in 1990.
* **Onsan disease** A pollution-related disease that occurred in Onsan in the early 1980's.
* **"Unification of Candidates" and "Critical Support"** The movement of citizens who demanded the unification of the two candidates, Kim Dae-Jung and Kim Young-Sam, in opposition to ending military dictatorship in the first election in 1987. At the time, Kim Dae-jung was criticized as a relatively more democratic leader compared to Kim Young-sam, but still brought together the public support through the "critical support" stance.
* ***Minbyun*** Abbreviation for Lawyers for Democratic Society. Established in 1988 by lawyers who served in defense of civil rights and human rights.
* **Guilt by Association System** The system before the modern criminal law that gives joint responsibility and punishes the person who has a certain relationship with the union criminal. Although the law prohibits the abuse of the past, when a family member or relative of the death penalty is revealed in the identity inquiry, they were not appointed as a high ranking public official.

1 My Encounter

2 My Life

3 My Accompaniment

4 My Destiny

To the Blue House

The taste of the 2002 Presidential election lingered - especially in Busan, the hometown of then-President-elect Roh Moo-hyun. After the election was over, it was difficult to contact the new President-elect. Consequently, I had to handle the incoming congratulatory calls. I was also responsible for thanking those who had helped with the campaign.

It wasn't as pleasant as one might think. Those who truly deserved my appreciation refrained from calling, concerned that they might impose upon me an unnecessary burden. Some, perhaps, thought that I might be too busy to answer. People with little to no involvement in the election victory called to request meetings. Navigating the slew of congratulatory calls was exhausting. Mr. Lee Ho-cheol, the President-elect's campaign manager, had managed every election in which the President-elect had run. He once told me, "After each election, I am under a heavy debt for years afterward." I empathized completely.

After the election victory, President-elect Roh called me. It was the end of the year. He invited me and my wife to come to Seoul for dinner.

It had been a while since I was in Seoul. My wife and I joined the President-elect and his wife for dinner. We dined at a high-rise hotel restaurant, where we could see the Pugak Mountains and the Blue House. The President-elect had reserved a room with a good view of the Blue House, and he and his wife yielded the best seats to me and my wife. The dinner was exquisite, and we exchanged compliments and congratulations.

The rapport between us was extraordinary. We shared news of the election with the ease of old friends reminiscing. Not a word about the Presidential Transition Committee (PTC)* or politics was uttered. When he told me that he planned to see all his children married before the inauguration, I thought that was just like him.

On January 13, 2003, I met the President-elect again, this time with Mr. Lee Ho-cheol. Somehow, a regional newspaper received word of the meeting and reported it. The meeting was held at a traditional Korean full-course restaurant near Sahjik-dong in Busan. There, the President-elect revealed that he wanted me to be The Blue House Senior Presidential Secretary for Civil Affairs (SPSCA)*. According to him, there was no one else to whom he would rather entrust the position. The President-elect also asked Mr. Lee to accept an appointment to any position of the President-elect's choosing.

I couldn't immediately accept the position. I asked for a few days to consider the offer. Mr. Lee Ho-cheol asked for time, as well. The President-elect must have been offended. Immediately after we spoke, he replied, "Since you pushed me into politics and made me a president, you should be accountable for your actions." I struggled with the decision for a week. At that time, I was a human rights attorney and made my living reprimanding those in power and holding them accountable for corruption. I felt that I lacked the experience required to undertake an executive role in the state administration. I was a legal expert, yet I viewed myself as nothing more than a naive scholar. I was ignorant considering insider politics. Though it was true that I held the position of the chairman of the Busan Regional Election Headquarters for the New Millennium Democratic Party (NMDP), I did this without joining the party.

I endeavored to understand why the President-elect wanted me for such an important position. I agonized over whether or not I could apply my legal knowledge in a way that would obtain the level of national reform he intended to accomplish during his presidency.

I couldn't immediately accept the position. I asked for a few days to consider the offer. Mr. Lee Ho-cheol asked for time, as well. Perceiving our reaction as lukewarm and indifferent, the President-elect went as far as to say, "You have driven me into politics and made me the president, so shouldn't you bear the responsibility?". I struggled with the decision for a week. Upon embracing the title of human rights lawyer, I acknowledged my sole engagement in critiquing power, devoid of any experience in national administration or governance. As a legal expert, my expertise was limited to the law, leaving me a complete novice in matters of statecraft. I was also unfamiliar with the political arena, having never participated in it. Even though I served as the head of the Busan campaign headquarters, I did so without becoming a member of the Democratic Party.

I deeply contemplated wheat the President-elect's intention was in asking me, with such a background, to serve as the Chief Presidential Secretary for Civil Affairs, and how I, in that role, could effectively assist in implementing the reforms he aimed to achieve.

The Office of the Presidential Secretary for Civil Affairs (OPSCA) was to carry out the initial task of forming a non-authoritarian Blue House. In the Participatory Government, "Ending Authoritarianism" became the new slogan for reform. The OPSCA had historically been a symbol of the authoritarian Blue House. This office had been abolished at the start of Kim Dae-jung's People's Administration. After reconsidering the necessity of the office, the People's Administration reinstated it. The office existed but was no longer authoritarian. Professor Kim Sung-jae, who was then the current director of the Kim Dae-jung Presidential Memorial Library of Hanshin University, was appointed as the Senior Secretary of the newly reinstated OPSCA. In the 1970s and 1980s, he played a leading role in the Democratic Movement, which was a nationwide anti-authoritarian movement led by academics, university students, and workers. He went on to become the Minister of Culture and Tourism. He was well qualified to be the Senior Secretary. When he was appointed, Senior Secretary-appointee Kim asked me to accept the Presidential Secretary for Civil Affairs (PSCA) position. He thought someone with a legal background would be appropriate for the secretarial position. He wanted me because I was a legal expert specializing in human rights cases. He also appreciated that I had no Supreme Prosecutors' Office (SPO) background. I declined his offer, because I believed that my daily legal battles for human rights would help Korea more than my potential position in the Blue House would.

Towards midterm, the People's Administration realized that the Supreme Prosecutors' Office needed better management. They returned to a system that appointed a high-level ex-prosecutor of SPO to the position of Senior Presidential Secretary for Civil Affairs. Even then, the Senior Presidential Secretary for Civil Affairs was appointed as a current prosecutor. When first elected, the People's Administration had gone as far as abolishing the OPSCA. There was an urgent desire to revive the spirit of that early stage of the People's Administration. There was an urgent desire to revive the spirit of that early stage of the People's Administration.

The next task was reforming powerful governmental institutions, such as the SPO and the National Intelligence Service (NIS). The reform wasn't meant to create a new system, but to prevent the Blue House from using government institutions as political tools.

The President-elect didn't mention our reform plan or acknowledge our concern about his superseding authority. He only spoke of his deep concern over the low-birth rate in Korea. He briefly reminded me that I was the one person he could appoint as Senior Presidential Secretary for Civil Affairs. In the past, we had frequently discussed our dismay concerning the vestiges of authoritarianism that lingered in the People's Administration. We both were upset by the OPSCA returning to its old role, and we bristled at the insufficient reform of government institutions. He didn't have to say much. I simply understood him.

The President-elect's decision to choose me for his cabinet wasn't merely based on our shared convictions. A man in power is apt to forget his convictions. The President-elect sought someone with the legal background needed to navigate the OPSCA. It was his intention to appoint as Senior Presidential Secretary for Civil Affairs (SPSCA) someone who didn't understand the SPO. My appointment as SPSCA would show the country that he had no intention to control the SPO.

I found myself running out of reasons to refuse. As I began to better understand the President-elect's agenda, I had to concede that I fit the qualifications needed to achieve his goals. I accepted his request, rationalizing that the position of SPSCA handled the administration's legal affairs, so my position as SPSCA was just an extension of my normal legal activities. I innocently believed that I could return to my previous position as a human rights lawyer, after working one or two years as SPSCA.

Then I told the President-elect, "Since I don't know politics very well, I don't think I can handle the role of making executive decisions in political affairs. However, I think I can handle the work of keeping and protecting the principles. If you think that that is my role to perform, use me." I added two conditions for my acceptance. First, I told him, "My involvement in the administration is only as far as the SPSCA goes and no more," Secondly, I added, "Don't tell me to go into politics." This was because during the President-elect's election campaign period, the

"Since I don't know politics very well, I don't think I can handle the role of making executive decisions in political affairs. But I think I can handle as far as the work of keeping and protecting the principles. If you think that that is my role to perform, use me."

President-elect had urged me to run for the office of Mayor of the City of Busan in 2002. The President-elect was very happy with my acceptance and agreed to my terms.

On January 23, 2003, I went to the Presidential Transition Committee (PTC) Press Room to announce that I had been appointed as the new SP-SCA by the President-elect. I began working immediately. It was urgent to set up the structure for the OPSCA. It was difficult for those who were appointed as senior secretaries to the President to control and manage their personnel appointments during the presidential transition period. There were many who had worked for years with the President-elect who had hoped to be appointed. After an organizational restructuring was set unilaterally with these people in the center, individual senior secretaries had little room to maneuver in terms of finding people to work under him. Due to the special circumstances concerning the OPSCA, however, my recommendations for personnel for the office were mostly respected by the President-elect.

Once I became Senior Presidential Secretary for Civil Affairs (SPSCA), I considered Mr. Lee Ho-cheol for appointment and immediately received his acceptance. Before I began working on the personnel, I met with the previous SPSCA of the People's Administration and asked for his advice.

According to him, 80% of the work dealt with by the OPSCA involved the SPO. He said that it was ideal to have those with SPO background in Senior Secretary and Secretary positions. He also told me that, of all the reports that go to the president, those of the SPSCA are of the highest priority. Thus, an ability to write good reports is one of the most important assets to look for in an SPSCA candidate. If I didn't find any ideal candidates, I could choose a highly trained prosecutor from the SPO and send him back to his original post later. I also met with the then-current SPSCA who had received accolades from President Kim Dae-jung for his excellence in writing reports. He had been chosen while he was still a prosecutor at the SPO and had returned to his old post when the Participatory Government began. He was of the same opinion as his senior.

I didn't follow their advice. Should any need arise for communication with the SPO, I thought either I or the Senior Presidential Secretary for Audit and Inspection (SPSAI) could handle it. There was no one as capable of carrying out the Senior Presidential Secretary for Civil Affair's duty as disciplinary Sergeant as Mr. Lee Ho-cheol. In fact, throughout the Participatory Government period, it was largely his contribution to that office that bolstered moral alertness in the Blue House.

Other presidential secretaries were also appointed by legal experts who could see eye-to-eye with the reforms initiated by President Roh and his Participatory Government. Mr. Park Beom-kye, an ex-judge and esteemed academic with a plan for SPO reform, was appointed as the Presidential Secretary for Civil Affairs (PSCA). He strongly pursued the removal of the SPO from the Ministry of Justice (MoJ). Some female secretaries to the President were intentionally appointed, as well. Attorney Hwang Ducknam, recommended by the Minister of Justice, Kang Geum-Sil, was appointed as the Presidential Secretary for Legal Affairs (PSLA). Mr. Hwang oversaw all the legal issues that pertained to the Blue House.

I paid the most attention when appointing the Presidential Secretary for the Civil Service Discipline (PSCSD) and the Presidential Secretary for Audit and Inspection (PSAI). We needed the position of PSCSD to be filled by someone who could make a clear distinction between public and private affairs concerning the appointees' verification processes. Whoever filled the position would also have to keep pace with the administration's policy agendas.

Mr. Lee Suk-tae, who was then-vice president of the Lawyers for a Democratic Society (LDS) and later became the society's president, was a long-time human rights attorney. He had a character that would never pander for his private ambitions. He possessed the intelligence and charisma of the scholars from the Koryeo or Chosun Dynasties in Korean history, known as seonbi.

I persuaded Mr. Lee to join the administration, repeatedly explaining how the Participatory Government's appointment selection procedure was different from the past and how important its appointees' verification was. My efforts to convince him to support the new PSCSD was later compared to those of Emperor Liu Bei of the ancient Three Kingdoms Period of China who had visited Zhuge Liang, the legendary strategist, three times in humility to finally persuade him to join his camp.

Although I was the SPSCA, Mr. Lee, the new PSCSD, didn't allow me to know the results of the appointees' verification. He sent the Appointees' Verification Reports directly to the Presidential Appointments Committee (PAC). He then reported to me, either in the afternoon the day before the PAC meeting, or in the morning the day of the PAC meeting. When I was too busy to receive or read his reports, I often went into the PAC meetings without knowing the verification results. The only time he discussed any details with me was when an appointee's verification result was too ambiguous to make a clear decision. On rare occasions, verification results were designated as an item of business to be discussed during the OPSCA secretarial meeting. That way, a consensus could be reached more easily. He did all this to avoid any outside influence, including that of the SPSCA, in the appointees' verification process. In doing this, he set a precedent; all his successors have followed suit.

For the position of Presidential Secretary for Audit and Inspection (PSAI), however, I wanted someone who had no contact with any of us to be appointed. That position was to audit and inspect the president's special relations, high level public officials and the Blue House inner circle. To be objective, this person needed to lack any prior connections to anyone from the President-elect's past. The PSAI needed to be ideologically impartial in order to handle audits without bias. Mr. Yang In-seok, a long-time retired lawyer and ex-prosecutor, fit that description perfectly. Mr. Yang had been the Prosecutor in the "Clothing Lobby Case*," so it was easy to find references. We collected Mr. Yang's reviews from various sources, including a review from the Ex-Special Prosecutor, Lawyer Choi Byeong-mo.

After two difficult meetings with him, I barely persuaded Mr. Yang to join the administration. The PAC was strongly against his appointment. Mr. Shin Gae-ryun, then-Chief of Staff of the President-elect, was especially against it. Mr. Shin's argument was that appointing a PSAI who was already on our campaign's side would significantly aid the administration's efforts. It was a logical argument. In retrospect, I sometimes think that Mr. Shin's argument was correct. Even in audit and inspection, a shared sense of trust should exist. I didn't see it that way then, however. I argued my point of view profusely and I swayed the cabinet with my convictions. For this reason, the appointment of PSAI was a bit delayed.

After many difficulties, we finished the appointment process for the new administration. To this day, I believe it was a perfect dream team. Due to our team's hard work, the Participatory Government's goal of expelling authoritarianism from Korean politics was realized. We were able to reform powerful government institutions and we established key moral tenets for the administration.

It was difficult to understand why there weren't systematic procedures set up during the time of the Presidential Transition Committee (PTC) to support the preparatory activities for the new administration's appointees. In case of the OPSCA, both the SPSCA and the PSCAs had to get involved with the appointments so that the Cabinet could be formed at the start of the new administration. This work was completely different and unrelated to the executive work for which we were prepared. Despite our lack of experience in assembling an administrative team, doing so was seen as our official duty, and we did it well.

Other than the PTC, our preparations for the new administration weren't subsidized. No salary was given. We paid our own office rental fees and funded our own gatherings and activities. We were so dedicated to our mission that we willingly made this sacrifice, but it was hard to believe that there still existed this sort of a systematic gap in a developed nation.

Difficulties continued, even after the official calendar for the new administration had begun. All the elected and non-elected government officials who worked for the Blue House had to go through the security clearance procedures before their official appointments. In the beginning of the administration, the security clearances were being done all at the same time and by early April of 2003, almost one and a half months after the start of the new administration, their official appointments were given.

Until their official appointments, all these people had been doing the work required for their positions. Despite this, they received no salaries for their labor. It was simply absurd and in direct violation of labor laws. The president was indifferent to this issue. When I advised him to pay the officials for the work they had done prior to their official appointments, he dismissed me, saying, "There's nothing that can be done. They should consider it as an investment to work at the Blue House."

Over time, I paid the transportation expenses of all non-elected employees in the OPSCA out of my own pocket. After this, I urged the Presidential Security Service (PSS) to expedite the security clearance process period. It was shortened to seven days, but the fundamental issue couldn't be resolved.

* **Presidential Transition Commission (PTC)** After the election is finalized, the President-elect is guaranteed the position until the official inauguration and takes over the regime to launch the next government. The Commission is a body set up to assist the President-elect and to carry out the tasks related to the presidency acquisition.
* **The Blue House Senior Presidential for Civil Affairs** A key position in the presidential secretary's office, identifying public opinion and trends, assisting with public affairs and social discipline, and assisting with legal matters. They also administer presidential relatives and verifies senior public officials, and overseas the following offices: the Secretary for Civil Affairs, the Secretary of Private Affairs, and Secretary of Public Office Discipline and Legal Secretary.
* **"Clothing Lobby" Case** IIn 1999, there was a suspicion that the wife of Shin Dong-A Group's president was accused of smuggling foreign currency and had lobbied high-ranking women with expensive fashion for her husband's clemency.

The Behind Story of the Participatory Government's Cabinet Appointment

The Participatory Government's cabinet appointments progressed at a breathtaking pace. The appointment of all cabinet members first required verification by the Office of the Presidential Secretary for Civil Affairs (OPSCA). It was, therefore, the first task I faced. I became deeply involved in coordinating the cabinet's social functions and quickly mastered the art of diplomatic communication. Sometimes, I gave my opinions directly to the President-elect. Other times, I followed the President-elect's orders and received his candidate choices. Sometimes, I met with the candidates alone and persuaded them to accept their appointments. I also arranged interviews between the candidates and the President-elect.

We received recommendations and suggestions through many different channels. The OPSCA of the People's Administration sent five possible candidates per position and all the verification data about them. The People's Participation Suggestion Center* initially functioned as a subdivision within the Presidential Transition Committee (PTC), receiving candidate recommendations directly from the people. All information collected by the PTC was sorted into departments directly relevant to the data received. The shortlisted candidates were discussed at the Appointment's Team Meetings.

These meetings were attended by the Chairman of the PTC, the Chief of Staff-appointee, the Senior Presidential Secretary for Political Affairs appointee, the Senior Presidential Secretary for Civil Affairs (SPSCA) appointee, the Senior Presidential Secretary for Personnel Affairs appointee, and other key members of the Blue House. We revised the shortlist of candidates again. The new number of candidates was transferred to the Presidential Appointments Committee (PAC)*. The OPSCA conducted its verification procedures for each person on the revised list. Out of the verification results, the Appointments Team selected two or three possible candidates and made its final recommendation to the President-elect. The President-elect also submitted his verification requests to the PAC.

The first cabinet appointment was exceptional. The appointments done in the social science area were especially outstanding. During the Civilian Administration (President Kim Young-sam's) and the People's Administration (President Kim Dae-jung's), I saw one or two progressive candidates appointed to conservative cabinets. The progressive candidates quickly resigned, unable to change policy in administrations that were stacked against them. I thought the only way to make it possible was for all the progressive and reform candidates to simultaneously attain key positions in the cabinet at the Blue House. The President-elect had the same thought. It was possible in the social science area. We had a pool of candidates for it. But we couldn't appoint progressives when it came down to foreign affairs, national security, defense, and economics. We didn't have a big enough pool of candidates. I admit that even I was unfamiliar with those subjects and could barely contribute.

The most exceptional appointment was Ms. Kang Geum-sil's to the Minister of Justice (MoJ), whom I recommended. She was a practicing attorney, and after her tenure as a judge, she became vice president of the Lawyers for a Democratic Society (LDS). I followed the President-elect's will, seeking a female legal expert for appointment. The President-elect had previously met her through his own involvement with the LDS but didn't know her well.

Initially, I didn't consider her for the position of Minister of Justice, but rather the Minister of Environment (MoEnv) or the Minister of Health and Social Security (MoHSS), as those were positions previously occupied by women. After asking in detail about Ms. Kang, the President-elect suggested we appoint her as Minister of Justice. I was astonished by the suggestion. At the time, our initial candidate for MoJ, Lawyer Choi Byeong-mo, was facing personal issues and could no longer be appointed. Even with that, this appointment seemed a bit too much.

I suggested to the President-elect that it would be better to consider Ms. Kang for the MoJ after she had gone through her initial appointment to either MoEnv or MoHSS. The President-elect had a different opinion. He wanted to break the stereotype that female cabinet members could not overcome the constraints of positional limits in the government between

MoEnv, MoHSS, and the Ministry of Education (MoEdu). It was the President-elect's opinion that women must be appointed to positions in the government that were then considered male-dominated territories. The President-elect's view on women was progressive. He believed that men and women were equally capable and that if a female was better qualified for a position than a male, she should be the one appointed.

Ms. Kang Geum-sil was ambitious. Until then, she hadn't accepted any cabinet appointment suggestions, but when I mentioned the position of MoJ, she agreed immediately. Despite his bold suggestion, the President-elect requested a direct interview with Ms. Kang. I assumed he wanted a chance to assess her personally. I sat in on the meeting. This was the only meeting the President-elect had with a cabinet appointment candidate where I was present. In the meeting, the President-elect discussed his plan to reform the Supreme Prosecutor's Office (SPO). I think Ms. Kang was a bit nervous and couldn't show her usual decisive demeanor. At first, I thought the meeting was for the President-elect to make a final decision regarding her appointment, but he intended to provide a clear direction for Ms. Kang should she accept the position of MoJ. He wanted her to be ready for her new position. He warned her that there would be adverse public opinions and strong opposition to the SPO when her appointment was announced and that she would be responsible for confronting those obstacles. He also offered her his encouragement and confidence.

Another woman was appointed along with Ms. Kang; it was Attorney

Park Joo-hyun. Ms. Park was less experienced and more suited to a secretarial position. Due to the President-elect's strong desire to appoint a woman Senior Secretary in the Blue House, Ms. Park was appointed as the Senior Presidential Secretary for the People's Participation (SPSPP)*.

The President-elect wanted to appoint Ms. Kim Myeong-ja, the last Minister of Environment from the People's Administration, as the Minister of Construction and Transportation (MoCT). It was done with the intention of creating a new paradigm of active participation of women in governance and construction policy and administration based on environmental awareness. At the time, the Saemangum Project and the Kyeong-in Canal became the sources of huge social conflicts, and her appointment was to resolve the difficult task of skillfully coordinating construction and environment. In the end, Ms. Kim Myeong-ja's appointment couldn't be confirmed because of an unfavorable opinion by Mr. Goh Kun, the Prime Minister's appointee.

The President-elect's enthusiasm for appointing female officials continued. Korea saw the first-ever appointment of a female Constitutional Court Justice, multiple appointments of female Supreme Court Justices, and the first-ever appointment of a woman Prime Minister in the history of Korea. I was actively involved in these decisions, and I felt a great sense of achievement. While away from the Blue House, I pushed for the first-ever appointment of a female Chief Justice for the Constitutional Court. However, my efforts failed due to the opposition of the Grand National Party (GNP, Korea's then-major opposition party). An appointment of a woman to

Chief Justice of the Constitutional Court would have opened a new door for women's social advancement. I was disappointed by the lost opportunity.

I was pleased with Director Lee Chang-dong's appointment as the Minister of Culture and Tourism (MoCT). During the 2002 Presidential Election, the president-elect received near-absolute support from the cultural and art industries. The artists started initiatives within their industries and continuously supported the campaign, sparing nothing in their efforts to spread the campaign among all the people. It could be said that the MVPs of the election victory were the artists.

Just as André Malraux*, who served as the Minister of Cultural Affairs of France, had presented a refreshing image to the world, we thought it would be a great idea to appoint a minister among our artists. The President-elect had the same idea. We asked for a recommendation from the cultural and art industries. After much deliberation, they recommended Director Lee Chang-dong and Poet Hwang Ji-woo without asking them if they were interested. When asked to accept a Ministerial position, Poet Hwang Ji-woo declined the offer, saying that Director Lee was a better candidate than he could ever be. Director Lee wouldn't accept the appointment either because of his love for artistic freedom. We persisted and asked others to join in persuading him to accept the appointment. He eventually agreed. On the day he received the certificate of appointment from the president, and even on his first day at the office, Director Lee's attire was casual. He became famous for going around in a no-tie combination fashion style.

Just as André Malraux,
who served as the Minister of Cultural Affairs of France,
had presented a refreshing image to the world, we thought it
would be a great idea to appoint a minister among our own artists.

Director Lee's first day as the Minister of Culture and Tourism caused all of us to laugh until our bellies hurt. On his first day, the Minister left for work before his official vehicle arrived at his residence. He thought driving was still his responsibility. He left his residence in his car, drove himself to the Office of the Prime Minister, and reported to the Prime Minister as the Minister of Culture and Tourism. Meanwhile, the MoCT was in a frenzy. The Undersecretary and the Director of Planning for the MoCT drove the minister's official vehicle to the Government Complex Seoul, where the Office of the Prime Minister was located, to escort Minister Lee back in his official vehicle.

They told him that they would drive him back to the MoCT. Minister Lee, not being used to this kind of treatment, asked them, "What about my car?" The Undersecretary and the Director of Planning replied, "Mr. Minister, we will bring your car to the ministry. Please, get in your official vehicle." Minister Lee replied, "I can drive my own car; there's no need for this inconvenience," and began walking to his car. The Undersecretary and Director didn't know what to do in this situation. They couldn't coax the minister into his official vehicle, nor could they sit in the car the minister was driving. There were no other cars they could use to get to the ministry before the minister's arrival... Minister Lee saw them standing awkwardly and told them, unable to quite understand their dilemma, "Hop in. Let's go together in my car," and drove them to the MoCT. This was indeed a rare scene in Korean politics: the minister was driving the car while the Director of Planning was sitting in the passenger's seat, and the Undersecretary was sitting in the minister's place in the backseat. All of them were "escorted" to the MoCT by the minister. In front of the MoCT building, a huge crowd of many journalists was camped outside, waiting to capture the scene of this film, the director-turned-minister's first day of work at the MoCT on camera. In the eyes of these journalists, what a comedic rare scene presented itself! The next day, the media reported the news of Lee Chang-dong, the newly appointed Minister of Culture and Tourism, driving himself to work on his first day at the MoCT in his private vehicle, a Hyundai Santa Fe, with the Director of Planning in the passenger seat. Thankfully, the Undersecretary in the backseat wasn't caught by those journalists because he hid himself in the backseat when he saw the journalists and got out of the vehicle only after all the journalists had left the MoCT premises.

Minister Lee didn't hold a special incoming ceremony. Instead, he visited every department of the MoCT and met with the employees - that was his incoming ceremony. Perhaps some dignified people may have frowned on this, but we at the Blue House accepted it as a natural part of the stripping away of authoritarianism.

Appointing Mr. Kim Doo-gwan as the Minister of Interior was shocking news to the press and was entirely the President-elect's idea. He wanted someone who had been a successful mayor of small local townships to be appointed to a top position to bring an intrinsic structural reform to a centralized administration. The President-elect's goal was to share and distribute power to regional administrative governments. It was a bold move on the part of the President-elect.

During his tenure as the Minister of Interior, Minister Kim Doo-gwan carried out his work successfully, and in the official Ministerial Task Performance Review and Innovation Review, the Ministry of Interior (MoI) achieved the top score. However, the main opposition party, the GNP (Grand National Party), kept criticizing him as a "local village mayor," meaning his inexperience in national politics was unbefitting to this position as the Minister of Interior and finally passed a motion of no confidence against him during a session in the National Assembly. The reason cited was Minister Kim's past participation in the student movement during the regime years. I thought it was completely unfair and a purely political decision with no legality, and I hoped Minister Kim would continue to keep his position and overcome their opposition. Yet, he voluntarily submitted his resignation to avoid further prolonging political tensions. In the end, the president accepted his resignation, but it showed how abusively domineering the "powerful" in Korean society were.

Another shocking appointment was Mr. Ko Young-gu, a long-time human rights lawyer, as the Director of the National Intelligence Service (NIS). From the very beginning, the President-elect wanted a broad NIS reform from the inside out and wanted to elect a human rights lawyer to its top position. Going further ahead with this objective, by appointing someone who was senior to the President-elect himself and notoriously principled, the President-elect created a protective measure over the NIS so that it wouldn't receive any politically motivated or illegal orders or favors from others, including those of the President-elect himself. I spoke with Mr. Ko on behalf of the President-elect, and when I explained the President-Elect's intent, Mr. Ko gladly accepted it.

Among the Blue House senior secretaries and advisors, the appointment of Mr. Chung Chan-yong as the Senior Presidential Secretary for Personnel Affairs was unique. The President-elect had a certain principle regarding the personnel appointments. He separated the processes for recommendations and verifications to prevent monopoly and maintain the checks and balances in government appointments. Coming from the Youngnam region (southeast of Korea, comprising the North and South Gyeongsang Provinces), I was in charge of verifications. Still, he wanted someone from the Honam region (southwest of Korea, comprising the North and South Jeolla Provinces) to be in charge of recommendations.

The Honam people consistently recommended Mr. Lee Hak-young, the Secretary-director of the YMCA Suncheon, and Mr. Chung Chang-yong, the Secretary-director of the YMCA Gwangju. Mr. Lee was the right fit for the job, but his past during the Democratic Movement period could expose him to a malicious attack from the ultra-conservative press. We selected Mr. Chung. The President-elect also knew him from his time teaching at Geochang High School. When I told him about appointing Mr. Chung for the position of SSPPA, the President-elect was pleased and accepted. I think the President-elect, too, had Mr. Chung in mind.

Among the economic positions, the appointment of Mr.Chin Dae-je as the Minister of Information and Communication was unique. At the time, the press talked about Mr. Jeffrey Jones, then-Chairman of the American Chamber of Commerce in Korea (AMCHAM), and recommended him for the position. According to Korean regulations, it wasn't even considered an option because a foreigner could not legally be appointed to any governmental position in Korea. I concurred with the critical consensus that a minister appointee should be considered from a global perspective. Yet, after appointing Mr. Chin, the press began pointing out the status of Mr. Chin's son being a double citizen as a disqualification. It was stunning to see this change of perspective within the same press that once had insisted on appointing a foreign national to the position. Of course, the standards of appointment verifications cannot universally be applied to all ministers. We determined that, even on the issue concerning the double-citizenship status of appointees' children, there should be a different application of the standards applied to positions for considerations like the Ministry of Defense, the Ministry of Justice, the Ministry of Education, or the Ministry of Information and Communication.

My idea was to appoint Mr. Lee Yong-sup, the former Commissioner of the Korea Customs Service (KCS), as the first Commissioner of the National Tax Service (NTS). He had no previous relationship with any of us. As we were contemplating possible candidates for the top positions of the four most powerful government institutions (the National Intelligence Service, the Supreme Prosecutors' Office, the National Police Agency, and the National Tax Service), considering taking into consideration regional impartiality, someone from the Honam region was an ideal candidate for the Commissioner of NTS.

Lee Yong-sup from Honam, Director of Customs Tax Office personal and ministry innovation evaluations, was a very good choice. There was also the intention of trying to reform the chronic problem of the NTS through a non-NTS appointment. I agreed with all who recommended him to the Appointment Committee. He reflected later that he was selected without having any relationship with us and expressed appreciation for the government's appointment philosophy.

When appointed Director of the National Tax Service, he created the Tax Policy Reform Committee (TPRC) chaired by Park Won-soon. He instituted many tax policy reforms, such as setting a ceiling on lobbying expenses and excluding golf and nightlife-related expenses from the lobbying expense list. The president highly appreciated his innovative ability, and since then, he appointed Mr. Lee as the Blue House's Senior Presidential Secretary for Innovative Management, Minister of the Interior, Minister of Construction and Transportation, and many other positions. It was wonderful to see him continuing his parliamentary activity as a current National Assembly member with a distinguished record of expertise.

There were times, however, when my appointment recommendations weren't well accepted. During the selection of the Blue House Spokesperson, we had no one prepared. I then recommended Ms. Park Young-sun, a reporter and a female anchor for MBC then. Someone familiar with the press recommended her to me. I also judged her to be an ideal candidate among the journalists in terms of gender, being an anchor with a good public image, combined with a sense of balance, problem consciousness, and critical thinking. However, since the press isn't a field I was familiar with, my recommendation wasn't accepted. Instead, another woman was selected. She, unfortunately, didn't know President Roh.

Unlike past press briefings, we wanted an open press briefing in which only what the Blue House wanted to say was being presented. We wanted our press briefings to be held regularly every morning and afternoon, explaining the contents and their background stories. However, despite her professional abilities, she couldn't handle this task since she didn't understand the president's thoughts. She did her best, and on some complicated issues, even the Senior Presidential Secretaries involved in these issues accompanied her to the *Chunchugwan* (the Blue House Press Briefing Room) and provided the "background briefings" on her behalf. It was still insufficient. Regrettably, this happened during the critical period of the beginning of the new administration. Since then, Ms. Park Young-sun has entered politics as a member of the Uri Party in the National Assembly and served as an active two-term assembly member of the Democratic Party. Perhaps it was better for her that she didn't take the position of the Blue House Spokesperson at the time.

Yoon Young-kwan, professor of foreign affairs at Seoul National University, was elected as the Minister of Foreign Affairs. It was the President-elect's decision. He served as the Department of Foreign Affairs

Unification and National Security secretary. He seemed to have a clear opinion on balanced diplomacy that eschewed a heavy diplomatic reliance on the United States.

During the transition period, the President-elect's special envoy was dispatched to the United States to discuss North Korean nuclear issues. Professor Yoon Young-kwan was most prominent in the activities of the special envoy, and I reported that fact to the President-elect. The president was debating over which position between the foreign minister and that of diplomatic adviser he would appoint the professor and finally concluded that Professor Yoon was best suited for the ministerial appointment. It was a massive risk for him since Professor Yoon's peers were only at the rank of deputy director general in the Ministry of Foreign Affairs. However, the president's willingness to reform the principles of Korea's diplomatic policies was stronger than adhering to the bureaucratic convention.

Unfortunately, after assuming the role of Minister of Foreign Affairs, Professor Yoon showed less reform than expected. He found himself surrounded by a solid wall of foreign ministry bureaucrats, a situation that he struggled to control. As a result, our diplomatic posture towards the U.S. remained largely unchanged. This was a source of disappointment for us, considering our initial hopes for his unconventionality at the time of his appointment.

The President-elect had a clear position that the Prime Minister's Authority of Agreement on the Cabinet Appointment*, which existed but only in name, should be protected and preserved. In other words, the Constitution must be upheld in this regard. He, therefore, sent Mr. Cheong Chan-yong, the president's personnel aide appointee, to Prime Minster appointee Goh Kun to discuss his agreement on the President-elect's Cabinet appointment. Mr. Goh worried about the unconventionality of the Cabinet appointment. Instead of receiving Mr. Goh's consent regarding his intention, the President-elect yielded his position to reflect Mr. Goh's recommendations for some of the Cabinet positions. Even the position of the Director of the Office of Cabinet Coordination, which wasn't a cabinet position, was appointed by Mr. Goh's recommendation. In some cases, people with very vague political identities became ministers of the first Cabinet of the Participatory Government.

It's the general view that the Prime Minister's Authority of Agreement on the Cabinet Appointment should be guaranteed for the sake of a presidential system with separation of power or a parliamentary system with a prime minister as primus inter pares. The President-elect also had the same firm conviction in this matter. It should be respected since it is stated in the Constitution. Yet, I also think it's not a policy befitting of a presidential system and very hypocritical in nature. Under a presidential policy, a president whom the people elected should be able to form his cabinet according to the political and policy characteristics he pledged to the people during the campaign. I think there is no legal ground for a prime minister who is not elected by the people to get involved with the cabinet appointment. Unless it is a coalition government, can there be a prime minister who would insist on the appointments of those whose political and policy ideas are not congruent with those of the president?

It appeared that the Prime Minister's Authority of Agreement on the Cabinet Appointment had disappeared from the Lee Myung-bak administration. Even if the Prime Minister's Authority of Agreement regarding the Cabinet Appointment is substantially guaranteed, in actual operation, it usually tends to be a "collaborative" formula that reflects the intention of the Prime Minister in the cabinet appointment. This is by no means a democratic system. I think it is sufficient to give the Prime Minister the authority to fire cabinet members if necessary for the Prime Minister's cabinet leadership. This matter is something to seriously consider when the right time comes to amend the Constitution as a whole.

There was a serious systematic gap even in 21st-century politics. Since we couldn't appoint a prime minister before assuming office, we couldn't also appoint cabinet members. We started the new administration with the former Prime Minister and Cabinet.

Fortunately, the National Assembly confirmed Goh Kun as the Prime Minister on February 26, 2003, the day after President Roh was inaugurated.

President Roh officially launched the official appointment procedure for the Cabinet after giving Mr. Goh the certificate of appointment to the position of Prime Minister on the 27th, the next day. He was able to finish the Cabinet appointment in a short time. Even then, a few days after the Inauguration, the gap was unavoidable. If the political situation was in turmoil or the National Assembly's confirmation of the Prime

Minister was delayed, the gap could have been even longer. Also, at the time of the Participatory Government, the National Assembly's procedural hearing for the Cabinet appointment was officially instituted, and the gap in the early stages of the administration could have been even more prolonged.

We revised the law on presidential succession for the next administration. The new law fixed the system to enable the President-elect to appoint the Prime Minister and the Cabinet and have them go through the National Assembly's hearing procedures so that the President-elect could give them the official appointment immediately after the Inauguration and get them to work immediately.

* **The People's Participation Suggestion Center** An institute established during the Transition Commission period of the Participatory Government, in order to receive a wide range of national ideas, policy proposals, and personnel recommendation proposals.

* **Presidential Appointments Committee (PAC)** High-ranking officer personnel recommendation and verification unit operated at the Blue House of the Participatory Government. The Chief of Staff usually participates as the head of the committee along with major chief officers.

* **Senior Presidential Secretary for the People's Participation (SPSPP)** An organization that expanded from the Public Participation Proposal Center of the Transition Commission, after the launch of the Participatory Administration. Later, its name changed to the Chief Office of Citizen & Society, and expanding its role.

* **André Malraux** A representative French novelist in the mid-20th century. Deputy Minister of Culture in the De Gaulle regime.

* **Authority of Agreement on the Cabinet Appointment** The Prime Minister has the right to request the president to appoint a new Minister to join the Cabinet.

Life in Seoul and the Blue House

At first, I thought some official residence around the Blue House was provided for someone appointed to a position, such as the Senior Presidential Secretary for Civil Affairs (SPSCA). There was an official residence for the Presidential Security Service (PSS) personnel. For the Office of the President, only the Chief of Staff had an official residence and nothing for all other personnel under him. I had to rent. Even after selling my Busan home, which was 3,558 square feet, the money couldn't even afford a 1,067 square-foot property in the Gangnam District of Seoul. I found a small tenement apartment in Pyeongchang-dong that I could rent.

At least, I could afford it with a little savings as a lawyer. Those like Minister Huh Sung-kwan and Minister Kwon Gi-hong, who came up to Seoul having been working as university professors in provincial districts, had a tough time finding apartments for rent in Seoul because of the expense. When government officials are being dispatched to provincial districts, they are given official governmental residences - even a police chief gets one. However, this isn't the case when one gets a government appointment in Seoul from a provincial district. Not even the ministers are provided residential housing, let alone the senior secretaries to the president. Those who go to the provinces from Seoul can rent out their Seoul residences and use that money to rent their provincial homes; those who come to Seoul from the provinces, if they don't have savings, have to get loans to rent space in Seoul. On the other hand, the governmental residential policy for government officials is reversed. This is an irony shaped by the Seoul-centered mindset.

There was no difference from my previous lifestyle except that the extended working hours eliminated my private life. There were no reasons for change, but many people marveled at it. Outside of work hours, driving my own car, eating at public eateries without separate rooms, waiting in line like everyone else, and using the economy seats on planes or trains were seen as surprisingly unique. There was something nice about living in a small tenement house, going alone without an assistant, and even encountering other citizens while on a holiday hike - all were considered very special. It was different from the image they had had regarding high-ranking public officials.

In fact, during the Participatory Government era, it was not just me who lived that way; it was rare for someone to have a personal driver or secretary outside of work hours. One rainy Sunday I had climbed Cheonggae Mountain and met the then- Minister of the Industry and Energy, Lee Hee-bum, who came to hike with his friend sharing one umbrella. Twice I had encountered Jung Chan-yong, the Blue House Personnel Advisor, during the hike on Bukhan Mountain. People said that the Participatory Government officials differed from the past.

The salary of the secretary of the Blue House was less than I had expected. The bureaucrats who have been dispatched from ministries and agencies in the same class had better salaries. The salaries for those non-confirmation positions were given in the 1st and 2nd Class categories, but only in its ranks. Their actual salaries were low. Towards the middle of the administration, they were allowed to mirror their past work experiences to their salaries, but this was only possible if their past works were clearly connected with official institutions and agencies. Therefore, their salaries were also lower than those who were in the same class in other ministries. Even when they retired, there were no pension benefits. Their titles sounded good, but financially, not that much.

It wasn't much better even for their bosses, who were the senior secretaries to the president. My income as a senior secretary to the president was lower than when I was a lawyer. I had to be frugal. In fact, during my tenure at the Blue House, I used up all my savings. So even as a high government official, my life was nothing different from other ordinary citizens.

President Roh often talked about Swedish Prime Minister Olof Palme in envy. He became famous by going to the market on his bicycle after work without security details. Eventually, he was tragically assassinated by someone shooting at him as he and his wife were coming out of the cinema without security detail. Still, he mostly led a private life of freedom outside of work.

President Roh's yearning for a life akin to that of the Swedish Prime Minister was palpable. He often pondered, if the leader of a nation could live such a life, how much more should senior secretaries to the president or ministers? In a society where the life of a high-ranking government official is starkly different from that of an ordinary citizen, it's hard not to question the normalcy of our own society.

Life at the Blue House was difficult. In addition to the heavy workload, I had to be mindful of daily media coverage of the government, and if there were any incidents, I had to field the journalists calling in for comments. They could call me directly on my mobile phone, and there were many sensitive and complicated incidents in which I knew not how to respond. But I couldn't avoid those calls. Along with my job as SPSCA, I had to handle the labor and conflict issues that the Blue House should pay attention to, and the amount of work was endless. The work didn't occur in an orderly manner; often, many things happened simultaneously. Frequently, it felt like I was functioning in overdrive.

Transitioning from a life as a lawyer, where I had grown accustomed to working late and sleeping in, to the demanding schedule of a high-ranking government official was a challenge. The early morning breakfast meetings were particularly difficult to adjust to. Despite my best efforts to adapt, I found myself perpetually sleep-deprived, a chronic condition that became a constant companion in my new life.

Even during the meetings, when the subjects in discussion weren't my field, I found myself struggling to stay awake. This was a common experience, even among high-ranking officials. During the first year at the Blue House, the Chief of Staff, Moon Hee-sang, and the Senior Presidential Secretary for Political Affairs, Yoo In-tae, were often seen dozing off during the meetings. Mr. Moon's allergy medication was a known culprit for his frequent dozing off. Mr. Yoo, on the other hand, insisted that he only had his eyes closed. It was a testament to their professionalism that they were able to stay informed about all the items discussed during the meetings, despite their occasional drowsiness.

There were times when journalists caught me dozing off during the meetings and reported it in malice, so I tried my best not to doze off. The president, however, never dozed off. It was impressive. Since the president attends meetings knowing fully well what items and issues will be discussed during the meetings, he could easily get bored of the repetitious contents. Once I asked him about this, the president replied, "Secretary Moon, you won't doze off once this becomes your work someday." To me, only my own field was significant, but to him, every item on the table at each meeting was his work, which he valued.

Even in the most unusual circumstances, such as a dental treatment with my mouth propped wide open, I found myself dozing off. The risk was real-if I closed my mouth while in slumber, I could potentially injure myself with the sharp dental equipment used in the operation. The dentist, understandably, often had to raise his voice to wake me up.

There were a few times I fell asleep while I was having a conversation with someone in a face-to-face meeting. It would have been quite impolite had he noticed me dozing off while he was talking, so I tried everything I could not to, but the rush of sleepiness that came over me from being extremely tired was relentless.

What was curious was that I was gaining weight with this killer workload. I gained 10kg during my tenure at the Blue House. First, I thought it was due to the lack of exercise. But later, I realized that it was due to eating too much and too many oily things. During working hours, it was almost impossible for me to have any outside meetings or negotiations. The only available times were during meal hours.

These were referred to as "luncheon meetings" or "dinner meetings." These official meetings had to be held in private rooms in restaurants, and because of this, we had to order a lot of expensive dishes. Ever since I was instructed not to leave any food on the plate, I regularly ate a lot, though I shouldn't have. After leaving the position, I returned to simple meals that I was accustomed to and returned to my previous weight.

I wasn't in good health the first year. I was not alone. Everyone's health was compromised because of the pressure to perform well regarding tasks, responsibilities, and lifestyles we had never known before. Furthermore, the president was a workaholic, so when it came to work, he had no consideration for those who worked for him. No one could handle this for too long. About a year later, everyone was knocked out. In retrospect, it wasn't something I should have driven myself that hard to do. I had to pace myself well. As I prepared to leave the office, I saw Chief of Staff appointee Yu Woo-ik of the Lee Myung-bak administration. He already had mouth sores because of fatigue. I told him about my own experience and advised him to pace himself well in the long run.

In the fall of 2003, the president's first year in office, there was a blood donation event at the Blue House. TV cameras and photo reporters were present, and the president was the first to donate blood. I was next in line per the request of the Office of the Personal Secretary to the President.

However, the president failed the health examination before the blood donation. His plasma was abnormal due to overwork and exhaustion. It was a normal condition if you were extremely exhausted. But it was embarrassing because it was impossible to show the president being a good model for donating blood. There was no way to report the president being unable to donate blood due to the abnormal condition of his plasma. After a brief discussion, we came up with a solution, saying that he forgot about the blood donation event and took medication in the morning.

I had to make up for the president in this event but was also disqualified to donate blood. My blood pressure was too high. I refused to accept the examination result. I had never been diagnosed with high blood pressure, and just a few months prior, during the medical examination for the appointment at the Blue House, my results were normal. After drinking a glass of cold water and calming myself down, I retook the examination, but the result was the same. I went to the hospital straight after that. It was true that my blood pressure got high during those first few months.

In ordinary work, the higher one's position, the less work there is. In the Blue House, it was the opposite. During my first year at Blue House, I had to have ten teeth extracted. Not only me but Secretaries Lee Ho-chul, Yang In-suk, and many others in the OSPSCA had to have tooth extractions. What was funny was that the higher one's position, the more teeth had to be pulled. We joked among ourselves that this was solid evidence of work-related issues.

The Special Prosecution of the Fund Transfer to North Korea

Shortly after the inauguration, a myriad of complex issues surfaced, notably the Special Investigation for the Fund Transfer to North Korea*. The investigation had already commenced during the Transition Committee* period, with discussions about its contents initiated by Hyundai. During the June 15th Summit Meeting*, a substantial fund as transferred to North Korea, allegedly prepared by Hundai. The rumor was that if Hyundai executed the transfer first, the North Korean government would compensate by providing special work projects, but this was not the case. The actual amount of the fund was soon revealed, fueling suspicion and leaving no room to deny the transfer. As the Supreme Prosecutors' Office (SPO) grappled with investigation procedures, the Grand National Party instigated the Special Prosecution just a day after the inauguration. Given the legal nature of the matter, the Office of the Presidential Secretary for Civil Affairs (OPSCA) was compelled to intervene.

The first option considered was to proceed without investigation. The transfer of funds to North Korea was illegal at the time, and it was undoubtedly considered a unique circumstance to ease the tension between North and South Korean relations. Furthermore, the approach facilitated the first-ever summit meeting held between the heads of the North and South Korean governments, leading to the historic June 15th Treaty. Broadly speaking, it was an action that could certainly be justified.

Per President Roh's decision, we exercised the veto against the Special Prosecution, giving special instructions that SPO should drop the investigation. Of course, through a press conference, I also had to appeal to the people. The only goal was to set President Kim Dae-Jung's "Executive Action*" in motion, aiming for a significant shift in the inter-Korean relations between North and South Korea. Of course, the theory of the Executive Action is an old legal theory from the authoritarian era, and most law scholars find it archaic these days. For the government that advocates for democratic reform, insisting on the Executive Action theory was placing a heavy burden on itself. It was painful, but there was no other way.

Even if we proceeded with the decision, there was no guarantee that we could manage the aftermath. It was evident that the Grand National Party (GNP) would exert all its efforts to push for the Special Prosecution through the National Assembly's actions, leaving the administration with no choice but to focus solely on this issue from the very beginning. However, if we had persisted in this manner, a simple fund transfer could have been perceived as more than a legal matter but a dark deal with North Korea in the eyes of the Korean people. Even if the president could veto the direct investigation of SPO, there was no way to prevent an investigation stemming from the lawsuits initiated by the GNP or those involved in this issue at court.

Still, President Roh decided to continue. There was one premise, however, to assert the Executive Action. Former President Kim Dae-Jung had to admit that he had instructed the fund transfer or either allowed or let it pass after receiving an action report. Only then could the case be made for an argument that President Kim had made the high-level Executive Action by his own determination.

Until then, President Kim's side explained that they hadn't previously known about the funds transfer to North Korea. President Roh ordered Chief of Staff Moon Hee-sang to inform President Kim of his intentions. President Kim, at a press conference, maintained that he had no prior knowledge in advance. It is unclear whether the situation was unavoidable because President Kim was not previously informed or if his advisors acted out of concern that it might reflect poorly on him. We believed that even if President Kim had directly initiated or permitted the incident, it would not negatively affect him. On the contrary, we thought it would further highlight his political skills and decisiveness. Nonetheless, President Kim's final press conference left no room for arguing that his governance was solely a result of his decisive actions. It was disappointing.

Now, the remaining choice was whether to conduct the investigation through the Special Prosecution or the SPO. President Kim's side insisted that we use a veto against the Special Prosecution legislation. Had we followed that request, we could have avoided the immediate accusation that we had abandoned political protocol. But if this went to the SPO, there was no guarantee that we could prevent the investigation from going forward.

There was no assurance that the investigation would be limited to the legality of procedure regarding the case of the transfer fund to North Korea. There was a possibility that investigating the remittance* partner's account or how it was being utilized would backfire and ruin the root of the inter-Korean relationships between the North and South. Also, while investigating the details of remitted funds, there was a more significant potential for investigation spreading through private corporate funding and split accounting. When the prosecution office uncovers the accounts of the officials concerned, there is a possibility of focusing the investigation strictly on political funds and other individual corruption scandals. It would be impossible to control it. Once the file was in the hands of the prosecution's office, we would not know where it would lead and when it might explode.

Meanwhile, our special investigation was confined to the purpose and scope of the legislation itself. Moreover, if someone with a keen interest in inter-Korean relationships were to become the Special Prosecutor, we could anticipate a more nuanced investigation. Fortunately, the executive members of the Korean Bar Association, who were tasked with recommending a special prosecutor, were individuals of integrity. From an independent standpoint, the investigation by the Special Prosecution was a much more favorable option. However, the difficulty of the decision lay in its political implications. The request from President Kim's supporters to veto the Special Prosecution added a significant political burden. On the other hand, the weight of exercising the veto power over the very first legislation from the National Assembly, the ensuing confrontation with the main opposition Grand National Party, and the potential for political deadlock were also substantial considerations. From the Blue House, with the exception of Senior Presidential Secretary for Political Affairs Yoo In-tae, everyone favored the Special Prosecution. I believe everyone was aware of the context and the challenges we were grappling with at the time.

The opposing opinion against the Special Prosecution was in favor in the cabinet. The opposition of the Minister of Unification, Chung Se-hyun, was especially strong. President Roh couldn't easily make a decision. He decided to make a final decision at the Cabinet meeting after listening to the opinions of the senior advisors. We prepared the president's public speeches in two versions: one for accepting the Special Prosecution and the other when the veto was exercised.

Many expressed dissent in the Cabinet meeting. After listening to all the remarks, the president thanked them for expressing their honest opinions. Even Minister Chung Se-hyun of the Ministry of Unification, who expressed the strongest opposition, the president said, "I think that it is natural for the Minister of Unification to oppose this as his duty. Had you not done so, I would've considered you not doing your job properly."

Despite the opposition, the president ultimately decided to accept the Special Prosecution.

The president felt it critical, though not mentioned in the Cabinet meeting, that the investigation should not damage inter-Korean relationships. In that regard, the president determined that the Special Prosecution was a better option than the investigation by the SPO.

Fortunately, as expected, the Korean Bar Association recommended someone respectable as a special prosecutor who could investigate this issue without damaging the Inter-Korean relationships. Special Prosecutor Song Doo-hwan conducted the investigation only within the scope of the procedural legality of the fund transfer to North Korea and was careful with contacting the press. We were able to minimize the wave of the investigation and did not cause potential damage to the inter-Korean relationships. I was sorry for those who suffered the consequences of this investigation and provided the presidential clemency as soon as they were found guilty. I think I made the best choice, given the circumstances.

President Kim and his supporters were quite upset about this issue for a long time. Even later, when I returned to the Blue House as the Senior Presidential Secretary for Civil Society and visited President Kim, he expressed his dissatisfaction with it. I explained our intent and sincerity regarding the issue every chance I had. I believe he understood us in the end. Because of the split between the Democratic Party and the Uri Party, the politicians in the Democratic Party repeatedly criticized us for this issue. I think they had more of a political agenda than anything else in doing so.

Even now, there are those who say that the Participatory Government's decision to accept the Special Prosecution was to politically oppress the People's Administration, distinguish itself from it, or deny the Sunshine Policy initiated by the People's Administration. Because of that, the Inter-Korean relationship was frozen at the start of the Participatory Government. It's not at all true. I would like to ask them to put it aside and let go of this misunderstanding.

The OPSCA's opinion was most influential in President Roh's judgment and decision at the time. The OPSCA made a detailed report concerning all the issues mentioned above. For this reason, even if President Roh's decision was wrong at the time, I was responsible for his decision, which solely relied on me, the SPSCA. It would have been me who misguided him. The OPSCA came to be in charge of this issue because it was a legal issue, but in actuality, it was a political issue of the highest altitude. It was the moment I painfully realized the difficulties of judgment in politics. It was indeed a difficult issue.

* **Special Investigation for the Transfer Fund to North Korea** Suspicion arose that the People's Administration provided financial assistance to the North while arranging for the 2000 Inter-Korean Summit. The National Assembly proposed a Special Prosecutor in 2003 to investigate the case.
* **Transition Committee** An independent investigative agency that temporarily takes investigations and prosecutions on behalf of the prosecution when high-ranking officials are found guilty of illegal charges. Initiated by the National Assembly and appointed by the president.
* **June 15th Summit Meeting** A historical summit was held for the first time between the North and South Korean chiefs-of-state. President Kim Dae-jung and North Korean leader Kim Jong-il met for the first time since the division in 2000 in Pyongyang.
* **Executive Action** The political actions of the president related to fundamental rulings of the national government. Because they are highly politicized, they are not subject to legal examination by the judiciary.
* **Account of the remittance** A company creating false accounting data during the settlement process, deliberately inflating assets or profits.

The Supreme Prosecutors' Office Reformation

During the early days of the administration, a unique and highly sensitive issue emerged-a conflict with the Supreme Prosecutors' Office (SPO). This conflict, which began immediately after the government's establishment on March 6, 2003, was centered around the Ministry of Justice's control over the personnel of the Directors of High Prosecutors' Offices. The SPO's dissent was not just a simple disagreement, but a systematic and organized resistance, earning it the monikers of "The Riot of Prosecutors" or "the Collective Revolt." This marked the beginning of what would be known as "The Dialogue between the President and the Prosecutors*."

At that time, the SPO's institutional complaint against the administration's personnel decisions was unprecedented. The SPO had a long-standing tradition that saw senior prosecutors who were bypassed in promotion resign. Even when a prosecutor was appointed as the Director of the SPO, his peers would resign from their current posts and retire. This tradition, which the Participatory Government deemed undesirable, was seen as a military culture that needed to be eradicated. It was not in line with the government's vision for the SPO's reformation.

We thought that to ensure the political neutrality of the SPO, it would be necessary to guarantee each prosecutor's status without having to line up politically every time a new administration comes into power. The tenure of the Director of the SPO was of the same issue. Even after the start of the new administration, President Roh had no intention of removing the Director of the the SPO Kim Gak-young, who was appointed to the position by the previous administration. Director Kim even asked me about the president's intention regarding his tenure as a director. I told him to fulfill the remainder of his tenure as a director since there was no intention of change. Looking back, I can't help but feel a sense of regret over the missed opportunities for SPO reform.

However, the high-ranking prosecutors had deep misunderstandings and victimized themselves. They probably thought the new administration would push them out like all the previous administrations had done. Particularly, those who were rejected from their positions as Directors of High Prosecutors' Offices fanned the embers of frustration over the personnel change. Even young prosecutors participated in the misunderstanding and joined the rebellion. Their rejection of the Minister of Justice, Kang Geum-sil, also played a big role.

Such a case should have been left alone and would have naturally resolved in time. It was an issue that could be handled at the level of the Ministry of Justice. However, the president's unwavering determination to reform the SPO was evident. He didn't shy away from tackling this issue head-on, viewing it as an opportunity to create rapport with young prosecutors and drive the SPO reformation forward.

There were other reasons also why the president felt differently. Before the personnel decision was systematically rejected, there were internal suggestions from the SPO regarding the SPO reformation from the level of local prosecutors in the field. Many of them supported the kind of SPO reformation we had in mind.

Through dialogue with the young prosecutors, the president demonstrated his patience and understanding. He aimed to resolve the prosecutors' misunderstanding concerning personnel decisions and to discuss the SPO reformation openly. This was how "The Dialogue between the President and the Prosecutors" was initiated. There, the president planned to accept what could be accepted and promised to review what he could not accept immediately based on what the young prosecutors had suggested or recommended. He also thought this would be a great opportunity to ask these young prosecutors about the SPO's internal objectives and efforts to secure its political neutrality. Through that, the president wanted to demonstrate and promise the people the consensus and vision for the SPO reformation together with lower-level prosecutors. He also wanted to use this process as the engine for the SPO's reformation.

I wasn't present when the problematic event in question was decided. It was the day the ministers and senior secretaries to the president were doing a workshop. I came to Busan to persuade Monk Jiyul, who was in the middle of his first fasting, to protest the construction of the Cheonseong

Through dialogue with the young prosecutors, the president wanted to solve the prosecutors' misunderstanding concerning personnel decision and to openly discuss the SPO reformation.

Mountain Tunnel. The president called me during the workshop. He asked my opinion about holding such an event. I mentioned that I would like the event to be coordinated in advance and not in a hurry. Nevertheless, the president announced the event and decided the date.

We hurriedly initiated preparations. When the conversations began, we thought the president's explanations could easily resolve all the misunderstandings and complaints about the personnel issue. During the remainder of the time, a sufficient amount of discussion will take place over the SPO's reformation. The president, too, diligently studied the SPO's reformation materials we had prepared for him.

When the event finally started, it was a sight for sore eyes and hard to watch. The young prosecutors participating in the event only repeatedly questioned the president over the personnel issue. Even though the president explained the whole issue sufficiently to the one who questioned him, another prosecutor would ask the same thing that had already been explained. The president needed to repeat himself many times. Besides their dissatisfaction with the personnel situation, no prosecutors prepared themselves to discuss the SPO's reformation. No wonder, after this event, a new word became trendy among the Korean people: "Prosecutor-ative." The noun "prosecutor" was morphed to form an adjective.

While preparing the event, I asked the Minister of Justice not to prevent prosecutors' complaints over personnel. We proposed that this event be a forum where the SPO reformation was the main topic of discussion, which had already been discussed among prosecutors in joining their ideas and perspectives. This was not the case, however. Each participating prosecutor was chosen per region or group. Each had their own set of questions ordered from the group that each represented. Everyone had the same set of questions revolving around the personnel complaint. Also, each seemed to have been told not to feel small in front of the president and fiercely argue his perspective concerning the personnel issue. The participants never discussed among themselves the different roles in the discussion they might be assigned. According to the group each represented, each one repeated the same questions.

The president's self-control was masterful. He got angry at times but soon regained his composure to continue the discussion. Something we probably would not be able to do until our anger had completely subsided. I had a bitter aftertaste. As a senior legal professional, these young prosecutors looked quite idiotic.

The stupid conversations continued, and the mood of the event turned awkward. The president tried to change the subject, but he couldn't discuss the SPO reformation that he wanted to. After the event, the people began saying, "The president won the discussion against the prosecutors," or "prosecutor-ative," but they were all useless. It was a shameful event before the eyes of the people. The president, too, greatly regretted the event. We, nor the president, had much time before the event, but we had put a lot of effort into the discussion concerning the SPO reformation. It was in vain. We lost an excellent opportunity to show the people a doable vision for the SPO reformation. It wasn't very pleasant.

Despite that event, the SPO reformation was promoted as planned. Most of the reform proposals were submitted by civil society organizations, such as the Lawyers for a Democratic Society and the Participation Solidarity. They have now been carried out. We all, including the president, saw the political neutrality of the SPO as the start of the SPO reformation. In other words, getting out of "political prosecution" was the core of the reform. This objective was seen as the problem of the culture rather than the problem of the system, in which political powers suppressed themselves due to their greedy ambition to use the SPO as their political tool and the SPO keeping themselves from being politically motivated.

Of course, one administration alone cannot be enough for this reform to take root. At least two or three more administrations would be needed for this culture to take root properly. We tried to lay a foundation to help eliminate this cultural problem.

Whenever there was an opportunity, the president relayed his will over this perspective issue directly and indirectly. The OPSCA also did not order an investigation or give instructions over any important incident. This principle was strictly maintained throughout the entire tenure of the Participatory Government. Even when the investigation led to inquiries of the Presidential Election Fund, scrutinizing the president's inner circle, we permitted the SPO to conduct their investigation in principle and conviction. Even while we were enduring the pain of cutting our own flesh, we guaranteed and protected the independence and neutrality of the SPO's investigations. We desired the political neutrality and independence of the SPO, which was structured in this manner, to continue to be preserved by the SPO themselves.

This is a side note, but there was a hotline between the OPSCA and the SPO. A standard telephone line connects the Blue House with all ministries in the Blue House. Uniquely, a dedicated line for the SPO was connected to the OPSCA. I ordered it to be cut off immediately. The SPO also provided a special vehicle at OPSCA. It is a vehicle of convenience provided by the SPO since the Blue House work vehicles were short in number. I ordered the vehicle to be returned to the SPO. They seemed like minor things, but I believed that these minor things were damaging the political neutrality of the SPO.

The abolition of the SPO's Department of Central Investigation (DCI) was a very important task for the SPO's apolitical status and political neutrality. Ironically, we couldn't touch this because of the demand for political neutrality. The SPO's DCI plays the most significant role in making the SPO political. All departments within the SPO, such as the Department of Criminal Investigation, the Department of Violent Crimes Investigation, and the Department of Espionage Investigation, take up the roles of directing the investigations for the High Prosecutors' Offices and regional Prosecutors' Offices pertaining to each department. Only the DCI has its own unique investigation function. Of all special cases, political cases are especially directly investigated by the DCI. Therefore, the political affiliation and bias of the SPO naturally arise from here. Unless the political power also has a firm resolve to secure the political neutrality of the SPO, it is difficult to resist the temptation to utilize the DCI. A case like the SPO's DCI cannot be found anywhere else except in Korea.

Even in Japan, too, the special investigation department of a regional Prosecutors' Office looks into political affairs. They don't have anything like the DCI. The Tokyo District Prosecutor's Office's Department of Special Investigation does not follow political cues in their investigation. While maintaining political neutrality thoroughly, it is famous for having made a more brilliant achievement than Korea's DCI in the investigation of large fraud cases. Political neutrality enabled such a thing. It was the reason why the abolition of the DCI was a very important goal of the SPO reformation.

However, there is a reason why the SPO could not abolish the DCI at the time. Before discussing the abolition of DCI seriously, there was an ongoing investigation into presidential election funds. The DCI conducted the investigation. The president and the Blue House guaranteed that the SPO could investigate this with conviction and principle. With this investigation, the SPO gained a lot of trust from the people. The abolition chatter of the DCI was diluted. Under such circumstances, if we had tried to abolish the DCI, it could have given the impression of political retaliation against his investigation of presidential election funds. We missed the timing and couldn't get a second chance after that. It was regretful. Even doing this, what we had preserved was the political neutrality and independence of the SPO.

However, when the Lee Myung-bak administration emerged, they quickly returned to the past. It is a pity that the SPO regressed once the Lee Myung-bak administration had begun. President Roh, who had been wholeheartedly attempting to guarantee political neutrality and independence without taking control of the SPO, became the target of a political investigation at the very same time by the SPO he had protected; I do not know of anything else in this world that is vainer than this.

* **The Dialogue between the President and the Prosecutors** President Roh Moo-hyun's public dialogue with public prosecutors, as prosecutors continued to oppose the prosecution reforms in the early stages of the Participatory Government, was live broadcast on TV to the whole country.

Reform of the National Intelligence Service

Compared with the Supreme Prosecutors' Office (SPO) reformation, the National Intelligence Service (NIS) reform was less burdensome. It was easy to reform since it was an organization directly under the president and had little administrative action involved with the general public. The president also had a strong intention to reform the NIS. Considering his track record as a human rights attorney, he had experienced heated debates with the NIS's torturous cross-examinations, observation, and surveillance methods. The traditional task of reforming the NIS involved abolishing human rights violations during its investigation and illegal intelligence-gathering methods. The People's Administration made significant progress in this regard. By restricting the scope of the investigation regarding the crimes against the National Security Law only to those of North Korea and its related issues, the Participatory Government attempted to prevent and eliminate any elements of human rights violations in the NIS's investigation from its foundation. Although it was a case that occurred at the time of the former administration, the so-called "NSP X-File Case*" became the starting point for eradicating the NIS's illegal eavesdropping. During the tenure of the Participatory Government, there wasn't a single incident in which the NIS was accused of human rights violations or illicit eavesdropping. The Participatory Government put its emphasis on NIS's de-politicization and de-powerment. The president demanded that politics be completely eliminated from the NIS's intelligence-gathering activities. He deeply hated the political reports consisting of accusations, such as "Assembly Member A said B about C issues" during an intelligence briefing. Such reporting almost disappeared during the time of the Participatory Government. Still, if, by chance, such information came up mixed with the daily intelligence briefing, the president sent it back down to the NIS, pointing it out as unacceptable. To depoliticize the NIS, the NIS agents were prohibited from constantly visiting any government institutions or agencies and the press buildings. In order to facilitate the de-powerment of the NIS, the president personally did not think of using the NIS for any political reasons, in addition to not giving the NIS any authority superseding the law. As part of this effort, weekly vis-à-vis and private briefings by the Director of NIS with the president were eliminated. Instead, the president ordered the NIS to share its intelligence-gathering results with all governmental departments and related agencies per relevant information, in addition to the president and the Blue House. The NIS intelligence information was made available to the entire government. To verify the status of intelligence sharing, the president ordered the NIS to mark all the relevant government institutions and agencies with which a certain intelligence briefing should be shared as "recipients." If any institution or agency that should be on the distribution list was missing, he sent the briefing back to the NIS, pointing out that it should be sent there as well. I had endorsed the president's measures to eliminate the weekly vis-à-vis briefings and private briefings, but I was worried that such measures would demoralize the NIS and jeopardize the NIS Director's control over the agency. There was a voice of discontent within the NIS if they continued presenting intelligence briefings that the president wouldn't be interested in. I was worried that this loss would create an appearance of fraud within the NIS and lower the ability of the NIS to grasp the organization's power and importance. It's because dissent was expressed within the NIS that the president was forced to continue reporting information, even when it bored him. The president's lack of interest in the NIS lowered morale within the agency. The fact that the president would not directly receive the NIS Director's briefing was interpreted as the loss of NIS's existential value by some in the National Intelligence Service. The president also clarified that he didn't want to receive only weekly vis-à-vis and private briefings. Still, should there be any issues to report or brief him about, the president would receive the NIS Director's briefings whenever they were needed. I arranged an irregular briefing once every month and allowed the NIS Director to use it as a monthly briefing. When the NIS Director wanted to report to the president in a private one-on-one meeting, I made everyone leave the room so that such a meeting could occur naturally, though for a short duration. Even in these moments, the president urged the Senior Presidential Secretary for Civil Affairs (SPSCA) to remain in the seat, leaving at least one to accompany him during the meeting. The president also cared about the NIS's morale. To boost it, President Roh visited the NIS directly to receive business reports and exchange conversations with employees. He visited the NIS twice during his presidency, and I accompanied him both times. I could feel that the NIS staff warmly welcomed the president's visit. The president's desire to make the NIS un-politicized and de-powered was so strong that it almost seemed as though he had issues against them. Some in the Blue House once recommended me as the Director of the NIS to the president. But the president would not hear of it. He determined that if someone whose loyalty and love for the president somehow came to a point of having an ambition to help the president by using the NIS, it was the way to go under. When appointing the director or the co-director of the NIS, after the official appointment ceremony, the president sincerely told them at the reception, "Don't even think about trying to do something for the president." I asked each new director of the NIS to send me any information or intelligence pertaining to the Blue House personnel immediately after receiving them without wasting time trying to verify their validities. The NIS Directors sent them to me in Top Secret envelopes with labels like "CONFIDENTIAL: SPSCA ONLY" or "CONFIDENTIAL: Chief of Staff ONLY." Among the intelligence reports, there was even some unverified tabloid news about me. Most of them turned out to be untrue when investigated, but from time to time, knowing and verifying them alone helped maintain the Blue House's moral standards.

* **NSP X-File Case** An MBC reporter investigating the wiretap tapes of the Agency of National Security Planning (current NIS) triggered a series of illegal wiretapping cases. At the time of the 1997 presidential election, a meeting between senior executives of the Samsung Group and the *Daily Joong-ang* reporter was publicized, discussing a plan to provide illegal support to a specific presidential election candidate.

Reform of Powerful Government Agencies

The core of the reform of the National Tax Service (NTS) wasn't to use it as a means of political control, like "retaliatory tax audit" or "targeted tax audit." The Participatory Government had never mobilized the NTS to do such things. It is regrettable to see that the Lee Myung-bak administration again returned the NTS to its past role to maintain power.

Instead of using the NTS as a political means, we returned it to its original purpose of establishing taxation justice. In the beginning, having the government and the civilian agencies join hands, we pursued many solid taxation reform programs. In May 2003, the Tax Reform Promotion Committee was established. The civilian chairman was Lawyer Park Won-soon. We set a 5,000,000 won (US $4,500.00) ceiling for single lobby expenses, excluding golf courses and nightlife entertainment. The cash receipt system was able to secure transparency of funds.

It was promoted simultaneously as the Special Prostitution Law, which was criticized for contributing to the economic difficulties. There was concern over setting a tight limit for lobbying expenses. Even the president expressed concern if the measure would be too radical. I insisted on going forward on principle. A half-joke, half-serious discussions went around, saying that the Participatory Government destroyed three major industries: the "Power Industry" due to the secret black money for power disappearing, the "Lobbying Industry" due to the new ceiling limit for lobbying expenses, and the "Sex Industry" through the introduction of the Special Prostitution Law.

The Office of Senior Presidential Secretary for the Economy daily checked the economic influence of these three new measures by monitoring the daily sales trends for each industrial sector. Often, those talks were just hoaxes. Overall, it is true that the purchases made by the powerful have a considerable impact on the real economy for a certain period of time. However, such revelations were necessary for us to obtain our economy's transparency. Had we not done so at the time, it could never have been possible later.

The direction of reform within the Board of Audit and Inspection (BAI) was also clear. In the early stages of the Presidential Transition Committee (PTC), the BAI was set to end the past auditing practice of "prescribing medicine after the patient is dead" and switch to preventive, evaluation, system, and policy auditing. A direction was established. The president expressed a strong desire for reform.

Until then, the BAI had been conducting legal auditing. It was necessary to ascertain if there were any violations concerning the provisions of the law during the time that specific ministries, agencies, and departments were conducting their business. It wasn't what the president wanted. For example, if several hundred billion were designated for a project, we needed to know whether or not the budget was put to proper use, whether or not there was a comparable result complimenting the budget, and if the project was properly executed. We also needed a systemized structure that could be applied to other similar projects to determine if the ROI (Return on Investments) yielded what was intended and would be a suitable preventive measure to avoid financial mismanagement and ensure accountability. These were the kinds of auditing standings we wanted to implement. We thought these principles were important for proper auditing. We considered this kind of auditing bickering and reprimanding over whether or not there was some mismanagement of funds would not change the intrinsic nature of auditing. Each ministry's individual auditing department largely implemented this kind of auditing protocol.

We also reviewed plans to implement the auditing command function in the National Assembly. It was the president's idea. The United States, for example, had placed the auditing agency under the control of Congress. They also executed the audit function neutrally and professionally, regardless of changes in executive administration. Their independence and neutrality were strictly protected. Sadly, this sort of system was not adopted here because of Korea's political situation.

Since the majority party would attempt to control the BAI according to their objectives just as they would easily change the Secretary-General of the National Assembly, I wondered if the BAI's neutrality could be safely guarded. We abandoned this idea, thinking our political atmosphere was yet too immature. Instead, we focused on changing the BAI's constitution through policy evaluation auditing. I had a particular interest in it because the BAI's constitutional improvement was the foundation of multiple reforms to be carried out in the Participatory Government.

Professor Yoon Sung-sik had delved into this field of research. In his book, *The Vision and Strategy of Government Reform*, he emphasized that the BAI should be changed from an auditing institution to an evaluating institution. He also argued that government reform was impossible without the BAI's reformation. The president commissioned Professor Yoon and the BAI's Reformation task force to study strategies together for the BAI reformation. When the BAI's Director Lee Jong-nam's term was completed, Professor Yoon was appointed as the new BAI Director. There were no grounds for individual disqualification. However, the Grand National Party refused to confirm Professor Yoon because he was part of the Presidential Transition Committee. This halted the BAI's reformation. Instead, we created an evaluation team within the BAI to handle evaluation and policy auditing, but it did not meet our expectations.

Managing Social Conflicts

An additional important task that also fell on me was managing social conflicts that occurred in the resolution process of a long-term unresolved national policy project. Our job was to listen carefully to the stakeholders and form an arbitration plan through rational dialogue and compromise.

The reason why these long-term national policy projects were unresolved was because they created serious confrontations. Regardless of which administration, it was, at best, status quo. Of course, it kept being postponed until later dates. These projects included the Return of the Wartime Operational Control (WT-OPCON)*, the moving of the U.S. military base at Yongsan to Pyeongtaek, the Radioactive Waste Treatment Facility (RWTF)*, the Sapae Mountain Tunnel*, and the Cheonseong Mountain Tunnel*. These were problems that required a minimum of five years and a maximum of ten or more to resolve.

The president said the Participatory Government would not avoid these pending issues, and he was steadfast about it. He was willing to go as far as possible to resolve these problems. It was the principle set during the PTC. Therefore, as soon as the Participatory Government began, we got to work. All the work of managing conflicts and conflict mediation was passed on to the OPSCA.

During the presidential election, the president pledged to review the Sapae Mountain Tunnel and the Cheonseong Mountain Tunnel issues. To follow up on this pledge, a route review committee was formed. The Pros and Cons Experts reviewed existing and alternative routes. In the case of the Sapae Mountain Tunnel, both sides were equally divided and could not agree on a consensus. The committee determined the Cheonseong Mountain Tunnel case, but the opposing side didn't accept it.

Neither tunnel's alternative solutions were satisfactory. The alternative solutions provided were not better than the existing ones regarding reducing environmental damage. Also, most of the routes connecting these two points were almost done, so not many options were left to consider. I visited these two sites several times. Sometimes, during holidays, I drove there myself, and in the case of the Sapae Mountain, I hiked up to the summit of the mountain to look down on the site. At the Sapae Mountain site, the highway bridge structure was already built all the way to the tunnel entrance, and even the decks were laid for the most part. Even if the route was changed, removing all these already constructed bridges and roads was no easy task.

We requested cooperation from the Buddhists. They, too, agreed that it was difficult to change the route in an environmentally friendly way, as the Buddhist community wanted. After several discussions with Monk

Bupjang, the Secretary-general of the Jogye Order, and Monk Sookyeong of the Buddhist Environmental Activism Coalition, it was decided that the president himself would pay a formal visit to the Head of the Jogye Order and ask for his cooperation.

On December 5th, 2003, the president visited Monk Bupjeon, the Head of the Jogye Order*, at the Haein Temple. He apologized to Monk Bupjeon that he couldn't keep the commitment to review the route. Monk Bupjeon graciously accepted the president's apologies and ordered the whole Order to cooperate with the government's national policy project. The Sapae Mountain Tunnel problem was solved in this manner.

When it came to the Cheonseong Mountain Tunnel, Monk Jiyul, who had led a fasting protest against the tunnel construction since the beginning of the administration, would not change his mind despite the instructions from the Order. He had undergone four different fasting protests during the Participatory Government. At first, he conducted fasting in Busan, but later, he began fasting in front of the Blue House. The fourth fasting lasted over 100 days - an extreme fasting that could take a toll on his life. The entire nation watched him, concerned that something unfortunate might happen to him. I visited Monk Jiyul to explain and persuade him at each fast, but it was useless.

One of the most important things the government needed to do was mediate conflicts. Even when the government is convinced of its policy, efforts to persuade dissenters are necessary, especially if the dissent is expressed by a group.

The entire nation watched him, concerned that something unfortunate might happen to him. I visited Monk Jiyul to explain and persuade him at each fast, but it was useless.

Because the Participatory Government existed during the time when authoritarianism was dismantled, there erupted many major social conflicts. I felt that it was necessary to have a national system to rationally and realistically control and mediate conflicts.

The Radioactive Waste Treatment Facility (RWTF) issue was a great matter of conflict. At first, we thought it was an easy issue to resolve and left it to the ministry. It made the matter more complex. We determined that the region that would accommodate the RWTF would receive 300,000,000,000 won (US $268M) for the regional support fund, the Proton Linear Accelerator Project*, and moving the headquarters of Korea Hydro and Nuclear Power (KHNP)*. We thought, on top of these, if other indirect social capital began flowing in the region, such as new roads, it would be greatly beneficial to the regional development and the residents' social security. We believed it would be a win-win situation for the government and the region.

Buan District of the North Jeolla Province applied for it. We later discovered that their bidding did not have a sufficient hearing session with its residents. The departments in charge of this issue made the mistake of not looking into the matter more closely. Since a lot of money was involved, they thought everyone would embrace this offer. The Blue House, not knowing this, thought we found a solution. Minister Yoon Jin-sik of the Ministry of Industry and Energy visited Buan and came back and told us that the region's reaction was positive and showed a willingness to host the RWTF in their area. The president had been brainstorming about how to create an economic boost in North Jeolla Province. This news was a welcome solution for him, so we decided on Buan as the RWTF site.

However, the work began to get crazy. There was an arbitrary aspect to the application procedure initiated by the mayor of Buan. It did not even go through the Buan Regional Council vote. There was a lot of opposition from civilians, and KHNP's persuasion of the Buan residents was quite inadequate. To this, environmental activists joined. Opposition and conflicts began expanding, and the Blue House had to step in.

I went down to Buan to look around. Unlike the reports from the Ministry of Commerce, Industry, and Energy (MoCIE), I felt something needed to be fixed based on the separate reports coming into the OPSCA. Without letting anyone know and receiving cooperation from anywhere, I went down there with my wife, who took shifts in driving during the weekends or holidays. Buan, as I saw it, was one beautiful place. The people had a deep sense of appreciation for the exceptionally beautiful natural environment in which they lived. Because they knew the importance of the environment, they exhibited an even stronger duty to protect it. I painfully realized that we were fundamentally lacking in our planning and sensitivity regarding the effects and demands that ensued.

As the protest against the RWTF in Buan was becoming increasingly fierce, the government attempted to persuade the Buan residents by increasing the initial amount of compensatory support for the region. After several T.F. meetings, we decided to expand the social overhead capital dedicated to Buan up to US $2 billion, which included a direct link for road infrastructure all the way to Buan. But it was too late to turn around the anti-mood of the Buan residents. In the end, the Buan residents' level of opposition toward the RWTF mushroomed into a riot, which caused a lot of injuries and even some arrests. We accepted some civil society NGOs' mediation and decided to determine this issue by a special vote. The result was an overwhelming no, and we ultimately abandoned the idea of pursuing the construction of the RWTF in the Buan region's Wi Island. We then received applications from other regions, and after going through their regional votes, we finally determined that the site of RWTF was Gyeongju. The extent of pain we had left on the Buan residents was very substantial in this process. I am sincerely apologetic for that.

The issue of the RWTF taught us an expensive lesson: When it comes to an issue with potential for opposition and conflict, these elements of opposition and conflict should either be resolved or minimized before the issue is pursued and further action is taken. In Buan's case, the district council's consent should have been obtained before anything occurred.

If the fact that the mayor had pushed this agenda without first going through the proper procedure was revealed, the right thing to do would have been to turn the whole thing back to square one. Instead, the government fell into a state of complacent optimism that the Buan residents would agree with the RWTF project since the government promised billions of dollars worth of support work and social overhead capital for the region. Even after it was revealed that the mayor of Buan did this without the consent of his constituents, the government continued to push for it.

Next, we should have visited the site. Even with the same proposal, each region may have had a different sentiment about it. In fact, only medium- or low-level radioactive waste, such as work clothes, gloves, boots, etc., is stored at the RWTF. In addition, it could have temporarily stored spent nuclear fuel. The risks are so low that they cannot be compared to nuclear plants that handle active nuclear fuel.

For this reason, the residents of towns with existing nuclear facilities, such as Uljin, Samcheok, and Gori, or those located nearby those regions, are accustomed to the idea of nuclear power plants and were comparatively less worried about the RWTF. Meanwhile, in regions where people are unfamiliar with nuclear power and pride themselves on their natural environment, one would become alarmed even hearing the word "RWTF" being uttered. It was wrong that we did not sufficiently explore such emotions in our planning.

I want to point out the culture of the Blue House and the bureaucratic society's partitioned business operations. It would have been better had all departments discussed important national and social issues with one another, but they simply did not.

The RWTF was also a massive conflict that the government had not solved in over ten years. The MoIE, the MoENV, the Government Information Agency (GIA), the Office of Senior Presidential Secretary for State Affairs Planning (OSPSSAP), the OPSCA, and the Office of Senior Presidential Secretary for Public Relations (OSPSPR) all should have participated in this discussion from the beginning. If we had divided tasks amongst different task forces for public sentiment, public relations, and environmental NGOs and worked together, the situation could have gone in a different direction.

We did not do this. We discussed this only between the MoIE and the OSPSSAP to handle the issue, and only after it was too complicated and too late to handle was when the circle of participation regarding the discussion expanded to include more entities. After the OPSCA joined the group, we saw that the public relations efforts undertaken by the MoIE and the KHNP were far less efficient than those by environmental NGOs that opposed the RWTF. The situation was that among the Buan residents, there was a misunderstanding that the temporary preservation of spent nuclear fuel and, finally, the work of reprocessing the spent nuclear fuel would be taking place at the RWTF. There was no need to transport the used nuclear fuel to the RWTF because there would be enough room for the used nuclear fuel to be stored after the medium and low-level waste had been transported to the RWTF. After giving up on Buan for the RWTF at a newly selected site, it was clearly stated as "Medium/Low-Level Radioactive Waste Disposal Facility" from the beginning to clarify that used nuclear fuel would not be stored and processed there.

The cases like the Iraqi Deployment and the ROK-U.S. FTA were the same. Although they were high-priority political issues that required all Blue House political advisors to participate in the discussion, only the offices related to foreign affairs handled them. Only after the situations worsened were these issues tossed to the Blue House political advisors to handle in the aftermath.

There must have been no precedent for the SPSCA to meet directly with the parties involved in conflicts and to establish negotiations with them. There were also internal objections. I always thought there needed to be someone to handle this task, even if it wasn't me. Even those who did not get any recognition from society strongly wanted to discuss critical social issues with others. It's a pity that so many voices went unheard. Letting them go unheard was not the image of the Participatory Government that promoted communication as its primary characteristic. I thought that approaching and lending our ears to the suffering and comforting them was one of the duties of SPSCA. It was the same when I became Senior Presidential Secretary for Civil Society. I always thought I should do this regardless of my social and political positions.

There were many I wanted to meet with and comfort. Unfortunately, all the tasks that demanded my presence in the Blue House prevented me from doing so. I heard that the family members of the fallen soldiers in the Battle of the West Sea were going through a difficult time financially and emotionally. At first, I planned to visit them, then changed my mind and asked the president to meet the families instead. Some were in bad shape financially, so we had to arrange employment for them.

The family of Mr. Nam Sang-gook, the president of Daewoo Construction, was also one such case. I really wanted to meet the family and comfort them, but I could not. It was regrettable that I only visited once I left the Blue House. I was heavy-hearted whenever I thought about how much they blamed us for their tragedy. Later, I heard that Mr. Nam's daughter was once a student of Senior Secretary Cho Gi-sook and that Ms. Cho sent our condolences to the family through the daughter.

* **Return of the Wartime Operational Control (WT-OPCON)** The right to control the operations of ROK forces in case of emergency in the Korean peninsula. At present, we have exclusive operational control in the peaceful period, but the control is given to the ROK-U.S. Combined Forces Commander in emergency situations. The Participatory Government agreed to transfer wartime operational control to the United States in 2006, but the Lee Myung-bak administration delayed the transfer until 2015
* **Radioactive Waste Treatment Facility (RWTF)** Radioactive material or substance contaminated by it is called nuclear waste. The radioactive waste disposal facility is a facility for the safe handling of this waste.
* **Sapae Mountain Tunnel** A mountain, 552m above sea level, between Uijeongbu-si and Yangjae-si Jangheung-myeon of Gyeong-gi Province. Environmental groups opposed digging the tunnel linking Songchu Interchange's and Uijeongbu Interchange's suburbs via the Seoul Outer Circular Expressway.
* **Cheonseong Mountain Tunnel** A mountain 922m above sea level in Yangsan City, Gyeongnam Province. As part of the second phase of the Kyungbu High-Speed Railway connecting Daegu and Busan, environmental groups opposed the passage of the tunnel through Cheonseong Mountain.
* **Head of the Jogye Order** The spiritual supreme leader of the Buddhist Order. The symbol of the sacredness of Buddhism in Korea, especially in the Buddhist Jogye Order of Korean Buddhism.
* **Proton Linear Accelerator Project** A high-tech project to accelerate proton proponents to identify the nature and structure of materials and explore new materials. It is used in the fields of ultra-fine technology, information and communication technology, biotechnology, space technology, and new material development. Advanced research facilities are promoted by scientifically advanced countries.
* **Korea Hydro and Nuclear Power** A public corporation specializing in hydro and nuclear power business separated from KEPCO in 2001

Labor Incident

Labor incidents were the responsibility of the Office of the Secretary to Presidential Secretary for Labor (OPSL), which was overseen by the Office of Senior Presidential Secretary for State Affairs Planning (OSPSSAP). However, the president distributed and arranged the work so that, out of the OPSL, the SPSSAP would handle the work related to labor policy while the SPSCA would take over the work related to strikes and labor disputes. Due to the nature of the work, the president saw that the OPSCA was more suitable for handling it than the OSPSSAP. Maintaining relationships with labor unions and labor organizations, understanding the current situations, and cooperating with SPO and police were closer to the work of the OPSCA. Also, the fact that I had long been a labor attorney and knew this area very well played a factor in this arrangement

By the president's order, I was in charge of dealing with significant labor incidents, such as the National Education Information System (NEIS)* strike by the Korean Teachers & Educational Workers' Union (KTEWU), the Korean Railway Workers Union (KRWU) strike, the Korean Freight Workers' Solidarity (KFWS) strike, the CHB Bank strike, etc. Because of this, I gained the nickname "King Senior Secretary" from the press.

I received a lot of criticism for being too soft in responding to illegal strikes. When labor work was added to the OPSCA's original workload, I was overloaded. Not only I but all the staff had an increased workload per person.

At the same time, I wished there was more that I could do. For instance, in the case of the KFWS, the problem was the structure that caused extremely low shipping fees. In the past, there had been a standard rate system for freight fees, which prevented the shipping fee from falling below a certain rate. However, during the beginning period of the People's Administration, its deregulation policy eliminated the rate system. During the IMF crisis, the workers who were laid off due to the corporate restructuring process rushed to be self-employed truck drivers, and the number of freight trucks substantially increased. In turn, the freight fees were dramatically lowered due to excessive competition. On top of that, because of the multistage structure of the freight transportation industry, 20 to 30% of each freight fee was taken as a fee for a freight management company that hired and commissioned their work to each freight truck. Based on our investigation, the actual rate that each freight driver was taking home was approximately 60 to 70% of what it was when there had been a standard rate system in place a few years prior.

To fundamentally solve the problem, we had to implement a policy approach to revive the standard rate system, improve the multistage structure, and reduce the number of freight vehicles. It wasn't under the jurisdiction of the OPSCA. I reported the problem to the president and recommended a policy approach to the related ministries and departments. Still, I became frustrated because we could not engage in the process beyond that.

There was also a problem with the government's response to the KFWS strike. For a long time, the KFWS side raised their grievances to the government and requested meetings, but the government ministries and agencies continued to dismiss them. The Ministry of Construction & Transportation (MoCT), which should handle this issue, considered this matter as a labor issue and pushed the work to the Ministry of Labor (MoL). The MoL, on the other hand, did not regard this as their work because the KFWS members weren't to be considered laborers in the strictest legal interpretation, and the KFWS, therefore, was not a recognized labor union.

The president was furious at the methods of the KFWS strike under the banner of "Stop Logistics, Change the World," attempting to impose their demands by blocking the import and export at the Busan Port. He ordered me to make a stern response and to review the option of the military personnel substitution program. And it coincided with the president's American trip. He urged me to handle this issue as he was leaving for America, and even during his state visit to America, he checked in daily to assess this issue and repeatedly ordered me to review the option

The president was furious at the methods of the KFWS strike under the banner of "Stop Logistics, Change the World," attempting to impose their demands by blocking the import and export at the Busan Port. He ordered me to make a stern response and to review the option of the military personnel substitution program.

of the military personnel substitution program. Yet, since the import and export freight coming through the Busan Port was primarily transported via land routes and only a small percentage of those was through the rail system, the stern response the president ordered was impossible. There were not many military-owned trailers, so even if we put all the military personnel to work, they could only handle as many moving containers within the perimeter of the Busan Port or its container yard. Also, using military personnel or substitute drivers to drive the freight vehicles that the KFWS members had parked along the road was illegal. The only way this would be possible was for the president to proclaim an Emergency Situation. Of course, even this extreme measure would have to be taken if the Busan Port were completely dysfunctional due to the strike. Leaving it as the final option, we had to continue negotiating with the KFWS.

Ultimately, we successfully negotiated with the KFWS, and the strike ended. Well, in truth, though we used the word negotiate, it actually was the government surrendering. As the cargo storage level kept increasing and having only one or two days to resolve this issue at that rate, it was the only way to resolve the issue. We accepted the majority of the KFWS demands. We agreed to implement what could be immediately implementable, and other time-consuming demands would continue to be implemented gradually over time. We also opened the door for the KFWS to an annual bargaining right, like a formal labor union with transportation employers. It was a great success for the KFWS. Their social status was raised, and the number of their members increased dramatically.

Seemingly intoxicated with their victory, the KFWS started the 2nd strike about two or three months later. Unlike the first strike, it was clear from the beginning that it was an impossible strike. The government did not negotiate. They were prepared to avoid another deadlock and had increased the cargo loading capacity of Busan Port before the strike even began. We had no choice except to respond according to laws and principles. It was disappointing. The KFWS leadership was arrested because of this. The conversations between the labor workers and the government for a more fundamental systematic improvement also ceased.

The railroad strike of 2003 had a similar outcome. It was a general strike in April 2003, barely two months after the Participatory Government had begun. Until then, we took their strike as a hopeful demand to a new administration to resolve the issues that could not be resolved in the past administrations, such as "the reinstatement of laid-off workers" and "the discontinuation of privatization." Despite being criticized as too soft, we accepted most of their demands. Within two months, however, the KRWU started their second strike to oppose the railway management turning into a government-owned company. A resolute response by police forces was the only option. Many were detained and dismissed. The problem associated with their reinstatement could not be resolved until after the Participatory Government was out of office.

In the early days of the Participatory Government, there existed an aspect of getting off on the wrong foot between labor and the government because of these collisions. Perhaps it was the labor sector's greed or impatience out of a certain expectation from the Participatory Government. Or perhaps the Participatory Government could not meet the tall orders of the labor sector. Whatever the result was, when it came to the labor issues, I think there was a reason that the Participatory Government's labor reformation was not accelerated, but its reform capability was greatly damaged.

The KTEWU leaders I met over the NEIS strike were truly dedicated people in every aspect, demonstrated through their demeanors and impressions. While tons of fundamental education reform tasks that the Participatory Government should initiate accumulated, they approached this issue in such a tragic and resolute manner that I described them as "those suffering patriots fighting for Korea's Independence from Japan in the Manchurian Plain."

At any rate, at the beginning of the Participatory Government, which was a critical time, the Ministry of Education and the KTEWU were stuck on this particular issue. They could not move even one step forward. After much time and effort was spent, the issue was resolved. However, the Minister of Education, who was considered an exceptional appointment in the very first Cabinet of the Participatory Government, had to resign without having done anything substantial for education reform. From this point on, the appointment could only head forward from exceptional to more stable. This is one of the reasons why the Participatory Government could not do as much education reform as expected.

* **National Education Information System (NEIS)** A nationwide educational administrative information system that connects elementary and junior high schools nationwide, the city and provincial offices of education, affiliated institutions, and the Ministry of Education and Human Resources through the Internet establishes a computerized environment for combined information usage.

Attitude Towards America

The ROK-U.S. relationship was a hot issue for the 2002 Presidential Election after several incidents like the *Yangju Highway Incident** (also known as the *Hyo-sun and Mi-sun case**) and the candlelight vigil. The relationship between the Republic of Korea and the U.S. was like a flip side of a coin, similar to the Inter-Korean relationship. From the time when he was a candidate, President Roh advocated peaceful resolutions concerning North Korea's nuclear weapon issue, continuous measures for reconciliation and cooperation with North Korea, the ROK-U.S. alliance, balanced diplomacy, and self-defense as major diplomatic security routes.

While emphasizing the traditional ROK-U.S. alliance, the President sought balanced diplomacy in opposition to excessive bilateral diplomacy. On that note, Yoon Young-Kwan was appointed Minister of Foreign Affairs, and Lee Jong-seok of the NSC* was appointed Deputy Director General.

When appointing the Minister of National Defense, the most important criterion was whether the candidate had a firm conviction for self-reliant national defense and military reform. The President believed "a civilian minister could inaugurate a full-fledged national defense reform." Therefore, at first, he made an appointment traditionally, and in the latter half of the term, he envisaged appointing a civil official as the Minister of National Defense. At first, there were not many candidates qualified for the job. When only two candidates were left, the President instructed his counselor, Jeong Chan-yong, to meet with both men to see what they thought about self-reliant defense and military reform. According to the counselor's report, Cho Young-gil was appointed.

In May 2003, the President made his first visit to America. At the beginning of the new government, the North Korean nuclear issue was becoming more critical than ever as some American neocons talked about bombing North Korea. The goal of the visit was to meet with the U.S. President, George W. Bush, and conclude with a peaceful resolution on the issue.

At the time, the United States drafted a joint statement that stated that the U.S. "does not rule out all options" regarding the North Korean nuclear issue. In other words, this meant they would "implement all necessary measures (including war)." Of course, the U.S. did not actually mean to use force but would have the option so they could use the alternative to check North Korea. Just mentioning such a possibility could raise anxiety and have an adverse effect on the economy, including foreign investments in Korea. Moody's lowered Korea's credit rating outlook by one grade just because the U.S. started talking about bombing

North Korea.

The security team tried its best to change the theme to "peaceful resolution through conversation." The NSC and foreign officials were sent to Washington, D.C., for negotiations two days before the ROK-U.S. Summit Conference. Even Minister Yoon was pessimistic about the U.S. accepting our demands. However, President Roh advanced determinedly, and our request was accepted during the Summit Conference. The President was greatly relieved and thankful to President Bush. His remarks the following day about the importance of the ROK-U.S. alliance, stating that "if it weren't for the U.S. during the Korean War, South Korea would not have progression this far," was his way of expressing gratitude. This remark became controversial in the progressive camp, which is understandable. It was an excessive and perhaps inappropriate diplomatic tactic to thank a country that had once considered bombing North Korea.

The President emphasized the ROK-U.S. alliance but thought that Korea needed to develop a self-reliant defense. Since November 2002, the Bush administration has been mentioning the possibility of U.S. troop reductions. As a member of the committee at the time, the President made a remark at *Gyeryongdae** and asked, "What kind of preparations did the Korean military commander have if the U.S. army suddenly withdrew its support?"

The public relations reporters softened the candidate's verbiage and intentions to avoid any controversy. However, the President's deliberate intention was to raise awareness in society. I, too, said that they did not have to do that. The elected also rebuked the PR team for such action.

Matters pertaining to the ROK-U.S. alliance and the U.S. Armed Forces in Korea (USFK) raised several issues in the first year of his term. While the Bush administration consistently pushed a new agenda, there was a hot debate and conflict between the ministries and the Blue House about effective countermeasures. As Senior Presidential Secretary for Civil Affairs, I also became involved in the issue of amending "Concept Plan 5029*" into "Operation Plan 5029*" and strategic flexibility for the USFK.

As such, the security issue triggered considerable disagreement even within the Blue House. Mediation was needed to close the gap between the Blue House and the ministries. After becoming the Chief Secretary, I arbitrated at the Security Policy Coordination Meeting, which was held every Thursday afternoon.

I think that the strength of Participatory Government was in the diverse opinions and deriving conclusions through uncanny discussions between ministries and the Blue House. One interesting thing was how the Ministry of Unification and the National Intelligence Service tried to understand from the North's perspective during the Security Policy Coordination Meeting, while the Ministry of Foreign Affairs and the Ministry of National Defense emphasized the ROK-U.S. alliance more.

Toward the end of the meeting, the Minister of Unification and the Minister of Foreign Affairs were exhausted from heated discussions. The Blue House mediated and coordinated for both parties.

* ***Hyo-sun & Mi-sun Case*** In June 2002, two female middle school students were killed by a U.S. armored vehicle. U.S.-ROK inequalities, such as the ROK-U.S. Status of Forces Agreement, were highlighted as a big social issue.
* **NSC** (National Security Council) Korea's highest decision-making body related to national security, unification, and diplomacy. Although it is an institution specified in the Constitution, its function wasn't well known until the Participatory Government strengthened its reputation greatly.
* **Neocons** (Abbreviation for "neo-conservatives") Refers to the American neoconservatives centered on the Republican Party, or their group of influence.
* **Moody's** International Credit Rating Institution in America.
* ***Gyeryongdae*** Integrated bases of the Army, Navy, and Air Force in Gyeryong-si, Chungcheongnam-do
* **Concept Plan 5029, Operation Plan 5029** U.S. military plans that assume the sudden situation of North Korea, such as coups, mass defection, or collapse of North Korean regime. "5" is the number the U.S. military attaches to the operation in the Korean peninsula. Unlike "Concept Plan 5029," which was somewhat abstract and general, "Operation Plan 5029" includes specific details such as mobilization of troops and deployment.

Painful Decisions

In the first year of the term, the president's most painful decision was sending troops to Iraq. The whole Blue House suffered tremendously. The defense and security lines of the Blue House and the Cabinet insisted that they should accept the U.S. request to dispatch, but the U.S. had not officially specified the size of the troops. Around 5,000 to 7,000 infantry soldiers were discussed off the record, but the diplomatic, national defense and security ministries were suggesting more than 10,000. Their reasoning behind such numbers was that the troops needed to be at least the size of a division to carry out independent operations by assuming independent zones or our people would be under the U.S. Army and their command.

On the other hand, other members involved with the political affairs of the Blue House, including myself, opposed sending troops entirely. It was difficult to see it as a just war, and if there were any military casualties of our soldiers, it would be challenging to take the criticism.

The president had a similar opinion. Personally, he didn't want to send troops and sympathized with those who opposed the dispatching of our soldiers. However, South Korea was in desperate need of U.S. cooperation for a peaceful resolution to the North Korean nuclear crisis. In some parts of the United States, neocons were discussing bombing North Korea or attacking with restrictions. Some even brought up measures like blockades against the North. A dark shadow of war was cast over the Korean peninsula. As Moody's lowered Korea's credit rating outlook by one level due to the unstable conditions on the Korean peninsula, there was a negative impact on the economy with foreign investments being withdrawn.

Nevertheless, the president clearly stated that he would oppose resolving the North Korean problem by force. His assertion that the North Korean nuclear issue should be resolved through diplomatic discussion was firm. To do so, though, the cooperation of the U.S. government was vital. We had to accept their demands to a certain extent, and the president was seriously concerned.

As if he had read the president's mind, NSC Secretary Lee Jong-seok proposed an idea just then. "We will accept the request of the United States to send troops, but the scale of dispatch will be minimal, with 3,000 non-combatant soldiers." The nature of the dispatch was not to carry out combat operations but to support postwar reconstruction projects, as clarified by Prime Minister Koh-gun. The president, who was struggling to decide, accepted the plan. It was the least we could do for an ally and the most we could do to prevent the casualty of our soldiers.

The dispatch location was also to be identified as a safe zone. With that, the president urged me to persuade the Blue House opposition parties and the civil society camp first. I agreed.

After the Ministry of Foreign Affairs and the Ministry of National Defense were sent to the U.S. to discuss practical strategies, Lee Jong-seok, the deputy at NSC, was sent to the United States as a negotiator. He reported that the State Department generally accepted the proposal, but the Defense Department was cynical about it. Our discussion about "dispatching more than 10,000 combat troops" had raised their expectations. Later, the Bush administration responded with appreciation through an informal route. They were also desperate for the alliance's participation in the war.

The Ministry of Foreign Affairs had prepared an official announcement concerning the dispatch plan. The initial draft included a statement that "this is a just war caused by Iraq's development of weapons for mass destruction, and our dispatch will be aiding with the reconstruction of their economy after the war." However, the president disagreed with it being a "just war" and discouraged the expression. The president stated, "I do not know if it will be economically beneficial for them, and I cannot send my people for such cause at the risk of their own lives." He was clear that economic benefits should not be the motivation for the dispatch. Instead, he insisted on disclosing the actual reason for a diplomatic decision for peace in the Korean Peninsula and the interest of the ROK-U.S. alliance.

It was a hard and painful decision, but with the dispatch of troops, the North Korean nuclear issue went as the president had hoped. The cooperation of the United States helped establish a multilateral framework called the Six-Party Talk, which became the assembly to discuss and resolve the North Korean nuclear issue diplomatically. We managed the crisis by alleviating the "tough policy," which considered bombing the North at one point. Sending the troops to Iraq was a big move that helped us. Later, the president said, "If it were just a personal decision, I, too, would have opposed it. But it was unavoidable for me as president." He added, "It wasn't a correct decision, but it was an inevitable one."

Progressive and reformist camps still refer to the deployment of troops by President Roh and the Participatory Government as representative of wrongdoing. I'm afraid I have to disagree. The opposition of the progressive and reformist camps helped the government decide on sending the least number of non-combatants. However, I cannot agree that the dispatch was a mistake, especially when it was proven to have contributed to resolving the North Korean nuclear crisis through the Six-Party Talk. Of course, the war in Iraq was unwarranted. It would have been better if we did not dispatch. Nonetheless, it was for greater national interest and management. I think the progressive and reformist camps should have been able to make such judgments in order to take power.

Pain

Internally, the most painful incident was the Nara Banking Corp incident* and the ensuing investigation of the presidential funds. Ahn Hee-jung and other presidential aides and the best contributors to the presidential election had to bear the cross. The president said he would openly be investigated for the matter. He wanted to break the election custom of that era with his own hands. Though it may sound grandiose, it was like cutting off one's own flesh, and he did. He publicly ordered the prosecution to investigate as necessary, which may have accelerated the investigation. It was not an issue to be avoided.

At the time, the recall process of the prosecution was a problem. In the case of Ahn Hee-jung, the arrest warrant was initially rejected. He was publicly embarrassed for nearly a month until finally, he was imprisoned after a warrant was issued. It was not just a disgrace but a witch hunt. I was so sorry to watch him, and I couldn't even imagine what it was like for his family. I still remember how Ahn Hee-jung appeared before the prosecutors. It seemed as if this unscrupulous bastard finally appeared in the prosecutor's office. Many reporters pushed and pulled him, making him look terribly "shabby." He became an evil criminal before the public eye and was insulted continuously. His human rights were violated. A minimum procedure for protecting the human rights of the main suspect has been established since then. Reporting inside the prosecutor's office was prohibited, and photo shoots were restricted to the exterior of the building.

The system still exists, but it should not be the fundamental solution. The suspect is innocent until proven guilty. Therefore, no media outlet or press release has the right to violate a suspect's rights by exposing him/her to the media during the investigation. This is not to be justified by excuses such as people's right to information or freedom of media coverage. At least until the prosecutor indicts, the suspect should be protected from media pressure.

Everyone under judicial action was treated unfairly, especially Ahn Hee-Jung. It was because he was responsible for the funds during the presidential election and because of suspicion regarding the case of Nara Banking Corporation. He did not come back to the Blue House because he was afraid of being a burden to the president. Some have suggested that he should have gone abroad for a while, but he was determined to confront the situation. It hit him in the face, and he suffered a great deal. He even took responsibility for things that he did not do. I regretted that I couldn't do anything but watch him and his family suffer. I couldn't help but feel sorry for those who suffered during that time, including Ahn Hee-jung, Gang Gum-won, Yeom Dong-yun, Jeong Dae-chul, Lee

Sang-soo, and Lee Jae-jeong.

I was also a campaign manager at the Busan division. The only difference was that I had a treasurer, so I didn't handle the funds directly. There were no fundamental differences between myself and those who were "unjustly" treated. I felt even more terrible.

Everyone made sacrifices to defend the president. Those were the people willing to bear the cross to honor the president's intentions to nullify old customs and remnants of a previous era. Their sacrifices brought a change in the election culture and enabled a revolution.

The case of Yang Kil-seung, the Chief Personal Secretary of the Blue House, was also heartbreaking. After he attended the ceremony for the restitution of *Cheongnamda**, he was invited to a friend's house for a drink, and somebody secretly took a photo and reported it as "a gathering of the private organization to prepare for the general election" and "receiving entertainment kickbacks and favorable treatment from inappropriate" persons.

I was on a late summer vacation in August when the incident became an issue. My vacation was supposed to be a week-long, but I would only take three days off with my wife in Mungyeong, Gyeongbuk Province, one of my favorite places.

I stayed at Bongam Temple for a day, where there was no reception. The next day, as soon as my cell phone worked, I got a call from a reporter. That was when I first learned about this incident. Later, there was an article accusing me of going on vacation and not responding to a phone call for a day.

Attending an alcoholic drinking gathering isn't appropriate conduct for the Chief Secretary, but he shouldn't have been blamed for anything more than that. If the criticism was based on rational, logical grounds, it would have made sense. However, it was a witch hunt, and he was blighted as if he were a shameless criminal. He resigned from his office. The media even suspected him of whitewashing the presidential office. It was absurd.

The press was all over it, and inside the Blue House, some people blamed him based on the media coverage without knowing the truth. I was so worried that I sent an email titled *Opinion of a Senior Secretary for Civil Affairs Regarding Suspicion Based on Insufficient Evidence concerning Chief Yang's Concealment*. Even inside the Blue House, people did not sympathize with the unfairness they were subjected to. The media reports misrepresented the truth, making it a publicOn the night of October 9th opinion trial. Further investigation revealed the facts, but it was too late to restore his damaged reputation.

* **Nara Investment Bank Case** Former chairman of the Bosung Group, Kim Ho-joon, was dislodged from his position as a major shareholder of the Nara Investment Bank after misappropriating two trillion dollars of public funding. It has been reported that he paid lobbying funds to Ahn Hee-Jung and Yeom Dong-Yeon around 1999, before his dislodgement.
* ***Cheongnamdae*** A presidential vacation house built on approximately 1,820,000m^2 of land, located near the Daecheong Dam in Chungbuk Cheongwon-gun, was named *Cheongnamdae* after *Cheongwadae* in the South. It was used as the presidential villa since the 5th Republic but returned to the National Recreation Facility on April 18th, 2003, during Roh Moo-Hyun's Participatory Government.

The President Asking for Renewed Confidence

The president visited Indonesia to attend the "ASEAN + 3" Summit from October 6th to 9th in 2003. During that period, the SK slush fund incident broke out. The prosecution announced the involvement of former Secretary General Choi Do-sool, who had summoned the investigation policy. The media was overwhelmed by the allegations concerning the former secretary. In fact, Choi's involvement had already been reported to the president long before. In August 2003, Chief Secretary Choi left office to run for the general election, but it was a preliminary measure for the Chief Secretary of Civil Affairs.

It was all anticipated. In reality, the impact was enormous. He was in charge of accounting throughout the president's political career and was called the "eternal deacon of the president." The morality of the Participatory Government was at stake.

The president seemed to agonize with the issue as he watched media reports in Bali, Indonesia. When he returned from his overseas trip, the president always had tea with the executive chiefs and aides in the residence. Welcoming his return, they discussed and reported the significant issues that happened in Korea during his absence. On the night of October 9th, executive chiefs and aides gathered together at the residence. There was a brief report on Choi's case, which was the most important. The president said that he would investigate the report himself. There was no mention of the content and method of his investigation or his position. We thought he would apologize and unveil his stance on the overall issue of the presidential funding case. Advisors dissuaded him from taking action when the investigation was still in progress. However, he said, "I will appropriately take care of it," and left.

The president called me when I was about to leave the residence. "Let's talk a little more if you don't mind." It was already late that night. Everyone assumed the president wanted more details from the Minister of Civil Affairs. When everyone left, and it became quiet, the president asked, "How do you feel about proposing a national referendum?" I was more than shocked. I could understand the president's feelings, as he regarded Choi's incident as his own responsibility, but it seemed like an overreaction. If anything, the country could fall into extreme confusion. I told him, and the president nodded and said, "But I've been thinking about this the entire time I was in Indonesia, and this seems to be the only way." At this point, I knew he was not asking for my opinion. He had made up his mind.

People think President Roh was very stubborn, but this wasn't necessarily the case. Many times, when challenged repeatedly, he would change his mind. Sometimes, it was necessary to give him some time. I said, "For you to regain public confidence, a referendum is the only way, but there are limited reasons for holding a national referendum under the constitution." I need to review if we could hold a referendum first, and even if it is possible, since there is an ongoing investigation underway, we should wait until it is over." The president seemed to agree with me, and I thought I had earned time.

Around 10 a.m. the following day, I received a call from the Office of the Private Secretary. The president was about to hold a press conference to ask for a reappointment immediately at *Chunchugwan**. I told them to stop him at all costs, even if that meant physically blocking him until I arrived. At the time, my office, the Ministry of Civil Affairs, was not in the Blue House but temporarily at the Ministry of Foreign Affairs and Trade. I immediately went to *Chunchugwan*, but the president had already started the press conference.

There was no script in this unanticipated press conference. However, the president's words stung my heart. "Until recently, Choi Do-sool has assisted me for nearly twenty years. Although the investigation will reveal the truth, I can't say that I didn't know about the charges. I will take responsibility if he has done anything wrong. I apologize to all of you and would like to take responsibility publicly. Whatever the outcome of the investigation, I would like to solicit public confidence regarding the problems of this government, including this issue. I give up all authority and power. Moral trust is the only foundation to lead the nation, which is at stake in this present time. With that, I humbly accept and put myself subject to your judgment... It is difficult for me to run the state of the nation on my own at this time, when the media, the government, and the regional civil environments are unstable. What was needed to overcome many of these issues wasn't simply greed for power but moral confidence concerning what I do. The problem I faced with former Secretary Choi's case makes it difficult for me to proceed confidently."

As his adviser, I was saddened. It was a press conference held without consulting his cabinet. Occasionally, President Roh would not provide opportunities for opposition when he anticipated objections from his cabinet. Such a thing was very rare, but the re-election announcement was a referendum, known as the Grand Coalition * proposal. I suppose he did this to maintain his intention. In any case, the result was generally not promising.

* ***Chunchugwan*** The press area inside the Blue House. Here, presidential speeches, interviews, and briefings from spokespeople are held.

* **Grand Coalition** The coalition government formed by the coalition of major parties of the National Assembly. On the other hand, the coalition of minor parties for a coalition government is called "Small Coalition."

A Freeman

As December 2003 approached, talks of the general election taking place the following year in April began to emerge. The Blue House had already sent out candidates for the general elections in August of that year during the restructuring of the organization and human resources affairs. Like the past regimes, it was either to greatly enjoy the "Blue House premium" when the general elections were imminent or, on the contrary, the policy was to block the Blue House administration from being affected by the general elections as much as possible. Senior Presidential Secretary for Public Affairs Lee Hae-sung, Secretary General for Public Affairs Moon Hak-jin, Secretary for Domestic Press Kim Hyun-mi, and Director Kim Man-soo, Senior Presidential Secretary for Civil Affairs and Executive Administrator Baek Won-woo were all gone by then. However, as the election quickly approached, my ideas and irrelevance for "mandatory appointment" emerged from the party. Both Head Chief Jung Chan-yong and I were the subjects of discussion. For the president to safely administer affairs of state, the majority of the seats within the National Assembly were essential, and qualified individuals with a competitive edge all needed to run for office and enter the National Assembly to help the president. The Uri Party in the Yeongnam region especially lacked qualified personnel, so people like me had to run. It was difficult to accept, but it was a reasonable request.

When I declared that I still didn't want to, the level of demand and verbalization from the party became stronger, later becoming harsh. Of course, they didn't talk directly to me but spoke to the press and the media and pressured me through the media reports. Later, they would use harsh words like "You want to enjoy the results but don't want to suffer for it" and would go to the stage callously criticizing me. I could make the assumption from the background. At this point, a part of the plan was to drive me out of the Blue House. While I was in the Senior Presidential Secretary for Civil Affairs (SPSCA) position, my principles, in many ways, were very uncomfortable for them. That was understandable as well. For a while, I heard complaints about me not helping with the prosecutor's investigations or not listening to the party's requests.

However, while I was at the SPSCA, it started to overwhelm me with how different it was from my normal life. Furthermore, I didn't have any thoughts of taking part in politics. Rather, I had the thought of quitting. In particular, though the president didn't say it publicly, it was obvious that he wanted me to run. Though he didn't say anything, I was able to sense it. I couldn't accept it and thought continuing was improper when I knew his desires. I used my health as an excuse to announce my resignation. Just then, the media and opposition parties raised preposterous accusations about the *Min Kyung-chan Fund Case**, and I used that as an opportunity to resign. On February 12th, I was officially receded from my position.

As I left, the stories that were swirling in my heart were discarded in the form of "the side of resignation." I expressed my remorse for the outrageous suspicions that arose from the *Min Kyung-chan Fund Case* and *Chief Yang Gil-seung Case* by saying, "I'm exhausted due to constantly unfounded accusations, suspicions, and tensions as if every day was a state of emergency. I felt incapable of responding to them one by one, feeling powerless." I told the truth about my health and the problem with my running for candidacy. "My health has significantly deteriorated. Recently, the escalating pressure to run for office has become an unbearable burden for me. My physical and mental energies are depleted for these and other reasons. I now wish to resign from this position and return to my original role."

Almost a year after my entry into the Blue House, I experienced a profound sense of liberation. I couldn't help but feel remorse for the president and those who were diligently working, but my departure was inevitable. The weight of the office had been lifted, and I was free to chart my own course.

The outside air was genuinely liberating. It was like a dream. My wife and I traveled to Gangwon Province right away. We had wanted to go there for some time and took a road trip there. We visited Yeongwol,

Jeongseon, Inje, Baekdangsa, and Sorak Mountain. Since I wasn't bound to anything, I went where I wanted to go and stayed where I wanted to stay. I wanted to scream, "I'm a free man!" like Choi Min-sheek, a Korean actor, did in a commercial.

* ***Min Kyung-chan Fund Case*** This is a suspicious case with no substance. Min Myung-Chan, the brother-in-law of Roh Gun-pyeong, President Roh's older brother, supposedly recruited 65 billion dollars in funds in early 2004.

Himalaya

On February 28th, I headed to the Himalayas in Nepal. I left the Blue House without any plans. I thought I shouldn't return to law for the time being and live quietly until I returned to being a lawyer again. I trekked in Nepal, Tibet, and North India, the places I dreamed of for a long time. I also tried to meditate and think about what to do next.

In the law firm where I worked, sabbatical leave was available for three months based on ten years of service and six months for twenty years. I was busy when it was my 10th year, so I didn't take a vacation. Then, in 1997, my 15th year, I took a three-month vacation. At that time, I went on a trekking trip to Everest in Ratak and Nepal, the stage of the Old Future written by Swedish ecological activist Helena Norberg Hodge. Without a guide or a porter, I traveled alone with a fellow pastor of my age who was on sabbatical, navigating by map. It was amazing. I wanted to go on a trekking trip again since then, so I have been looking for the right time. I decided to go to Annapurna this time since I went to the Everest last.

Trekking in Annapurna usually starts in Pokhara, the second city in Nepal. It had a warm, subtropical climate at an altitude of 900m above sea level. There was a natural lake called Pewa, with many hotel lake houses.

Nepal has changed so much over the last time. In Kathmandu, the capital of Nepal, there were many soldiers with rifles on surveillance. In the meantime, the brother of the King had succeeded to the throne as a result of a shooting that occurred in the court from which the King and his son were killed. The democratic measures that the former King had initiated had regressed significantly, and the public's perspective was agitated. With Maoists, anti-government armed rebels, being more active, soldiers with guns guarded the capital city.

While my wife and I were in Nepal, the Maoists issued a general strike order for all the people. Almost everyone in the provinces except Kathmandu seemed to follow the order. There were no cars other than military vehicles, ambulances, and ones labeled "Tourist Only." Kathmandu didn't have a general strike, but I was told they were suffering because of the lack of food and vegetables from other provinces. According to the tour guide, participation in the strike escalated only because the government retaliated against those who didn't participate in the general strike. There was also an actual retaliation case, which increased public fear. Even so, the participation in the rural provinces seemed too extensive. If the government did not catch the public attention with drastic democratic measures, it seemed like the monarchy would be in jeopardy.

Trekking in Annapurna usually starts in Pokhara, the second city in Nepal. It had a warm, subtropical climate at an altitude of 900m above sea level. There was a natural lake called Pewa, with many hotel lake houses. Between February and March, the southern blossoms bloomed in the hotel courtyard, and the exotic harmony of the scenic mountain is breathtaking. It was an excellent place to rest for a while. Several decades ago, a recently deceased author, Park Wan-seo, made a journey to Tibet and Nepal and published a book titled *Blasphemy*, which described Pokhara. Ever since I read the book, I have wanted to go there.

Initially, I intended to climb to the base camp at 4,700m above sea level in Annapurna. When I went to Everest and Lattak in 1997, I trekked up to 5,900m above sea level. I just wanted to go to a place called base camp more than I wanted to go up high. However, I wasn't confident I could make it, so we decided to trek to 3,500m and traverse mountain villages. One week seemed enough, but our schedule was shortened to five days. I was in such bad shape I struggled a lot.

Through a travel agency, I had a tour guide and a porter. The guide had a job in Korea, so he could speak some Korean. I asked for two porters since it was cold and I had a lot of things to carry, including sleeping bags and luggage. But only one porter showed up at the trekking point. It seemed like he wanted to decide whether two porters would be needed. The guide said he had experience being a porter for Korean climbers going to the Himalayas. He was petite but very fit.

After looking at our luggage, he said he could do it alone. According to the Nepal Labor Law, porters are only supposed to carry 20kg each, but often, it was not enforced, and they'd carry 30 to 40kg. The guide also recommended tipping the porter for carrying all of the luggage. Our bags just contained parkas and sleeping bags, nothing too heavy anyway.

Still, the combined weight of the two seemed to be well over 20kg. More than anything, it was almost as big as the porter's body. I couldn't leave it all on the porter and climb the mountain empty-handed. I was also a strong man, so I decided to take half of my luggage. It was a backpack weighing less than 10kg but very heavy. I couldn't hand it back to him again, nor could I give it to my wife... I carried it all the way, and it was painful. The porter showed no sign of fatigue and continued forward. He got impatient sometimes, waiting for us to catch up. My wife also didn't struggle as much either. The only problem was me, who was so proud of climbing up to 5,900m. After all the fuss, I enjoyed the scenery of the Himalayas, the beauty of the mountain village, the stars in the night sky, and the clear air. It was worth the trouble.

There was another significant accomplishment. I quit smoking in Annapurna. I had been smoking since high school. If I followed the building code for public buildings being designated as non-smoking areas, I would have already quit smoking while in the Blue House. I used to smoke with the president at first but stopped doing that because it did not seem respectful or courteous to the president. The First Lady didn't like it. I always thought it was a good idea to quit smoking, but I could not do that while I was in the Blue House. Instead of quitting, I kept it to about half a box per day before entering the Blue House, but it became a box a day during my time in executive service.

I felt the need to quit smoking when I was scuba diving. At first, I was taking scuba diving classes with my wife. Compared to hers, the breathing barrier of my snorkel turned yellow due to nicotine. I realized that I was releasing nicotine not only when I smoked but also when I breathed. I thought about quitting since then and finally did it while walking through Annapurna.

After hiking and sweating, I missed having a cigarette in places with a good view. But the air was pristine; I would feel ashamed smoking there. Because trekking was so strenuous, I might not have realized that I was experiencing withdrawal symptoms. In the end, I was able to quit smoking there.

When I reminisce about the Himalayas, everyone is curious about high-altitude illness. Perhaps the professional climbers might get that at 8,000m, but my body adjusted to the altitude as I was climbing slowly to somewhat average altitudes. People usually get sick from altitudes at about 3,000 meters above sea level, especially if they are moving fast on a vehicle or airplane or just walking really fast. Instructors in Annapurna advised people to walk very slowly, literally in manbo (or easy walking) in Himalayan.

However, Korean people like to climb, especially at a fast pace. Those who trek in the Himalayas have probably been climbing for a long time. Therefore, the trekking tour time for Koreans is often shortened by half compared to that of Western people. They just climb much faster. High altitude illness takes different forms, including headache, vomiting, and diarrhea, depending on the constitution. These symptoms will disappear when one comes down or stops for a little bit to adjust. Being Koreans of strong will, though, Koreans just go on, however painful it is. It's also because they don't want to cause inconvenience to others. The symptoms will worsen until they cannot get down on their own. When I was in Annapurna, two Koreans were removed by helicopter. The guide said, "Koreans say 'quickly, quickly' so many times when they climb. It's because they say 'quickly, quickly,' they get so ill." It would be nice if people took it slowly and enjoyed nature while they were out there.

I had a similar instance when I was trekking Mt. Everest in 1997. Mt. Everest had lodges and mountain villages scattered at high altitudes, up to 5,800m above the level. There were even markets similar to the "5-day" market of Korea. In particular, "Namche Bazaar" in Namche village, about 4,000m above sea level, is famous worldwide. It is held every Wednesday and has local products, food, tourist souvenirs, etc., from towns in higher and lower altitudes. Mountain villagers gather in markets with enormous amounts of goods in backpacks. It was unusual to see people wearing suspenders on the forehead, not over the shoulders. Foreign people would wait a few days to see the market, but Koreans were only interested in climbing up. I thought it would be nice if Koreans were as interested in the culture as in trekking.

After trekking in Annapurna, we went from Pokhara to Chitwan National Park for an elephant safari and bird exploration. We rode an elephant around the park and watched wild animals like rhinos and subtropical birds. On a canoe, visitors could watch crocodiles and birds along the river. While we were returning from the safari to the nearby airport, the reformists issued a general strike order. Even the bus stopped running and could not get to the airport. The guide quickly picked up a jeep, and a few people went to the airport together. The driver wrote a big sign on the windshield, saying "Tourist Only." There were no other vehicles than ambulances, military trucks, and occasionally vehicles that said "Tourist Only" like ours.

Trees and old tires were burning all over the roads, and vehicles passing by were being searched. The jeep chauffeur seemed to be making excuses every time he met people going to the checkpoint, and he finally said he could not do it anymore, ten kilometers from the airport. Our guide brought a rickshaw from somewhere and took us to the airport.

Unexpected News at Kathmandu

I accidentally heard about the news about impeachment during my visit to Kathmandu, where I was visiting markets and nearby temples. After I left the Blue House, I broke off all news updates. I was determined that it would be normal for them to ask for requests when I would contact and meet them sometimes. I wanted others to realize that if they requested something from me, I would be a regular person who wouldn't be much help. When I went to Nepal, I didn't notify the Consulate or even take my cell phone. So, I wasn't exposed to much Korean news for a long time.

During my stay at a hotel in Kathmandu, a newspaper printed in English would be left under my door every morning. I remember it being the International *Herald Tribune*. Though my English was insufficient, I was able to skim through the headlines while eating breakfast. "South Korean President Roh" was in bold letters and caught my attention. When I looked closer the word "impeached" followed. I didn't know what that word meant. When I thoroughly read the article, I was able to assume that it meant the opposition party in the National Assembly initiated the prosecution for the impeachment of President Roh. I was shocked.

I didn't think it was that serious because the Grand National Party discussed impeachment within a month after his inauguration. Even before I quit, Jo Soon-hyung, a representative of the Democratic Party, talked about impeachment. It was a repetitive political attack, so I thought this, too, was a political offensive. I did not expect the impeachment motion to be passed.

However, though they say it was a political offense, if they passed the impeachment motion, it could be assumed that the country would be in a difficult situation. Under such circumstances, I was not able to continue with my vacation. I needed to return to see the situation first and then continue with my vacation. Since there was no direct flight from Kathmandu to Seoul, I had to transfer from Bangkok or Hong Kong. While I spent a couple of hours in Bangkok, waiting for my connecting flight, I saw that the same article was on the main page of the *Bangkok Post*.

Soon after returning, there was a presidential press conference. The online articles showed that the public's opposition to the impeachment was overwhelming, and a withdrawal of the impeachment motion was discussed based on the president's apology. I thought the press conference would be compromising and propitiatory, where the opposition party would express their regret and dispose or clearly withdraw the impeachment motion.

But that wasn't the case. President Roh revealed his stance on principle in an unyielding manner that straightened the fighting spirit of the opposition party. It was something President Roh would do. The president's temperament was shown through the press conference, where he would become stronger when put in difficult situations and breakthrough when stuck.

Surely, his advisers suggested a base compromise, but I could imagine the president not listening. Anyway, the opportunity to compromise was gone. The president said what he wanted to say, and the only thing left was to wait for the results.

In the interview that day, mentioning the actual name of the former president of Daewoo Engineering & Construction Co., Nam Sang-gook, was the excuse for Nam's suicide. When I later pointed out that "it was wrong," the president didn't remember it. He said that he never mentioned his real name. When I said that he did, he asked for the press conference recording and checked for himself. At first, the president didn't mention the man's real name, but he did while answering the reporters' questions. After the president confirmed the truth, he was filled with regret for a long time.

Impeachment Representative

Eventually, the impeachment proposal was approved by the National Assembly. The president asked me to compose a team of impeachment representatives and to take charge of the first half of the overall legal proceedings. A team of representatives was formed. Even when we think about it now, it was the best organization we could arrange. The team selected to serve were neutral, known for their reputation, and highly skilled.

After consulting with various people, I pleaded with them to join by visiting each person. Everyone who had been asked to do so readily agreed except one person who personally knew the president. He said that he was willing to help in whatever way possible. He gave a lot of advice and provided support from behind the scenes. I am so grateful for every one.

I started work in earnest and first filed a business registration. Since I went to the Blue House, I stopped being an attorney, so I submitted a re-business registration. It was the second time that we met as a client and attorney since the arrest of Roh Moo-hyun regarding the Daewoo shipbuilding case. Since I wasn't a Seoul attorney, I didn't have an office. I got a temporary office in Seochodong. Those who joined as impeachment representatives were well-known in the legal profession. They knew each other well and were in good spirits.

These people had good legal capacity and were satisfied with each other. The meeting atmosphere was filled with confidence and commitment when they first got together. I was convinced that if we did it legally, we would win. The impeachment seemed absurd legally and was only a numerical tyranny of the majority party. It was a coup d'état of the opposition party against the people and a crisis against the democratic Constitution. If we did not rectify such a fiasco, the future of our Constitution would be very dark.

We distributed responsibilities. Attorney Yoon Hyun-suk acted as chairperson, and Attorney Han Seung-hun assumed the role of general director. The rest of us shared the discipline by topic. Attorney Lee Yong-hoon was responsible for some fields, and Park Si-hwan was responsible for others. They came up with topics and wrote essays on their own.

They also divided the courtroom defense. The judges discussed the details of the number and order of representatives to speak at each trial, the contents to be spoken, and responses to sudden situations.

Jo Yong-hwan and Baek Seung-hun are two of the most prominent and meticulous members of the Lawyers for Democratic Society (LDS). Instead of acting as representatives, they were devoted to legal research and practical support. Before the two came on board, they helped set up a framework

I was responsible of the promotion as a substitute manager with a practical role. Public opinion was also important. The role of the press was critical. Every time we went to the Constitutional Court, we had to stand in front of cameras and explain our position or issue on the day's trial.

for our legal defense and studied the impeachment trial system. Attorney Kim Sun-soo also helped. They firmly believed that the members of the LDS shouldn't reveal themselves or act as representatives.

I was responsible for the promotion as a substitute manager with a practical role. Public opinion was also important. The role of the press was critical. Every time we went to the Constitutional Court, we had to stand in front of cameras and explain our position or issue on the day's trial. At the end, I explained and commented on the proceedings that day. There were cameras everywhere, so many reporters overwhelmed me. I couldn't see the reporters because of the lights from the cameras. In front of the cameras, I realized how difficult it was. It was like this for representatives of the impeachment trial. I couldn't even imagine being summoned to that position as a suspect. Does the media really have a right to forcibly place a person on camera and demand an answer? I think our society should become more respectful of the honor of others.

I also tried to gather opinions against the impeachment of attorneys and legal scholars, including constitutional scholars. Because the Constitutional Court couldn't afford to have a political character, it had to stand on the opinion of experts. Many people voluntarily gathered their statements against the impeachment in the name of society or in the name of the majority. Professor Ahn Kyeong-hwan from Seoul National University of Law played the most important constitutional scholarship, which most of the other junior scholars supported.

I often attended candlelight vigil demonstrations against the impeachment during the impeachment trial. I also wanted to be part of the demonstrations as a citizen. Given the political nature of the impeachment trial and the constitutional judges' conservative tendencies, the public opinion was necessary to be overwhelmed. It was as important as the court defense. Considering that the will of the people is the Constitution, it was part of preparing for the defense. Candlelit crowds flooding the streets in front of City Hall every day was spectacular. It reminded me of the "June Struggle." People held candlelight vigils against the impeachment, calling it the "Second June Struggle." The media reported that my wife and I participated in the candlelit vigil, and some internet media covered my comments.

"What is the Constitution? It's not in some far-high place, is it? It is the most universal and simple desire for democracy that the people have, the symbolic representation of the Constitution. In the final analysis, the interpretation of the Constitution should start with democratic consciousness and the legal attitude of ordinary people. It must be reflected in the Constitution. So, as a candlelight vigil against the impeachment by the citizens took place, the impeachment trial had already shown the direction to go."

The president and his representatives gathered together in preparation for the trial. The president invited us to express his gratitude. There was no need to talk about the trial. Mostly, we discussed the president's first court appearance. The opponents requested immediate attendance at the president's court appearance, to which he said he would. It could

I often attended candlelight vigil demonstrations against the impeachment during the impeachment trial. I also wanted to be part of the demonstration as a citizen. Given the political nature of the impeachment trial and the constitutional judges' conservative tendencies, the public opinion was necessary to be overwhelmed.

be helpful, but we told him it wasn't necessary. Later, the Constitutional Court did not accept the request either. The president didn't lose his sense of humor despite being tired most of his long life. At the end of the conversation, I asked the president, "Do you have anything to tell us?" He said, "Please let me do it again." It could have been a serious meeting, but everyone was able to break up smiling.

On April 15th, during the impeachment trial, there was a general election for the 17th National Assemblymen. I supported the campaign at several electoral districts in the Busan area at the end of the election. As a result of the election, the ruling Uri Party won 152 out of 299 seats. The Democratic Labor Party also won eight seats in proportional representation and ten in total, becoming the third biggest party. Without "Negative Remarks*" from Assemblyman Chung Dong-young, the Uri Party would have won more seats and become an overwhelming majority party. A general observation was that a few seats could have been added from the Yeongnam area. In short, it was a terrible judgment resulting in imminent impeachment. I thought this general election would put a wedge in the progress of the impeachment trial in terms of the Constitutional Court.

On May 14th, the decision was finally made. It was dismissed. All of the representatives embraced each other in joy. Reporters asked about our impressions. "I'm incredibly glad. I hope our political culture advances one step further and this becomes a chance to unite people. As the Constitutional Court accepted some of the reasons for impeachment, it was necessary to respect and humbly accept the decision. The decision of the Constitution was generally as expected. I think it was a legal explanation of the common sense of the people."

There was sad news. Attorney Yoon Hyun-suk, who acted as a chairperson of the representative team, fell after making the closing argument and eventually did not get up. He passed away on May 25th after living his entire life as a human rights attorney. He burned his last flame at the impeachment trial. On the day of the Constitutional Court decision, the representatives visited the ward to give him the good news, but he was already in a coma and had to tell his family without seeing him. During the funeral mass, I attended as a civil society leader and conveyed my condolences to the president.

There is one thing about the impeachment trial that I pondered. Fortunately, the impeachment proceedings against Roh were dismissed, but what if they were not? In fact, three of the Constitutional Court judges upheld the impeachment. If many judges had the same opinion, the president would have been impeached. But who gave them that authority? Where is the legitimacy of the authority to impeach a president elected by the people? It is not the people who have elected them as constitutional judges. Are they the best judges in Korea? Not necessarily. At least three of the nine Constitutional Court members are elected by the National Assembly, the president nominates three, and at least six are politically appointed.

In the past, there were cases in which people who contributed to political parties were appointed, or even those who did not get nominated were appointed Constitutional judges. Impeachment is a high-level constitutional system designed to defend the Constitution and democracy, but judges in charge of constitutional trials could be appointed through lax procedures. The political decisions of those judges can even expel a president elected by the people. It could be used to destroy the Constitution and democracy. The impeachment system is necessary. However, I believe that the current system of appointing the members of the Constitutional Court is really dangerous.

* **Negative Remarks** Assemblyman Chung Dong-young made the statement, saying that the younger generations, who are in their 20s and 30s, need to vote because they will be the future leaders of the country. He continued to say that he thought it was okay that citizens in their 60s and over do not need to vote because there's no need for them to decide the future for the young generation. He later apologized.

Senior Presidential Secretary for Civil Society

Three days after the impeachment trial, I returned to the Blue House—this time as the Senior Presidential Secretary for Civil Society (SPSCS). My role was to oversee the reform of the Blue House organization, particularly the expansion of the existing People's Participatory Office to the Reformation of the Civil Society Office. The president established this office with the aim of improving our engagement with civil society, and he asked me to take the position. This was not the only reason for the reform, as the existing office had reached its limit. However, the president's request was compelling, making it difficult to refuse.

When the president created a new civil society office, and I took the position, there was something we both aimed for. The strength of the civil society established the Participatory Government. During President Roh's presidential campaign, he was elected with the support of civil society rather than the Democratic Party's support. However, due to the troop dispatch to Iraq, the Buan incident, the Saemangeum problem, and the issues with transferring the Pyeongtaek U.S. military base, the relationship with civil society was severely damaged. The disappointment was so great that many turned their backs on him.

However, the civil society once again gathered in a candlelight vigil to save the president from impeachment. During the April 15th general elections, they made the Uri Party into a majority party. Now was the time to join hands with civil society again. Just then, the word "governance" was becoming a fad. We dreamed of having governance with the civil society. The president recommended books that dealt with "governance" to his advisers in the Blue House.

The president said I was the first qualified person to be part of civil society since I was part of the civil society activities in the Busan area for a long time and knew many civil society personnel well while being the Senior Presidential Secretary for Civil Affairs. I tried my best to meet his expectations. Important assignments on social conflicts were divided amongst the secretarial offices, with the Blue House paying direct attention to them.

The "Presidential Commission on Sustainable Development" was a conflict coordination mechanism for the national conflict resolution system. It was a key platform for promoting sustainable development in our country. The government also enacted the Basic Law on Conflict Management for legalization. This greatly expanded civil society participation enactment in which organizations such as the National Energy Commission and the Sustainable Development Committee discussed national policies.

Looking back, our efforts were not enough. But the direction was correct. The reason the government was not excessively hypertrophying as national welfare progressed was that it handed over the functions that the government had done in the private sector. It was a way to foster the health of civil society.

However, since the duties of the office of the Secretary of Civil Society were not standardized, unlike those of other offices, there were drastic differences depending on who was in charge of the work and how it was done. The challenge was to overcome those problems.

One of the memories I especially remember from my time at the SPSCS was my mother's reunion with her separated family members. In July 2004, my mother was chosen for a North and South Korean family reunion and met her younger sister, who lived in North Korea at Geumgang Mountain. My mother was the eldest daughter of six siblings, and her younger sister was the last flesh and blood in her family. My mother had been applying since Roh Tae-woo's government, but it wasn't my mother's application that was chosen but her sister's from the north side. The family reunion was held during my absence from the Blue House, and the event was held after I had become the SPSCS. I brought my mother to Geumgang Mountain and enjoyed meeting my aunt. She knew I was in the Blue House and asked about my position. Of course, I answered, saying that I was the Senior Presidential Secretary for Civil Society, but no matter how hard I tried, I could not explain to my aunt what I did so that she could understand.

I could never forget Deputy Prime Minister Lee Ki-Joon's Personnel

One of the memories I especially remember from my time at the SPSCS was my mother's reunion with her separated family members. In July 2004, my mother was chosen for a North and South Korean family reunion and met her younger sister, who lived in North Korea at Geumgang Mountain. My mother was the eldest daughter of six siblings, and her younger sister was the last flesh and blood in her family.

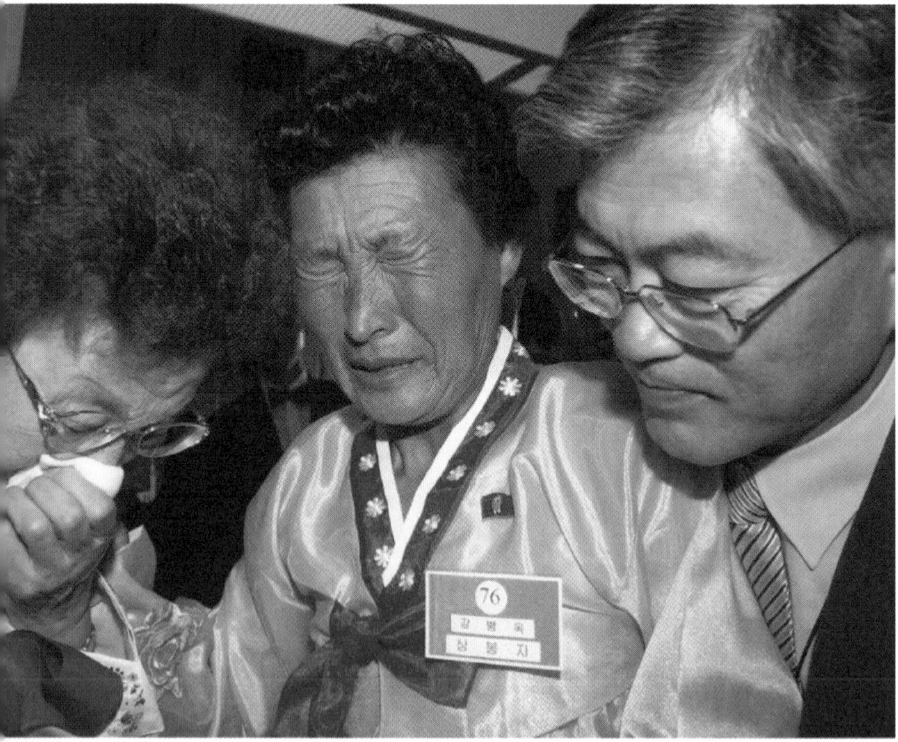

Crisis*. It was the biggest failure case concerning the Participatory Government's personnel. The crisis was triggered by a series of issues and controversies surrounding Deputy Prime Minister Lee Ki-Joon's qualifications and performance. It was not like we were not aware of his deficiencies during the verification process. Though it was all confirmed during the verification process, it was not deemed a reason for disqualification.

The decision was made when I was not part of the personnel recommendation meeting that day. While I was in the Blue House, I only missed the weekly personnel recommendation meeting once, and that was then. Personnel recommendation meetings were one of the most critical meetings not to be missed. However, on that day, there was an important event that needed to be taken care of in a rural area, and I was unable to return on time. I would have delayed the meeting if I knew I would be late, but I did not expect to be. Also, if I was the Senior Presidential Secretary for Civil Affairs who was in charge of personnel verification, I would have asked them to wait until I arrived. However, since I was the SPSCS, they held the meeting and made a crucial decision.

It was unfortunate that I would have been against it if I had been present. It was something that did not fit my standards. I also remembered that his fault was a problem at Seoul National University, and the media criticized it. If someone pointed out such a problem, everyone would have agreed. Since the Secretary-General knew and recommended him well, it was overlooked without anyone thinking seriously about it. With that, the Secretary-General, Senior Secretary for Civil Affairs,

Senior Secretary for Personnel Affairs, Senior Secretary for Public Relations, and I resigned. Though the Senior Secretary of Civil Affairs and Senior Secretary of Personnel Affairs quit, it was a great burden for all of us because we provided incompetent verification for the president.

Apart from that incident, the Participatory Government's personnel recommendation and the verification system were commendable. It was a mutual control system that separated recommendation and verification and was determined via agreement at a meeting. This system was designed to ensure transparency and fairness in the selection and appointment of government personnel. The most important thing was the president's willingness to respect the system.

The system would quickly be neutralized if the president's intentions were preceded. President Roh consistently respected the system. Sometimes, the president would ask me to review someone during an introduction. There were other times when he would speak in terms of an appraisal. When you keep the president close, you become naturally aware of the president's thoughts toward people. We would try to consider the president's intentions and include the person the president highly evaluated and liked amongst the candidates.

However, no exceptions were made in the verification and verification evaluation. Even though the president ordered a review of certain people, even those he had in mind for candidates, if their evaluations were low or if there was a problem with their verifications, they were excluded. When we reported the reasons why they were excluded, the president accepted them. There was never a time when he insisted on his intentions. That was why the Participatory Government's personnel system worked so well.

* **Deputy Prime Minister Lee Ki-Joon's Personnel Crisis** Deputy Prime Minister and Minister of Education and Human Resources Development Lee Ki-Joon took office in January 2005 but resigned two days later due to criticism concerning morality and public opinion, such as his son's dual citizenship, concurrent position as a non-executive director and chancellor of the Seoul National University, and excessive use of official expenses.

The Grand Coalition

Upon my return in January 2005 as the Senior Presidential Secretary for Civil Affairs, I was driven by a renewed sense of purpose. The initial strictness of the government's inauguration had begun to fade, and a more relaxed atmosphere prevailed. It was in this context that Lee Ki-joon, the minister of Education, took responsibility for the upheaval of personnel as the Secretary for Civil Affairs and Personnel and resigned. I, too, felt the need to return to my first intentions and contribute to fixing the mood, hence I returned to the job.

One of the most significant and painful events during my second term of the Participatory Government was the president's proposal for the Grand Coalition. This proposal, while aiming to remove regionalism, had the potential to shift power and compose the Cabinet of the Grand National Party. The shock of this idea reverberated among the supporters of the Uri party, who had worked tirelessly to make it the ruling party and had stood by the president during the candlelight vigil against impeachment. The civil society camps were disheartened, and people in the Honam area felt betrayed. We, the advisers, were also not convinced and had voiced our objections. The president later admitted that it was the biggest mistake during the Participatory Government.

The president's initiation of the Grand Coalition was not intentional. At the time, there was a regular consultation between the party, government, and Blue House officials every Friday evening over a dinner at the Prime Minister's Residence to discuss the state of affairs. The chairperson and/or the head of the party; one or two of the ministers among Chung Dong-young, Kim Geun-tae, Chun Jung-bae, and Chung Sye-kyun from the government; Chief Secretary, Policy Director, and myself from the Blue House attended the meeting. It was called the "Eight-Person Meeting," but since the members were not fixed, one or two more, such as the Chairman of the Party Policy Committee, occasionally attended. In rare cases, the president would make an appearance, saying, "Let me take a look at your faces."

At the end of June 2005, the president came to the meeting. We discussed many things, and one of the topics was the Grand Coalition, which was on the premise of the electoral system reformation to demolish regionalism. The president had mentioned this before, but the situation was different then. In the past, when the ruling party was hardly a minority, it was understandable, but at that time, it was difficult for many to understand. The majority lost their seats through the election, but we were still the majority in tandem with the Democratic Labor Party. Everyone was distressed about the president. It was so sudden that we could only listen. The president said, "Please do not think I'll do it immediately, so give me some time and think about it." When the president left, everyone said it can't be. Prime Minister Lee Hae-chan told all the attendees not to speak about the proposal.

A few days later, a newspaper covered the story as a scoop. It was presumed that someone from the party leaked it. When we saw the report, all of us from the Blue House suggested that we clarify by saying it is still only an idea. However, the president had officially proposed the coalition in a public letter to the members. When the advisers objected, he wrote the public letter and posted it online. The impact was out of control.

When the president came up with some ideas, he often reflected by telling his close advisers and listening to others' ideas. This process organized, revised, and redeemed the president's ideas. Those who did not know the president sometimes misunderstood his intentions from his initial statement before it was refined, which was precisely what happened at that dinner concerning the Grand Coalition. The president just started a conversation without having any specific plans. Later, the president told me that since the collapse of the Uri Party made the opposition party the majority and the Grand National Party proposed the dismissal of the Minister of Defense Yoon Kwang-woong, he regarded the political situation of the time as highly sensitive. If not for the media coverage, the president would have concluded his thoughts or consulted the advisers to assess the situation appropriately. If so, then his thoughts may have changed or at least been reflected upon in a more organized and timely

When the president came up with some ideas,
he often reflected by telling his close advisers and
listening to others' ideas. This process organized,
revised, and redeemed the president's ideas.

fashion. However, the unintentional media report made the president's intentions appear suspicious. The normal course of discussion became impossible with the agitated responses from the political parties as well as the public opinion. Even if the coalition proposal was ignored, at least the attempt to remove regionalism by reforming the election system should have remained confidential. Even that failed.

It was not the first time the president had proposed a link between electoral reform and coalition to do away with regionalism. A few days after the presidential election on December 26, 2002, President Roh attended the Central Democratic Party leadership training seminar and proposed a revision to the electoral system, stating: "I'm willing to concede anything to break the regional confrontation even if that meant my power as a president decreased." On January 18, 2003, in a TV interview, Roh responded, "I will not allow any one party to win more than 70-80% in one area to overcome the regionalism. Once that is achieved, I will follow the example of the French government and enable the majority party to decide the Prime Minister."

President Roh continued his statement at the National Assembly in the first speech after his inauguration on April 2, 2003.

"The regional dominance of one party must be resolved. Our politics cannot advance even one step in this manner. From the General Election next year, I would like you to revise the election law in agreement so that no political party will have dominance in any one area by more than two-thirds of the seats. If my proposal is realized in the 17th General Election next year, I will transfer the constitutional authority of the Cabinet to the political party or political coalition that holds the majority of seats. This transfer constitutes 50% or more of the presidential authority, which aligns with the decentralized system many people demand. Some claim that it is contrary to the Constitution. Still, it is possible that the recommendation rights of the Prime Minister, which are necessary to appoint a cabinet member under the current system, will be respected. It is my sincere proposal for the future of this country. Your consent and approval are greatly appreciated."

The result was the Grand Coalition.

The president consistently insisted on reforming the electoral system, which separates the constituencies from regionalism. He expressed that he was willing to concede his power to appoint a Prime Minister and organize the Cabinet and proposed coalition so that the reformation could be accelerated. However, the political parties showed no response to President Roh's repeated request for electoral reforms. The same was true for the civil society camp. They agreed it was the right thing to do but didn't provide much support. From my perspective, the civil society camp in Seoul wasn't interested in tasks such as regional development, demolition of regionalism, decentralization, and balanced national development. They agreed that those were the right things to do but also said, "Those do not have priority." "It seems that the president is too buried in the problem of less priority, such as the demolition of the regionalism, when problems need urgent attention, like solving polarization." This showed the present perspectives of the progressive and reformist camps.

* **Deputy Prime Minister Lee Ki-Joon's Personnel Crisis** Deputy Prime Minister and Minister of Education and Human Resources Development Lee Ki-Joon, took office in January 2005, but resigned two days later due to criticism concerning morality and public opinion such as dual-citizenship of his son, concurrent position as a non-executive director and as chancellor of the Seoul National University, and excessive use of official expenses.

Justification Over Investigation

In October, the prosecution investigated Professor Kang Jung-koo of Dongguk University's violation* of National Security Law. The issue at hand was the pursuit of ways to issue an arrest warrant. In this context, Chun Jung-bae, the Minister of Justice, took command of the investigation* and ordered a non-constraint investigation of the Prosecutor General's chief prosecutor, Kim Jong-bin. This decision, in line with the relevant laws of the Prosecutor's Office, where only the Prosecutor General had the authority to direct and supervise certain cases, underscored the importance of adhering to the rule of law.

Chun's decision to exercise the non-constraint investigation was not just because it seemed reasonable but also because it was in accordance with the belief that our criminal justice procedure should follow the principle of non-detention pursuant to the criminal procedure law. Whether the case would be investigated as a non-detention was an important threshold for setting the principle of non-detention. However, Prosecutor General Kim submitted their resignation in protest of the Minister's investigation command. Deputy General Jeong Sang-myung, now the Prosecutor General, and I tried to persuade him, but Kim did not give in. Opponents of the Participatory Government praised him as a hero.

I couldn't understand his behavior then, and I still don't. It was especially so when I compared the Participatory Government with the one before and the one following. Before the Participatory Government, it was very common for the Minister of Justice to command the Prosecutor General, and there was no need for an investigative procedure. The Minister just had to say what he wanted. How about the government now? Even though the Minister of Justice can only command the Prosecutor General, it was found that the Minister and his executive have commanded the Prosecutor General for an investigation over a phone call. There was no such thing in the Participatory Government because they followed the law. Therefore, the investigation command clearly indicated that the Minister of Justice did not interfere with the Prosecutor General.

The Prosecutor General's decision to step down after publicly releasing the contents, if they believed that they were secretly imposed unjust pressure and demands that were too difficult to endure, is a testament to his unwavering commitment to maintaining the political neutrality of the prosecution. However, Minister Chun's public and official procedure raised questions about this neutrality. At this point, the Prosecutor General needed to resolve the matter, even if it was different from his own conscience. He could have separately declared his personal conviction. It was not like Minister Chun hurt the prosecution's "face" or "pride."

Moreover, it was the perfect opportunity to establish a custom, in which the Minister of Justice directs the Prosecutor General through an official procedure of investigation. Kim's resistance brought back the inferior past practices. Considering that keeping the term of Prosecutor General was an important measure to ensure political neutrality of the prosecution, it is still hard to understand that Kim had given up his term at such a time when the term had not yet been firmly established.

On the other hand, the wisdom of Chun's conduct of the investigation is questionable. Since the time of Kang Kum-sil, a Minister of Justice from the non-prosecutor's office was seen as desirable, but the practical challenges of reconciling the two organizations were immense. This was why a minister with a non-prosecutor background was a rarity. Despite Chun's strong will to reform the prosecution, he was confronted with the same difficulties. The resignation of Kim and the issue of the investigation command only widened the gap between the prosecution organization, leaving the reconciliation and the prosecution reform unrealized. The command investigation, in the end, resulted in significant sacrifices.

* **Professor Kang Jung-Koo's National Security Law Violation Case** In October 2005, Professor Kang Jung-Koo of Dongguk University said that "The Korean War was North Korea's war for unification and freedom of the country" through Internet media, and was reported for violating the national security law.

* **Command of Investigation** Article 8 of the Prosecutor's Office of the Investigation and Supervision Agency states, "The Minister of Justice is the supreme supervisor of the prosecution office, and in general, conducts and supervises the prosecutor, and conducts and supervises only the prosecutor-general for specific cases."

Opportunity of Jurisdiction Reformation

The judicial reform, which was initiated while I was in the office of the Ministry of Civil Affairs, was still on the way when I returned, and it was the biggest issue I had to deal with. Fortunately, the Participatory Government has succeeded in legislating most of the judicial reform measures, which helped with the advancement of the judicial system of Korea. Both the civilian and the People's governments have made great efforts, but it never became more than a discussion. Obviously, we were not successful in everything. As for the reform of the military judicial system, we made plans but did not get to legislate due to insufficient time. The Supreme Court's effort to form a policy court did not get unified. Upon the foundation laid by the Participatory Government, any government with a willingness can make progress. Maybe the public did not actually feel the need because it was a judicial system reform. However, as a lawyer, I felt a great sense of achievement for successfully establishing and overseeing judicial reform.

Judicial reform is a task that must be done with the Supreme Court, so it's difficult for the government to pursue it on its own. Therefore, it was not a pledge during the presidential election, nor was it included in the national reform agenda that was selected during the transition. Judicial reform was, in some sense, an initiative by chance brought by the dynamics of history. It may be said that it was the result brought by the expectations of the reforms in the Participatory Government.

In August 2003, there was a justice wave in the Supreme Court. The Blue House and the Supreme Court were in a very difficult situation because of the recommendation of the Supreme Court justice. At the time, there was a strong public opinion demanding that the rights of humans, women, and minorities be guaranteed in the constitution of the Supreme Court. Young judges strongly called for diversity in personnel that reflects reform and change, not seniority. It was also the direction the president always emphasized. When the Chief Justice of the Supreme Court started working on the new Supreme Court Justice candidacy, I delivered the president's perspective to the Supreme Court. The president wanted to ensure diversity in the composition of the Justices, in whichever way it guaranteed human rights, women's rights, minority protection, and so on. However, the Supreme Court must have assumed otherwise or misunderstood his words, for the nominated candidate was in accordance with the traditional standards. The nominated candidate was successful, but the demand for diversity caused great opposition. Prosecutor General Kang Kum-sil, who attended as the recommendation committee to the Supreme Court justices, and Park Jae-seung, the chairman of the Korea Association, opposed and left. The judges, not to mention the legal system in the jurisdiction, also raised the problem. Park Si-hwan, the Chief Judge of the Seoul Central District Court, who was trusted by reformers, submitted his/her resignation. Some judges filed collective intentions and distributed online petitions in opposition to the recommendation procedure of the Supreme Court Justice.

It wasn't realistically possible for the Chief Justice to withdraw the recommendation. And it was not easy for the president to accept the Supreme Court proposal, which did not reflect diversity. If the president had refused the proposal, the Court would have suffered significantly from an unprecedented situation. Amid such a dilemma, former Chief Justice Yoon Kwan arbitrated and presented a solution discussed with the Court. The proposal stated that "if the president accepts the proposal of the Supreme Court, first, the Supreme Court will take the lead and push for judicial reform with the Blue House. Second, the Court will recommend the next Constitutional Court candidate based on the diversity criterion. The Court promises to convene a national judicial meeting to promulgate opinions and publicly announce that it will apply the diversity standard to appoint the next constitutional and Supreme Court justice." The president confirmed the willingness of the Court and accepted the proposal.

The first female constitutional judge in Korea and the first female justice officer were approved as a result. After that, efforts to diversify the constituency of the Supreme Court and the Constitutional Court made a steady and significant progression during the Participatory Government. Despite frustrations caused by the opposition of the Grand National Party, the first female Constitutional Court Chief was nominated.

On the other hand, after several preliminary discussions in October 2003, the Supreme Court and the Blue House formed the "Judicial Reform Committee" (senior commissioner) and entered the fora of judicial reform. Attorney Cho Joon-hee took on the chair position of the committee. After the discussion, the Supreme Court and the Blue House formed a "Judicial Reform Promotion Committee" and started establishing legislation based on the discussions of the Judicial Reform Committee. Attorney Han Seung-hun became the chairperson.

Rearranging Past Affairs

Among the things that started when I was first Secretary of Civil Affairs, organizing work on history was an important assignment. After some complications, the "Basic Law for Organizing Past History" was passed in the National Assembly. The "Past History Committee for Truth and Reconciliation" (Past History Committee) was also established. In this process, the strength of the civil society striving to organize history was crucial.

For a long time, a lot of effort was devoted, but due to the Grand National Party's opposition, though the legislation was delayed and the contents became ragged, there was great significance in passing it. Of course, the temporary activities of the "Truth and Reconciliation Commission," created by the special law, were not enough to reconcile the entire history. Hence, we came up with a solution. Although the Truth and Reconciliation Commission should do the legal final summary, each institution in the government would support it by clearing relevant historical events.

The plan was to have the institutions clear past events in parallel and have the Truth and Reconciliation Commission collect the results. It was effective. The National Intelligence Service (NIS), the police, and the military, which have the greatest need to clear the past, have each established their own committee. There was internal rebellion, but we persuaded them. In the end, the institutions successfully cleared their past historical events.

The courts cleared the history by reviewing previous court rulings. The committee's decision to investigate the truth has corrected many cases, and many are still being corrected.

The prosecution was the group that did not get to make reconciliation, though it was necessary. There was a reason for the delay. Often, the cases that were manipulated by public power or infringed fundamental rights were investigated by the NIS or the police first and then charged by the prosecution. Therefore, the NIS and the police first had to clear those manipulation cases, and the court had to declare innocence before the prosecution could process order and reconcile. The Participatory Government did not last to see this. Many cases were found to have been manipulated and found innocent by the court. Even though the nation was indemnified for tremendous damages, the prosecution did not seem remorseful.

April 3rd* was a single event resolved by the government and directly by the president. It had been discussed since before the People's Government and was an extension of clearing a painful historical event. All they wanted was the restoration of honor. A comprehensive report came out during the Participatory Government. The report alone helped considerably.

The president did not stop there. Roh considered it as a touchstone to settling problems of the past. Two public apologies were made. First, the Prime Minister attended the ceremony and officially apologized on behalf of the government. The president, unsatisfied at all, visited Jeju in 2003 and 2006 to apologize as the head of state. The bereaved families poured out their sadness and tears in front of the president after decades of endurance.

The Truth and Reconciliation Commission revealed the truth about 8,000 cases over five years, including those related to anti-Japanese independence movements, civilians' sacrifice before and after the Korean War, history of overseas Koreans, human rights abuse by anti-democratic and anti-human rights acts, violence, genocide, etc. In particular, it uncovered both the "Press Alliance" investigation that massacred thousands of leftist activists during the Korean War and the genocide of civilians by the army without due process.

It also identified civilian massacres by leftists or the People's Army. It was a great achievement that unburied historical truth.

Many things came to mind after watching the work of the Truth and Reconciliation Commission. After all, the nation has done a terrible thing to so many individuals, ruining the lives of many. The manipulation cases resulted in the imprisonment of many young people until

The president, unsatisfied at all, visited Jeju in 2003 and 2006 to apologize as the head of state. The bereaved families poured out their sadness and tears in front of the president after decades of endurance

they were all old and gray. The lives of their families were destroyed, as well. Shunned as a family of espionage, people were denied any employment, not just public service. The nation accused and broke those families.

Even though the state acknowledged its mistakes, restored the victims' honor, and compensated them with money, people's deprived lives were irrecoverable. The most important thing is the country's sincerity in acknowledging mistakes. The state can truly reconcile the perpetrator and the victim by sincerely apologizing for the mistake and restoring their honor. It is also necessary to reconcile and integrate people. In order to do so, we named the organization "Truth and Reconciliation Commission." The objective was to simultaneously pursue the incompatible values of "truth" and "reconciliation". I wonder how much of its goals have been accomplished.

This was a tremendous advancement in our history for the time being. Many countries have painful histories like ours, and they all make similar efforts to clear the past. However, not many are successful in clearing the past like we are. The same is true for Spain, South Africa, and Argentina. It is disappointing that the Lee Myung-bak administration has stopped all of this.

The filing period for clearing historical events is limited. For laws of a similar nature, such as the Presidential Truth Commission on Suspicious Death or Gwangju Compensation Law, the reporting period was extended with the Second or Third Amendments. The reporting period should have been extended for this matter, too. However, with the change of government, everything has stopped.

* **April 3rd** A People's Uprising in Jeju Island from April 3, 1948, to September 21, 1954. It occurred in the process of opposing the social problems of the U.S. military regime that ruled the Korean Peninsula after the Japanese defeat and the establishment of a South Korean sovereign government. In the process of suppression by the U.S. military, many civilians were killed. Statistics are uncertain, but victims are estimated to be between 25,000 and 30,000.

The National Security Law

Reflecting on my two terms as the Senior Presidential Secretary for Civil Affairs, there were several things I regret no accomplishing. Among them were the inability to establish a Corruption Investigation Office for High-ranking Officials (CIO)* and the inability to abolish the National Security Law. These failures have had a profound impact on our political landscape.

At the time of the presidential election, not only former President Roh Moo-hyun but also presidential candidate Lee Hoi-chang made the same pledge to establish the anti-corruption investigation and indictment authorities. The pledge of Lee Hoi-chang might have been closer to the legislation pursued by the Participatory Government. Candidate Lee Hoi-chang wanted to have the anti-corruption investigation and indictment authorities under the Corruption Prevention Committee at the time, and candidate Roh wanted to make it a separate organization. Later, the government pursued placing it under the Korea Independent Commission Against Corruption, so it was more similar to candidate

Lee's pledge.

At that time, the public's anger and demand for special countermeasures due to the corruption of the president and the power disclosed at the end of the Civilian Government and People's Government were palpable. The pledge to establish anti-corruption investigations and indictment authorities was a direct response to the people's needs. Despite the ample support and promises from both candidates, the bill faced numerous obstacles. The National Assembly, in particular, was a significant hurdle as it did not allow the investigation to target the presidential aide, relatives, and people around the Blue House who were exposed to power and corruption-related risks, as well as other senior officials and members of the National Assembly.

The National Assembly's resistance to the bill was significant, almost leading to a strike. Despite the need for balance, the bill should have been pursued more assertively. If the government had been more determined to pass the bill, it could have considered removing the members of the National Assembly from the investigation target. As elected officials, this was a viable course of action. However, we failed to demonstrate the necessary flexibility in this situation, a shortcoming that we must all reflect on.

What was even more painful was the National Security Law. We most definitely tried, with utmost effort. Even the president did. However, the ruling party only began the preparation after the president remarked on the abolishment. The subsequent process was disappointing. The party said it would devise an alternative but ended up dismissing the task force. The leak of internal documents and the "press play" of some members of the National Assembly were the excuses, but they were due to the failure to reconcile differences within the party. At that time, the ruling party could not reach a consensus even with a majority of seats and the absence of negotiations with the opposing party. They did not appeal to the public to form a popular opinion. They were not the only ones to blame, though. We must all reflect on the issue and realize our contribution or lack thereof.

I strongly criticized the People's Government for not abolishing the National Security Law because I knew they weren't trying hard enough. Such criticism backfired. Failure to abolish the National Security Law* is considered to be a symbol of the progressive and reformist camps' lack of overall capacity.

* **Corruption Investigation Office for High-ranking Officials** A separate agency that professionally investigates bribery or abuse of authority by high-ranking public servants

* **National Security Law** A Special Criminal Act was established to "secure the national security and the survival and freedom of the citizens by regulating anti-state activities endangering the state's safety." It was actually exploited as a means of regime security and ideological control. The United Nations Commission on Human Rights and the domestic community have posed it as a serious problem of constraining human rights.

My Resignation

In May 2006, I resigned as Senior Presidential Secretary for Civil Affairs. My resignation was accepted several months after I announced it to help the regional elections. I was greatly scolded for being caught up in gossip when I went to Busan and tried to help with the regional elections. During the five years of the Participatory Government, that was the only time that I was talked about inside and outside of the Blue House. It was then that I felt even more disillusioned and frightened about politics.

The Uri Party held a press conference at Busan City Hall, and I was invited to attend. Since the provincial board of elections in Busan was very frustrating, they asked me to speak aggressively for the election. The Busan City Public Relations Department spokesman and other spokespeople were there. The reporter asked, "How do you expect this local election to turn out, and what kind of election do you want?" to which I intentionally criticized the localism of the Busan people. "I expected the election of President Roh to be an opportunity to ease the regionalism of

Busan, but I'm sorry that it has become stronger. Since the president is from Busan and has a lot of affection for Busan, one would think that the people in Busan would support this government. I don't understand why the Busan people do not regard the Participatory Government as a Busan regime. I hope this election will dismiss such strong regionalism." It's not 100% verbatim, but I said something along these lines.

At first, this remark didn't receive much attention because only local reporters in Busan were there. However, the next day, one newspaper company that didn't even attend the press conference extracted the word "Busan regime" and accused me of instigating regionalism. This accusation, despite its lack of factual basis, significantly tarnished my reputation and further fueled the regionalism debate.

After they saw the article, the people of the Uri Party started blaming me. They criticized my remarks as encouraging regionalism, insulting the public, and disparaging the support of the Gwangju and Honam people, to whom the launching of the Participatory Government is indebted. Then, almost all the media covered it extensively, and it became a huge thing in an instant.

I was really embarrassed and apologetic. I regretted that I made highly controversial comments like the "Busan regime" and stimulated so many possible misunderstandings and arguments. I also regretted attending the press conference, thinking I would be helping the election. However, what was even more embarrassing was the Uri Party. It was a press conference held by the Busan City Party of Uri, and even though there was a spokesman and a public relations officer, they did not check the statement or my intentions but went straight ahead and reproached me. Even though it was not sensible that we, the victims of regionalism, would stir such a thing in the Yeongnam region, no one even questioned the verity.

The surprised Busan City Party announced that the statement and my intentions were not actually like that. It was no use. Even if I made a mistake, if they had a little bit of comradeship, especially since it was an election period, they would have attempted to explain and minimize the aftermath... Instead, they made it even bigger.

The aftermath of this incident was a painful experience for me, leaving a lasting scar on my mind. I found myself questioning my role in politics and feeling a deep sense of regret. I was informed that my remarks had led to some people being attacked by candidates of an opposing party in the Honam region. This news filled me with profound shame and I offer my sincere apologies to those who were affected.

During the remainder of the Participatory Government, I refused to return to being an attorney but decided to just rest. The president appointed me Special Affairs Secretary a few days later, a position that, despite its title, came with no salary, activities fees, vehicle, room, or even a work phone. There was no actual activity nor any request. They gave me a new business card, but I had no occasion to use it. Until I became the Secretary-General, it was the Special Affairs Secretary service, but the only time I did something as a Special Affairs Secretary was when I visited Ecuador as a special envoy.

The envoy for the inaugural ceremony had nothing to do but attend the ceremony. However, the Ecuadorian people must have regarded the title of "special" as a high-ranking official of the White House.

Alternatively, perhaps our local ambassador exaggerated my position. I was treated with the utmost honors compared to the ministers of other countries. When all the ministers went to the conference hall in one vehicle, I was given a separate car equivalent to the vice president's. The greeting and shaking hands at the inaugural ceremony were followed in the order of heads of state and vice presidents of other countries. I was ahead of the U.S. Secretary of State.

President Correa interviewed me alone as his first official duty the day after the inauguration ceremony. The inaugural ceremony was the first meeting and the interview time was 30-minutes, which is relatively long. I was impressed with how much he prepared before meeting with me.

Before formal conversations asking for economic cooperation and support, I told President Correa that his name had the same pronunciation as the name of our country in Korean. Then he said, "I don't think it was long ago that Koreans came to Italy and started using Correa as a last name." He added that their ancestors had gotten the same last name because of their relationship with them and emphasized a special relationship with the Republic of Korea. He also talked about Professor Chang Ha-joon, whom he studied with at the same university. Recently, the president read a book called *Kicking the Ladder* and highly recommended it. I was impressed that he prepared so much for our meeting. After

The envoy for the inaugural ceremony
had nothing to dobut attend the ceremony.
However, the Ecuadorian people, must have regarded the
title of "special" as a high-ranking official of the White House.

returning from Paraguay, even Paraguay's Foreign Minister took preventive measures. It was the same there. I could feel Korea's reputation among the South American countries was great.

Serving two terms as the Senior Presidential Secretary of Civil Affairs, including the position of Senior Presidential Secretary for Civil Society and the Chief Secretary, I spent almost four years in the Blue House, but I had never accompanied the president on his overseas visits. This wasn't directly related to my duty as the Senior Presidential Secretary for Civil Affairs and Civil Society. It wasn't impossible to make an occasion, such as visiting the communities of overseas Koreans, but the Participatory Government did not do that.

If I became the Chief Secretary, I should be protecting the Blue House in the president's absence. Instead of following him around, I was busier taking care of emergencies. Though in name only, I benefited from the position once.

On October 13, 2006, while I was resting, the news reported that former Foreign Minister Ban Ki-moon had been elected U.N. Secretary-General. I was glad to hear such good news, as it was also one of the ongoing projects while I was in the Blue House.

The president and the Blue House have not made diplomatic efforts from the outset with Ban in mind. Initially, the U.S. Ambassador, Hong Seok-hyun, dreamed of the position. Because we were anticipating the next Secretary-General to be from Asia, he was putting a lot of effort into becoming the one. Then, there was the "ANSP's X-file" tapping incident, and he became unseated. Instead, it made Minister Ban to be eligible. It was a great opportunity for Ban. The Participatory Government has made diplomatic efforts to "do whatever it takes" since then. The president asked for Ban's support in all rounds of diplomacy, and the same applied to the Prime Minister's overseas visits. The president sent the Chief Policymaker, Kim Byung-joon, to major countries as a special envoy and asked for support. When the election was imminent, he called many other nations.

Such efforts did not go unnoticed, but the high-level diplomacy didn't play a decisive role. The cross-governmental diplomacy effort was only the final step in the process of "picking flowers." The reason for the election of Ban was due to the balanced foreign policy that the Participatory Government consistently pursued. Support from China was essential to be a Secretary-General of the U.N. from Asia. China has highly valued and trusted the balanced diplomacy that President Roh and the Participatory Government employed. If it weren't for balanced diplomacy, gaining China's support wouldn't have been easy. Other third-world camps were in a similar situation. Of course, it would not have been possible without the help of the U.S. and the West. The firm alliance with the U.S. from sending troops to Iraq resulted in the gain of broad support.

In addition to Secretary-General Ban's election, the Six-Party Talks, including the North Korean nuclear issue, received a lot of cooperation from China. Without China, it would not have been easy to persuade North Korea. We paid our price, though, with the case of the Dalai

Lama*. Usually, as a sovereign nation, it is permissible, but because co-operation with China was so critical and necessary at the moment, we did not allow the visit.

The president was delighted to hear about Ban's election. On the phone, he congratulated him and extended warm words of blessing. That was all. Even though he could have made it his credit, he told the Blue House and the ministries not to. The president ordered the government not to disclose the efforts taken thus far nor celebrate the event.

Even When KBS hosted an "Open Concert" to celebrate the election, the president advised the government officials not to join. There was only one reason: now that Ban was an international leader, he had to be let go of for the world. The president feared that if the government made a big deal of it, it might somehow hurt Ban's position as the Secretary-General.

* **Dalai Lama** Tibetan spiritual leader who established the Tibetan exile government. Continues to develop the Tibetan independence movement in a non-violent manner. Awarded the 1989 Nobel Peace Prize.

The Last Chief Presidential Secretary

In March 2007, during the last year of his presidency, the president called again. I, the Blue House's last Chief Presidential Secretary in the Participatory Government, was hesitant. It was the third time I entered the Blue House, and I seriously did not want to take the position. I knew that being the last chief secretary of the president meant that I needed to be there until he retired. Honestly, I yearned to be free and return to my place. However, the president's political situation was extremely difficult. The change of regime was already expected. That was why the completion was even more critical. In the latter years, it was more challenging to choose personnel. It was not easy for the president to make other choices. *What are we going to do? Let's spend the last days together with the president,* I thought.

I had no choice but to summon brave determination. When you look at generations of governments, in the beginning, they do not let go of tension and are able to maintain their initial intentions and discipline. As the end approaches, the tension decreases and relaxes, so that's why

I had no choice but to summon brave determination.
When you look at generations of governments, in the beginning, they do not let go of tension and are able to maintain their initial intentions and discipline. As the end approaches, the tension decreases and relaxes, so that's why there are a lot of failures.
The top priority was not to repeat it.

there are a lot of failures. The top priority was not to repeat it. I thought that it was essential to maintain principle, initial intentions, and tension until the end, and I was determined to do so.

In my inaugural address, I laid out three key requests for the employees. 'First, let's have confidence and pride in the success of the Participatory Government. Second, until the last day of the president's term, no day should be spent in vain, negligible or slacking. Third, let's protect morality till the end.'

Then I said, "Many compare the latter half of the term to "hasan" (descending from a mountain). I disagree. There's no hasan in the Participatory Government. We must endlessly continue to reach the top, and on the last day of the term, we eventually are at the summit." I believe that the employees truly worked with that in mind until the day of the president's retirement.

The duties of the Chief Presidential Secretary were quite different from those of the Senior Presidential Secretary for Civil Society and the Senior Presidential Secretary for Civil Affairs. When I was the Senior Presidential Secretary for Civil Affairs, it felt like an extension of the laws I had dealt with my whole life as an attorney. As the Senior Presidential Secretary for Civil Society, thanks to being active in the area of civil society, I had many relationships and a sense of friendliness with that side of the people. Keeping that as background, I felt I would be able to do it.

The Chief Presidential Secretary's role in state affairs was very important. At that time, the Blue House, relatively early, got rid of the position of the head of the State of Affairs Committee and had the Chief Presidential Secretary take on the role. It was the most burdensome job I could think of, and I didn't have the confidence to do well.

In retrospect, I didn't think getting rid of the head of the State of Affairs Committee was a good thing. Though the president's willingness to strictly separate the party from the Blue House, I thought it was necessary to have intimate communications with the political communities, especially the ruling party, in different forms from the past. When getting rid of the head of the State of Affairs Committee, the Chief Presidential Secretary took over the general affairs functions, while the policy director was to take charge of the National Assembly's legislation of policy. However, I didn't think it was effective.

It is true that in the situation of separation of the party from the Blue House relationship with the parties were difficult. As soon as the president took office, he emphasized the separation of the party from the Blue House principles. The separation of the party from the Blue House was the promise he made during the 2002 presidential election. It was essential for new politics and political reform. The purpose was to change the disappearance and subordination of policies that were served by both the imperial presidency and the governor. It was the starting point of the party democracy. It was not the election promise made by the president's particular beliefs but rather the people's general demand.

The president was comprehensive of the separation of the party from the Blue House from the beginning. He was determined to adhere to this philosophy and commitment. The key to separating the party and the Blue House was giving up appointment rights and voting rights. The president said he would remain as an essential member of the National Assembly. As promised, he did not participate in appointing or nominating officials, party decisions, or the party's legislative decisions. Instead, he concentrated on policy and legislative consultations by actively engaging in the discussion between the party-government-Blue House and party-Blue House, respectively.

Although he did not meet them privately in person as he did in the past, President Roh communicated with party leaders and members of the National Assembly on various levels. Despite the effort, many complained that "there is no two-way communication, but the Blue House is communicating one-way." The problem was the protocol within the parties. Poor political function of the Blue House staff was also a major cause.

Later, the president and I both regretted that the separation of the party and the Blue House was premature. I had regrets then and still do now. The ruling Uri Party became the majority due to the impeachment backlash. At first, it overturned the majority, but it was not efficient or powerful. It was not prompt in making legislative and policy reforms. Mutual cooperation with the ruling party was necessary for more drastic and swift reform.

President Roh entrusted Ministers entirely unless the matter required combined effort and discussion. Important matters were decided by hearing the opinions of Ministers and related secretaries. Otherwise, things would just pile up and become overwhelming.

There were many political issues in the last year of Roh's term. In January 2007, the president proposed a "one-point reform." He requested the political party to discuss the constitutional amendment, in which the presidential term is changed to match the term of the member of the National Assembly; he proposed a "four-year presidential term." This was unfortunate. Political ramification was expected from this move. However, the president's proposal for an amendment is not of great importance. It is the president's constitutional right, and the political parties may agree or disagree with it. It was not like the president's authority was at stake if the amendment was withdrawn due to the dissent of the political party. Moreover, the media consistently insisted on the need for such an amendment.

It was an opportune time for the proposal because there was no advantage or disadvantage to the president, and it would not have been possible at any other moment. The president's "one-point reform" was of national importance, as the media repeatedly suggested.

Internally, the Blue House came to an agreement rather easily regarding the necessity and justification for the amendment. However, people who have been talking about the constitution were unresponsive. The press sold it out as being a political scheme. Not to mention the Grand National Party (GNP), even the ruling party showed little interest.

The GNP tried to avoid anything that could be risky because they thought that the next government would be their share if all went just as they were. Even though they would benefit first from the amendment, the GNP did not want to take action. The ruling party, on the other hand, strongly felt that they need not do a favor for the GNP. It is a shame that everyone has missed such an opportunity for the nation to pursue their own interests.

According to the agreement between the GNP and the ruling party, they promised to push forward with the amendment in April of that year when the 18th National Assembly opened. However, the 18th National Assembly did not keep the agreement, and the media never even mentioned it. The political party acted strangely; so did the press.

The issue of the pressroom became more problematic during the time of the presidential election. When I got appointed, staff in the Blue House had already finished reviewing and discussing the matter and were about to start implementation. I learned about the issue when the Secretary of Public Affairs and the National Intelligence Service began reporting specific plans to the president. The purpose and contents were all good. I could see the need and reason behind combining the pressrooms of departments, which were operated rather exclusively, into an integrated, open briefing room, establishing new rules and opening it up to more media and journalists.

The problem was the timing. Even though it was the right direction, there was little time left for the government. It was not a matter of simple measure or small budget. I thought it was demanding in many ways. I asked the president three times to reconsider the matter. The president was determined, though. He firmly believed in a basic system that could control the adherence of power and media, the wrong practices from the past, and the unjust tyranny of the media. I couldn't persuade him. It was especially difficult because I had no expertise in the topic.

I regretted that I didn't persuade more as I watched the situation get worse. If my understanding and perceptions were clearer, I could have opened up the discussion to the entire cabinet, and perhaps the president might have thought otherwise if other chiefs also suggested reconsideration of the matter. The president and the entire Blue House Office paid much for it. Too much was lost in the last year of the presidency.

In the last year of my office as Senior Presidential Secretary for Civil Affairs, the Blue House was still busy. There were a lot of big and small issues, and we pushed forward until the very end. According to the people who have seen other presidents, it was a rather uncommon situation. The last year of the presidential office is usually "completely hands-off" or "open without business," not because they were lazy but because of the criticism from people, party, and the press, as well as a serious lame-duck phenomenon.

The reason why the Participatory Government could be different was because we kept our morality until the end. I think it was also how we did not lose power completely. The president was determined to finish all reform tasks before the end of the Participatory Government.

Many say that the government must be able to do what it can do when it is first in power. They also say that if you fail to reform in the first few years, you will not be able to do so in the second half. There is a reason, which is not wrong to a certain extent because policy-making takes longer than overnight. Simple matters can be started and finished in a short time, but some matters are made into legislation at the end of the term after years of discussion. Sometimes, they even get passed to the next government. Therefore, working for the first couple of years and then finishing up what you started in the last couple of years does not sound like an appropriate state management. Whatever people say, we did what we needed to do according to our roadmap and principles.

ROK-U.S. FTA

The ROK-U.S. FTA that was promoted at the end of the term caused a lot of controversy. The approval and disapproval of public opinion were clearly divided. The president and the Participatory Government were always thinking about the national interest from start to finish. The Lee Myung-bak administration's principles were undermined, and diplomatic considerations destroyed the principle of national interest. The fact that the Lee Myung-bak administration had to make considerable concessions towards the U.S. requests proved that the Participatory Government had done well when negotiating with the U.S.

In the ROK-U.S FTA, it is impossible to overlook Kim Hyeon-jong, the Minister of Trade. The president had been briefed by Kim Hyeon-jong when he was a presidential candidate. It was not eloquent, but the contents were good. The president was satisfied and thought the Ministry of Trade would fit him well. However, it was unreasonable to appoint him to the General Director when he was a non-bureaucrat, considering his career and age. So, he appointed him as a mediator under the general manager. I then asked him to regard it as a process of adapting, integrating, and evaluating the Ministry of Trade.

He was always the representative of the International Bargaining Forum and received good reviews from the headquarters. Afterward, he was recognized for his skills and competence and appointed as a General Manager. Then, he announced his plan to "promote the Korea-U.S. FTA" but was not able to participate in the FTA negotiation process. After considerable progress in the negotiations despite civil society opposition, he started getting involved in the detailed discussion.

The president always emphasized the "shopkeeper logic" and "always act for the national cause." He stressed that negotiations can be stopped or not pursued if it counters national interest. Such an approach has given great power to the negotiating team. It gave them guts and determination. The president called the negotiating team the night before leaving for the Middle East, saying, "I'll take full responsibility if the negotiations fail or succeed. The general manager should thoroughly negotiate with the mind of a merchant and never think about the ROK-U.S. alliance or political elements. I will take all political responsibilities."

With support, our negotiating team maintained its composure and maintained the stance that "the U.S. negotiating team can leave any time tonight. We are not desperate." They were even ready to use a concession card when the negotiation was on the verge of breaking, but it wasn't necessary at all.

There was nothing that could've been done to those who opposed to the open economy. However, though many acknowledged the unavoidability, many opposed the idea of the FTA because they weren't convinced that our government could negotiate all terms successfully to promote and protect national interests against the U.S. government. I would like to highlight that "we have tried and were successful in pursuing national interest against the U.S."

North-South Summit Conference

The most significant event during my term in the cabinet was the North-South Summit Conference in October 2007. The basic principles of the Inter-Korean Summit of the Participatory Government were to be formally promoted through official organizations related to North Korea, such as the NIS and the Ministry of Unification. The president was adamant that he would not pursue such a strategy as he did in the past. He was also firm that the talks, which did not guarantee performance, would not be held. Therefore, at the Six-Party Talks, it was concluded that the North-South Summit could be held only after the North Korean nuclear issue was concluded. It was not desirable to pursue the Inter-Korean Summit before the conclusion of the Six-Party Talks.

There were many steps before the summit was held. On June 5, 2005, the 5th anniversary of the June 15th Joint Declaration, the president sent Chung Dong-young, Minister of Unification, to Pyongyang as a special envoy to meet with Kim Jong-il. I sent a letter of intent that said all the matters should be discussed with the special envoy, Chung Dong-young, who visited North Korea on my behalf. At this time, Chung resumed the Six-Party Talks early on to resolve the North Korean nuclear issue peacefully and conveyed the president's intention to open the Inter-Korean summit meeting. Kim Jong-il was in a good mood and proposed setting a date soon.

At the Six-Party Talks in September 2005, the September 19th Joint Statement was adopted to resolve the North Korean nuclear issue. However, as soon as the Bush administration adopted the September 19th joint signatures, it froze the North Korean accounts in North Korean Macao's main bank, the BDA*, which clouded the September 19th joint statement. Despite the multifaceted efforts of our government, the U.S. and North Korea failed to find a way to solve the BDA problem. North Korea committed to a nuclear test in early October following the July 2006 missile test. The Inter-Korean Summit had been pushed further back.

Before the summit, Ahn Hee-jung and Mun Sung-keun also made contact with North Korea. However, the North first sent the proposal to Ahn Hee-jung and he went to the North to discuss it further. It was Fall 2006. According to Ahn Hee-jung's judgment, he did not feel any weight. He informed the National Intelligence Service (NIS) and was finished with it.

Mun Sung-keun also went to North Korea in the Fall of 2003 with a presidential letter. It wasn't to promote the summit but to understand Roh's sincerity in the Inter-Korean relations. Such contact would have helped create a peaceful atmosphere.

In November 2006, Kim Man-bok took office as the head of the National Security Agency and announced his intention to promote the Inter-Korean summit. The president did not put much weight on it and asked not to overdo it. It was a warm afternoon on May 17, 2007, after the president and I visited the Gwangneung Arboretum. Baek Jong-cheon, the head of security, was waiting for the president in the residence. We reported that we would prepare a report in the next two to three months and report plans to close the Inter-Korean summit around August 15th. The president ordered the secretary general, the security chief, and the head of the NIS to make concrete progress. Then, the three met every Thursday. It was called the "Angol Meeting." As a practitioner, Park Seon-Won, a strategy secretary, attended. Secretary Baek was supposed to resolve the BDA issue and resume Six-Party Talks; Kim Man-bok, the NIS director, decided to start contact with North Korea.

Both sides made their progress quickly and efficiently. In early June, the BDA issue was resolved by our initiative. Kim Man-bok signaled that he intended to send a special envoy to the North to discuss the inter-Korean summit. Initially, Director Baek and Director Kim thought that I should go as a special envoy in case there was a response from North Korea. I expressed that observing the situation and letting things take their natural course would be best. I reported the progress verbally to the president whenever there was special advancement. Since it was mentioned that some form of contract was expected around the end of

July, I had been hopeful since mid-July.

On the evening of July 17th, there was rapid news from Afghanistan. Twenty-four ministers, evangelists, missionaries, and devotees who were engaged in missionary activities were kidnapped by the Taliban. Baek Jong-cheon, head of security, who waited for the North to come in contact, was dispatched to Afghanistan on July 22nd as a special envoy for the presidency. In late July, the North contacted the South and requested for a meeting. I had to oversee the resolution of the hostage situation in Afghanistan, so Kim Man-bok went to North Korea.

Kim, who visited North Korea, had agreed to push for the summit. From then, there was a quick break. While maintaining extreme security, more people began to work more on practical matters. I also made practical contacts. The summit was scheduled to be on August 28th. It was a very tight schedule. Once I informed the public and made the announcement, almost all of the Blue House personnel started preparing for the summit.

When the preparations for the talks were in full swing, there was a flood in North Korea. The North proposed a postponement of the talks. There were regrets, but we were able to make the preparations much more thoroughly. In the meantime, Kim Yang-gum, the head of the Unification Front, came to Seoul to discuss the preparations for the talks. However, little has been proposed about the major agenda that we previously agreed on. The president blatantly expressed disappointment. He ordered the North Korean version to be made and delivered to present the contents of our intentions and viewpoint for North Korea. Fortunately, the North accepted it and the outcome was very fruitful. and viewpoint for North Korea. Fortunately, the North accepted it and the outcome was very fruitful.

* **BDA (Banco Delta Asia)** A small bank in Macau, it has been North Korea's only foreign exchange billing counter since the 1970s. Business with North Korea froze in 2005, after the U.S. named the bank a money-laundering counter.

Beyond the Yellow Line

One of the most pivotal decisions post the Summit Conference was the mode of transportation for the president's visit to North Korea. President Dae-jung's arrival in the North by airplane for the June 15th Summit, with Kim Jong-il welcoming him at the airport, created a powerful symbolic image of the meeting. We wanted to choose a method that could facilitate progress in North-South relations, and the most ambitious approach was through railways, which at that time, was primarily used for cargo passing through the railroad connected to Kaesong, but not for people. If the president were to travel by train, it would signify the reconnection of the previously disjointed railroad between the North and the South. We strongly appealed to the North, and they gave it serious consideration. However, the track north of Kaesong to Pyongyang was in poor condition and couldn't be repaired in a short period. Finally, we agreed to send the Inter-Korean joint supporters to North Korea by rail for the Beijing Olympics.

The remaining road was the land route. It would have been meaningful if the president had crossed the military demarcation line by land and the North Korean people had witnessed the president's procession to Pyongyang. The problem, however, was that the image of the president crossing the military demarcation line in a passenger çar did not have a great impact.

Even if he were to leave a farewell message to the citizens in front of the Military Demarcation Line, it seemed the act of crossing the line itself seemsed unlike to lose its blandness.

During our discussions, Oh Seung-rok, the Executive Secretarial Protocol on the North Korea Working Group, suggested a momentous idea. He proposed that the president walk across the military demarcation line.

It was a brilliant idea that simply required a change in perspective. I asked what the military demarcation line looked like and what kind of barbed wire there was. The answer was that it was just a paved road without a physical line. I asked, "How can we show that the president is crossing the line then?" "We can ask the North to temporarily mark the line," he said, adding that the North has been very cooperative. I thought if the North didn't accept our proposal, maybe I would talk to the National Intelligence Service Director to consult with the Unification Front of the North. I thought that was perfectly plausible, and I decided to do so.

The remaining issue was the president himself. He had always been averse to staged events and ceremonial displays, and during the inter-Korean summit, due to the pressure of needing tangible outcomes, he expressed that he would not engage in any events upon his departure.

Seeing the president and the First Lady crossing the yellow line that day was a memorable sight. The president gave his testimony before the line. "I'm going across this forbidden line as a president this time. When I come back, more people will come and go. Then, finally, the forbidden line will gradually be erased."

He even said that he wouldn't make a national address from the Blue House before departing to North Korea. His stance was that it was inappropriate to create a spectacle of his departure as if the mere act of holding the summit was an achievement, especially when it was uncertain whether it would yield any results. Despite numerous explanations from various individuals, including myself, arguing that the continuation of the conversation between the South and North summits was a significant achievement in itself, he remained steadfast in his view.

President Roh repeatedly emphasized not to do any event at the departure and even scolded such a suggestion. Everyone was worried that the president would not do it. In fact, the Secretarial Protocol Oh Sang-ho was scolded when he first spoke to the president about the idea. At last, I stepped up and reported to the president that the North had already agreed during a meeting. He then accepted reluctantly. Luckily, after my report, the North side agreed to mark the military demarcation line and allow President Roh to cross on foot. I was able to avoid false reports.

Seeing the president and the First Lady crossing the yellow line that day was a memorable sight. The president gave his testimony before the line. "I'm going across this forbidden line as a president this time. When I come back, more people will come and go. Then, finally, the forbidden line will gradually be erased." Then he waved his hand to the people who greeted him near the line and walked forward and beyond the line to the north. We watched from the south that the president and the First Lady were welcomed with bouquets from the North. After we could no longer see the president and his party, we took photographs of ourselves standing on the yellow line, being extremely careful not to cross it so people would not use it to make an argument against us.

The effect of the president's walk across the military demarcation line was phenomenal. It seemed more dramatic when the military demarcation line was painted yellow. The scene repeatedly appeared on T.V. several times until the president returned from the meeting. Especially until the other footage arrived from the North, that image kept being replayed in the media. The group that visited the North was also thrilled to see the image on T.V. when they arrived at the Pyongyang Baekhwawon Hall. Domestic and international broadcasts covered the issue every hour. Ultimately the scene became the symbolic image of the October 4th Inter-Korea Summit.

The president was delighted with the event. Later, when he was awarded the honorary commissioner of the October 4th Summit, he awarded Oh Seung-rok, who first proposed the idea. Oh said it was the family's honor that he received the Service Merit Medal. It is rewarding for me as a chief to be able to leave such a historical scene as well.

During the first anniversary of President Roh's death, more than fifty senior artists held a memorial exhibition in Seoul. The exhibition's name was Over the Yellow Line. I attended the opening ceremony and gave my greetings, and I remembered how overwhelming it was to watch the president cross the yellow military demarcation line and the stories behind the event.

I was extremely eager to watch the summit in Pyongyang. However, as the chairperson of the summit preparatory committee, I oversaw comprehensive matters, from preparing the agenda to joint statements and any agreements to be discussed by the two leaders. Moreover, while the president was in the North, I had to guard the Blue House and remain on stand-by for emergencies. I had to be fully prepared to cope with any sudden situation. I waited for the news to come from the North with both anxiety and expectation.

A few hours before the summit meeting, the Chief of Security, Baek Jong-cheon, contacted me. He sent me a working-level agreement with the North, which was progress at that time and a remarkable achievement. He said the text would be a little more polished.

I told Baek, "When you return, you must go to the Kaesong Industrial Complex, possibly with North Korea's Leader, Kim Jong-il, or with Kim Young-nam, if not." A few hours later, a final consensus was reached. The agreement contained most of the agendas we were trying to pursue in many areas. I wanted to go somewhere and scream in joy. I was so thrilled about our achievement. The only issue we did not achieve was the regular summit meeting.

The president was skeptical about the feasibility of regular summit meetings from the beginning. However, considering that the next government will be less active in Inter-Korea relations, we should take a big step to avoid any retreat. I told the president about this and repeatedly requested Minister Baek and Director Kim to pursue the agenda, but it was unsuccessful. I asked why when they came back. They replied that we made an offer, but the North expressed disapproval. Regular summit meetings implied that the leaders of the North and the South would visit each other alternately, but Kim Jong-il was not able to do that. If Kim Young-nam had visited instead, it would have been criticized that he was not the representative of the summit. The North did not want to pressure Kim Jong-il to visit, and I regretted that we did not convince them further by proposing our visit to the North until they were ready.

As the Summit Return Report at Dorasan Station took longer, the president's return to the Blue House was delayed. The president, who arrived late that night, didn't even know he was tired and was smiling. Everyone congratulated him. The president spoke about many anecdotes, including his witty response when Kim Jong-il proposed he stay for a few more days and episodes behind the story of the "secret of the yellow line," which continued the conversation.

I still regret that the Inter-Korea Summit couldn't have been held sooner. It could have been if it were not for the U.S. Treasury Department's freeze on the BDA. It put an abrupt pause to the Inter-Korea Summit when the Six-Party Talks was resumed and created a promising atmosphere for the summit. A year passed without progress. If the summit had been held without any gaps, the inter-Korean relations would have gone much further.

What is worse was the ratification of the National Assembly. The summit ended with success, but there wasn't much left in the term. It was necessary to solidify the accomplishments before moving on to the next government. Legally, the agreement between the two Koreas is treated like a treaty between nations. The October 4th Joint Declaration was a treaty that placed significant financial burdens on the nation and its people. So, I stressed that it would be a good idea for the National Assembly to accept the ratification agreement on the summit agreement. At that time, it seemed promising as we had the support of the U.N. General Assembly. If the bill were submitted to the National Assembly, then it would have been difficult for the GNP to dare to oppose it.

However, the Then-Prime Minister, Han Duk-soo, did not proceed. He argued that it wouldn't be too late to take action after the size of the financial burden was set through follow-up agreements. We lost the opportunity, and with the change of government, the agreement between the summits was abandoned.

Looking back at the summit's abundant achievements, I was reminded of many events pertaining to the North Korean relationship, which had troubled the government since its inauguration. In fact, the North Korean nuclear issue troubled the president and us the most. President Roh's philosophy, patience, and political power, which helped manage the North Korean nuclear issue peacefully and diplomatically, should be deeply appreciated. I think his wise leadership saved the country in that period.

As soon as he was elected president, the North Korean nuclear issue was in a state of sudden crisis. Following the suspension of U.S. heavy oil supply, North Korea withdrew its nuclear non-proliferation treaty, resumed its nuclear program, and expelled nuclear inspectors...the Republican Bush administration neocons poured out tough arguments. They even mentioned a North Korean attack.

Even before the inauguration, Roh had a firm diplomatic attitude when his position was just the president-elect. "The North Korean nuclear issue must be solved diplomatically through dialogue; there should be no mention of an attack or possibility of an attack on North Korea, especially without the consent of South Korea," he asserted. Furthermore, he clearly expressed his opposition to the U.S. blockade policy.

The conservative camp and conservative media made a big deal of having a different opinion from that of the U.S., but he did not hesitate nor cared.

The president was so strong-willed that the Bush administration could not but abandon its hardline policy toward North Korea. Finally, they took on the diplomatic solution through dialogue. In the process, we also raised the framework of the Six-Party Talks by dispatching troops to Iraq to help the U.S. and enhance confidence. Through the Six-Party Talks, a complete denuclearization agreement was drawn, and a discussion structure for the peace regime on the Korean Peninsula and the permanent peace of Northeast Asia, along with the abolition of all North Korea's nuclear programs, was created. Because the North Korean nuclear issue was resolved peacefully through the Six-Party Talks, so was the Inter-Korean Summit.

The summit was the fruit of a long process of continuous patience and trust-building with North Korea. Peace between the two Koreas is achieved through trust. If one does not have confidence in the other, the relationship cannot move forward even one step. What we realized as we prepared for the summit was a remarkable improvement in the confidence between the North and us. Beyond the Inter-Korean summit, everyday interaction and exchange between the North and South improved greatly during the Participatory Government.

The Thing About Politics

The thrill of the Summit Conference did not last long. The country was in a full-scale presidential race. Many events were taking place that were too embarrassing to report to the president from the Blue House position. It was something all political communities had to deal with. We were forced to endure helplessness.

The president, a figure of authority, was not immune to the unfair treatment demonstrated by the ruling party members. This mistreatment had been ongoing, even before the Summit. The political landscape was devoid of loyalty and humanistic duties, with causes and principles taking a backseat. The support for the president and the Participatory Government seemed to wane, and the next presidential election appeared bleak for the party. Those in leadership positions began to oppose the president and the Participatory Government, seeking to establish their own grounds. The president, while enraged, was also deeply saddened by these events.

During the 2002 Presidential Election, former President Kim Dae-jung had a low approval rating, even lower than that of President Roh at the end of his term. At that time, many people claimed "reform" and tried to build up their positions by attacking and differentiating against President Kim. President Roh always objected to that and never attacked or disrespected Kim.

It may seem that the public supports the behavior of "differentiating" at a glance, but it is not true. The nation sees above and beyond. Such behavior is rather disappointing to the public, for they know it is an aspect of betrayal. It is no different from self-denying that engulfs oneself. President Roh behaved in such a way, although he was not from the Dong-gyo-dong camp*.

The president was deeply hurt by the strong objections of the central members of the Uri Party. He felt a tremendous sense of betrayal, which left a lasting wound. Chairman Chung Dong-young's actions devastated Roh, as the president had placed the greatest expectations on him.

The president had special attachments and expectations for Chairman Chung. He was always thankful for the close race with Chung during the presidential election. Roh did everything he could to help Chung. When Chung was Prime Minister and Chairman of the party, Roh told the Blue House advisers to make their best effort to help Chung as needed.

Roh and Chung had an important meeting when the Uri Party was approaching a crisis. Chung requested that I arrange this meeting for him. I still don't understand his attitude and intentions. At that time, members of the National Assembly on Chung's side were leading the

However, this time, the central members of the Uri Party made the strongest objections. The president felt a tremendous sense of betrayal, leaving a deep wound.

defect from the Uri Party. I thought that his intention for this meeting was to ask for the president's understanding and cooperation to prevent a complete dissolution of the party. Or I hoped they would have a serious and sincere conversation to clarify any misunderstanding.

However, upon meeting, it turned out not to be the case. In response to the president's question about defection, he continuously reiterated, "I believe that the issue of party membership is not the essence." That statement indicated his intention to leave the party, and ultimately, the meeting took on the appearance of being convened to announce his departure. It was an unpleasant conversation. As I attended the meeting, I couldn't help but feel bad seeing such an important meeting closing without any gain. When the two were talking about ordinary topics in the beginning, I actively engaged in the conversation to keep it going, but after the topic had shifted to defection, I couldn't say anything. I couldn't understand why Chung wanted to see the president if all he wanted was to notify defection to the president, who was so worried about the very issue. In addition, we promised to keep the meeting secret, but Chung, for some odd reason, not only revealed the meeting to the media but also the fact that he proposed North Korean support of former President Kim. It marked the worst ending of all.

That day, the president did not specifically intend to hear him say, "I will not leave the party. I will firmly stand by Uri Party." If Chung had shown his struggle as one of the founding fathers of the party and said something along the lines, "I will not be the one who destroys the party" or "I won't be the first one to defect," there would have been room for further discussion. I thought Chung would defect immediately, but he did not until about two months later. It remains unclear why he rushed to ruin his relationship with the president. It was a regrettable loss of the last opportunity to prevent a split within our camp. I predicted that the presidential election would be hopeful only if the two were cooperative. Chung Dong-young needed to get votes in the Yeongnam region, in particular. After that day, there was no more chance to reconcile the two. It was greatly unfortunate that they were never able to overcome their differences and misunderstandings.

The president agonized over the division of the Uri Party. He thought of it as a failure of his political life. What the president regarded most painful was not the defeat in the presidential election. "If one doesn't have enough support or fortune, one could be defeated. However, one must hold onto the values and principles even in defeat, for there will be no tomorrow without value or principle. Suppose one gives up values because it seems disadvantageous at the moment. In that case, there is no hope, let alone the defeat." That was the president's perception of our camp breaking away from the Uri Party. President Roh always emphasized that "an uncalculating, straightforward politician, in the long run, is following the best path for one's interests as well."

He also demonstrated the truth of that statement himself. If one looks at the long term, it is a principle clearly visible to the public, yet it remains inexplicable why politicians fail to see it.

The president also emphasized this: "I can lose in the presidential election. Winning is good, but it's not always possible to win every time. However, if I were to lose, I shall lose in hope. It is only possible if there is a great cause and principle. In particular, one must not forget the cause. Without cause or principle, winning or remaining hopeful will be difficult after you lose."

The philosophy of the Uri Party, which was to go beyond the regional limitations of the Democratic Party in the past and to make the nation one party, regressed due to the breakdown. The president was worried that such a consequence would take away hope from people. Despite his belief, he stopped people who defended the Uri Party till the last moment. Although he knew that the breakdown of the party was not desirable, nor was it the right decision, he did not want any more division in our camp.

* **Donggyo-dong camp** Supporters of Kim Dae-jung were associated with the town called "Donggyo-dong," where Kim lived.

U.S. Beef Importation

The current Deputy Minister of Foreign Affairs, Min Dong-seok, was the head of the ROK-U.S. beef negotiation during the Lee Myung-bak administration. In his book Life of an Official in the Republic of Korea, he stated that President Roh violated a promise he made with President Bush on March 29, 2007. He claimed that the former president refused to open the beef market in accordance with international standards. His claim was unfounded.

On that day, President Roh spoke to President Bush about the beef import problem as follows:

"And now, with regard to the issue of beef, we have, in principle, the willingness of the international bodies to respect the import conditions, hygiene, and openness of beef and to open it to a reasonable level. We are also willing to end the proceedings in a reasonable period of time in good faith and without malice of prior confirmation of such quarantine conditions.

I'm well aware of the suspicion of the U.S. due to an unreasonable decision by the agriculture and forestry authorities regarding the bones in the beef during importation. In the future, the president was willing to make decisions so that similar matters were managed reasonably.

With the fundamental principle of resolving the beef problem, I would like to make two requests to your Excellency*. Just as it is an important matter to you, I would like to begin by saying that it is also very important to me and the Korean government, especially with the upcoming presidential election. So, I would like to request a procedure in which I can speak to the U.S. government and the people about my willingness to resolve the issue rationally.

Although we will negotiate according to the recommendations of the International Water Agency, this issue is very sensitive to national pride, so our people will react very sensitively to the comparison with the conditions of Japan, Taiwan, and Hong Kong. There is a possibility that the party may utilize this as an issue for the presidential election; I request that you consider balance and strategy for the election."

This statement is found in the ROK-U.S. summit conversation.

In summary, President Roh's promise to President Bush was not about importing unconditionally according to the standards of the International Bureau of the OIE (Office International des Epizooties), but in principle, it respects the standard and will "open up to a reasonable level."

In other words, the president promised to consider not only the OIE standard but also the standards, the level of implementation of the U.S. ban on feed, the level of trust of the Korean people in U.S. beef, and the criteria of import hygiene in Korea when deciding the range and time.

In addition, President Roh took one step further. Since Korea cannot expand the scope of its opening despite the OIE standard, it must meet the timing and magnitude of the openings of Asian countries such as Japan, Taiwan, and Hong Kong.

After the call in May 2007, the OIE classified the United States as a country needing "mad cow disease risk control." However, since August 1, 2007, spine or SRM (special remnant material) has been found in imports of U.S. beef, and import quarantine of U.S. beef was discontinued. On October 5, 2007, trust in compliance with the sanitary conditions of U.S. beef deteriorated rather than improved, as the quarantine ceased after a backbone was discovered again.

At the time, Japan imported only 20-month-old beef (including bone), while Taiwan and Hong Kong allowed imports of boneless beef less than 30 months old. These countries did not expand the opening until December 2007. Not to mention the enlargement of the opening, they had not even negotiated to expand it.

Nonetheless, the Open Party bureaucrats, such as Prime Minister Han Duk-soo and the head of Trade Kim Jong-hoon, constantly pursued the expansion of U.S. beef import opening within the term of the Participatory Government. Of course, all the officials in the Blue House were against it.

On December 24, 2007, President Roh held a meeting with ministers of affairs and summarized the final stance of the Participatory Government on the matter. Director Kim Jong-hoon divided the U.S. beef import and export measures into two stages at the meeting. In the first stage, the OIE standard was accepted for those less than 30 months, and in the second stage, the OIE standard will be accepted completely if the U.S. announces reinforced feed prohibition (expected to be Feb. - March of 2008 at the time).

After the meeting, the president drew the following conclusions below:

- The lifting of restrictions on imports of beef that were 30 months or older should be taken very seriously, considering the public consciousness of mad cow disease and negotiations and trends of neighboring countries.
- Allowing imports of bone beef younger than 30 months is a large concession. If the U.S. agrees, proceed with the discussion only on that matter.
- Importing beef that is 30 months or older should not be discussed at this stage.
- It is inappropriate to process the beef issue before ratifying the FTA. If this is the case, the FTA ratification agreement may be adversely affected, and the early U.S. ratification cannot be guaranteed.

Even after deciding the government's official position at the ministerial meeting, Minister Han Duk-soo and Minister of Trade Kim Jong-hoon asked the Policy Chief to review the issue again. Since then, the Minister of Trade has made practical business contacts with the U.S. side; the U.S. Ambassador presented a better position than in the past.

After reporting this to the president, I convened a meeting on American beef-related affairs on January 21, 2008. The conclusions from the ministerial meeting on December 24, 2007, were kept. In the same book, Min Dong-seok argued that the president's Chief Secretary had overturned entirely the terms decided on the ministerial meeting, which was completely false.

On the other hand, President Lee Myung-bak made a courtesy visit to President Roh twice during his candidate years. During my term, I asked Roh to help me ratify the Korea-U.S. FTA and resolve the U.S. beef issue.

At that time, President Roh told the elected Candidate Lee that 70% of the respondents favored the FTA, while 70 % of the respondents opposed beef. Furthermore, he explained that it was taking longer than anticipated because the U.S. was requesting more than what was agreed; one of the conditions was balance with neighboring countries.

In addition, ratifying the FTA and postponing the beef negotiations is desirable because beef could become a great obstacle. He said the beef negotiation should be exchanged with the U.S. FTA ratification.

The elected-Candidate Lee Myung-bak, also expressed agreement with the president of the Republic of Korea.

During such a series of processes, the beef instance in the Lee Myung-bak administration was already being promoted by the open bureaucrats at the close of the Participatory Government. It does not seem like a coincidence that former Prime Minister Han Duk-soo and Kim Jong-hoon, head of trade negotiations, were leading the way in the Lee Myung-bak administration for a long time.

* **Your Excellency** An honorific title used to address summits of other nations in dialogues and documents to show diplomatic respect.

That Winter

On December 21st, with the rights of the Presidential Chief Secretary, I went to congratulate Candidate Lee Myung-bak. He treated me with kindness when I congratulated him. He promised, "I will hold the respect needed towards the former president," and asked me to deliver his message to the president.

Afterward, Candidate Lee expressed the same sentiment to President Roh during two courtesy visits to the Blue House. I held onto his words, hoping for the best. Despite the differences in our factions, I believed there would be a shared understanding among presidents. Just as we had drawn from former President Kim Dae-jung's experience in the North-South Korean Summit Conference, we anticipated that our past would guide the Lee administration. This, I believed, would ensure the continuity of government administration.

These expectations began to crumble during the transition period of the Lee Myung-bak administration. The government reorganization plan they initiated was a point of disagreement, but not one that warranted conflict. The real issue was their request for President Roh to promulgate a revision bill of the National Government Organization Act, a request we could not support. This led to a clash between the new and old governments, with the Participatory Government seemingly hindering Lee Myung-bak's administration from fulfilling their objectives.

To be honest, we thoroughly handled various work for the next government. It was the task of sorting out vast records of our time. First, it was a dimension that left a history of what we did, but we thought it was necessary for the next government. The intention was not to have inefficiency in the continuity of the governmental administration, and it was our sincere desire.

The policy documents passed by the Participatory Government included the history of the policy as well as the discussion process. When we did it, many previous government policies continued, and there were many times when we wondered about the history of the policy and the process of discussion. Though they might be policies that ended with the previous government, they were often referenced. There were socioeconomic phenomena common with past governments, and there were common considerations for countermeasures. Anyway, the vast records we left were primarily for the next government to reference to.

The records we passed along included the Participatory Government's personnel verification manual. The disclosure of government officials' assets got in trouble and was denounced by the public for personnel verification, and it has been in every government since the civilian government. Experiencing that, the Participatory Government developed a personnel verification manual. If it was correctly referenced, it would not be necessary to go through the trial and error of the Participatory Government. Even at the end of the Participatory Government, President Roh made the Korean Independent Commission Against Corruption Committee to create an upgraded manual that supplemented the Participatory Government's personnel verification manual.

Since verification criteria cannot always be the same, judgments about importance can differ from generation to generation. In February 2008, the Korean Independent Commission Against Corruption Committee reported the new personnel verification manual to the president right before his retirement. It was a manual made for the next government. The verification manual was needed not only to do good personnel verification but also to announce the verification criteria in advance so that candidates for public or high-ranking offices can self-manage accordingly. However, the Lee Myung-bak administration did not even refer to the personnel verification manual left by the Participatory Government.

It would have been understandable if they had created their own verification manual separately. However, the Lee Myung-bak administration did not have a personnel verification manual until Kim Tae-ho's candidacy for Prime Minister. After Kim Tae-ho's candidacy, it was rumored that he made a manual or vertical checklist of 200 items. It was difficult to understand how this could still be the case despite repeated disappointments with appointments since the beginning of the government's tenure.

Our efforts to avoid any inconvenience or trouble that we experienced to be handed down to the next government were significant. The vacancy in the appointment procedure of the prime minister and the new minister was an inconvenience that we experienced, so we supplemented the institutional deficiency. Even when Lee Myung-bak's election was confirmed, he proceeded without regard for such matters.

President Roh even repaired the small, prefabricated bathhouses while hearing the secretarial staff swear at him. He even remodeled the walk around the presidential residence. At the end of 2007, the next government would come in, and he thought they would not be able to do it right away, so he hurriedly organized it. It would take a lot of time for the new government to do it. Since it was a budget problem, it was burdensome. We wanted to pave the road so that the burden on the next government would be reduced. But all work was in vain.

His Retirement

Two months from the presidential election to the date of his retirement, the president was busier than before. It was for the preparation for history rather than some preparation for himself. He carefully organized the records and requested that all should be transferred as soon as possible.

What was left at the end, inside the five-year history, were records. That was why the president had been obsessed with documenting since the beginning of his term. The five-year record of success and frustration would hopefully be used by the following governments as well as be a source of historical evaluation. I had to lead the work. There were a lot of complaints from secretaries as well as administrators. Though they understood the deep meaning behind the president's wish, the amount of work was so voluminous that they would need to stay up all night for weeks. Many said it was pure torture. I encouraged them, and the work was completed.

On the other hand, he was busy preparing for his retirement. It had been a long time since the president decided to go to his hometown,

Bongha village, after his retirement. From the beginning, the president thought of ways he might be helpful after retirement, considering regionally balanced development. That is why he decided to go to the province after he left the Blue House.

Since about 2005, they have been scouting locations. They even considered choosing one of the villages designated as 'Livable Rural Areas.' Due to their keen interest in forestry, they also asked the Head of the Forest Service to recommend suitable places.

However, they had to consider realistic matters, such as securing land to build a private residence and obtaining a living base. Eventually, he decided to go to his hometown. We heard that there was suitable land in Daedong village in Gimhae near my hometown, but he finally decided to go to Bongha village. That was around the second half of 2006.

We asked the late architect Jung Ki-yong to design the private residence. Though the land was cheaper than Seoul's, a loan was needed for construction costs. I thought that if the president wrote a book or gave lectures after his retirement, he would be able to pay off the loan.

I, too, was slowly preparing myself for retirement. I hadn't thought about staying in Seoul from the start. I think it's a real problem that high-ranking governmental officials do not return to their hometowns after retirement. For example, there were many Busan natives who were ministers in past governments, but I only know of Oh Gu-don, who was the former minister of Maritime Affairs and Fisheries and who is currently the president of Haeyoung University in Busan. He and I will be the only two.

Though it was natural to return to Busan, I wanted to go to the countryside near Busan rather than Busan itself. I was very exhausted, and my heart was damaged. I thought I had, but everything was in vain. Whether we admit it or not, the evaluation of the Participatory Government was cruel. The presidential support was low, and the party was broken. The recreation of a regime was a terrible failure. The entire progressive camp collapsed at once. Of course, our responsibility to the government administration was the greatest. I wanted to live quietly while distancing myself and the world. It felt like sending myself to self-banishment. So that was why I looked for a place to live in the countryside.

There were also the economic circumstances. Though we didn't originally have a lot in our savings, I squandered it all when I was in the Blue House. I wanted to take a break from being an attorney, but I couldn't afford to. I had to find a place where I could commute to the law firm. So that is why I chose the place I am currently living in, Yangsan Maegok.

My wife was a Seoul woman and was urbanized, but since I was having such a hard time, she agreed that it was best to go to a quiet place and take a break. We bought an old house. It was a space used as a workshop by someone who painted and sculpted in Busan. The inside was small, and the rest was used as working space. It was not a suitable place for residence. However, the yard was spacious and the surrounding natural environment could not get any better.

When I went to Yangsan, I thought I would visit the president at

Bongha occasionally. As the last Presidential Chief Secretary, I thought I had to accompany the retired president to official functions or attend them. I could not imagine having to go so often.

Leaving the Blue House

The last few days were a whirlwind of departure preparations. As I took individual commemorative pictures with the chief, secretaries, administrators, administrative staff, and female workers, a profound sense of gratitude welled up within me, threatening to spill over. Our time in the Blue House, particularly in 'Roh Moo-hyun's Blue House,' was not without its challenges. We had to tread carefully, be patient, and face criticism. Yet, my colleagues persevered. These photographs were my humble attempt to express my deep appreciation. I hoped that one day, when they revisit these images, they would be flooded with memories and a sense of pride.

On the night of February 24th, the president graciously invited everyone above the vice ministers' status to the Blue House for the last meal. After the dinner, I returned to the official residence of the Chief Secretary. My wife had already left for Yangsan with some of our belongings. The realization that it was my final night at the Blue House filled me with a bittersweet melancholy. I spent the evening in deep reflection, unsure of what the future held.

On February 25, 2008, I had the honor of accompanying the president to the next presidential inauguration ceremony held at the National Assembly building in Yeoido. It was a grand inauguration ceremony for the incoming president, but for the outgoing president, it was a lonely exit without even a farewell ceremony. I couldn't help but compare this to my experience as a special envoy to congratulate the President of Ecuador on his inauguration. There, a farewell ceremony for the outgoing president was held just before the inauguration ceremony, attended by the majority of delegates. The outgoing president's speech, listing his accomplishments, was long but meaningful. Our culture of presidential departures, in contrast, seemed starkly different and perhaps lacking.

Going to the presidential residence, I escorted the president and his esteemed wife toward the front of the residence. The distance from the presidential residence to the Blue House was quite long, and all of the Blue House employees were lined up. There were people applauding the president for his hard work, some waving their hands, some bowing deeply and greeting him, and some saying farewell with their tears. We left them behind and headed toward the venue, the atmosphere heavy with the weight of our departure.

When the event was over, we went to Seoul Station. The president and I were to take the KTX (Korean Train Express). Many people gathered at Seoul Station for our farewell. Among the massive crowd was a group of people who were incessantly crying, sending the president off, which caught my attention. They were Chinese compatriots. Perhaps it was in 2003?... When they were pleading for the suffering and hardships they went through conveyed via a hunger strike, the president showed his support despite the objections, including those of the Department of Justice. They were grateful for that incident and came to Seoul Station to say farewell.

The president politely greeted those who came and got on the train. Many people got on to ride together with the president to Bongha village. Even though the president said it was unnecessary, many former and current office workers and the Blue House employees rode with us. They tried not to be depressed amid the chaos. The president wanted to brighten their mood, so he walked around, laughing and joking with them. Many people also greeted us at Miryang Station. Already, a great crowd had gathered at Bongha village. The president seemed to be in a better mood, thanks to many people. At the welcoming ceremony, the president shouted, "Hey~~ I'm feeling good!" at the end of his greetings, and I screamed silently in my head. *Hey~~, I'm free!*

Once I saw the president and his esteemed wife enter their residence, I headed home. I arrived at my Yangsan home late that night. I was a mess. Since I was busy until I left the Blue House, I could not help with the relocation. Since the internal construction was not completed, there wasn't a place where we could unpack, and there wasn't a place to sleep. But it was good. I was happy, just feeling freedom.

On the night of February 24th, the president graciously invited everyone above the vice ministers' status to the Blue House for the last meal. After the dinner, I returned to the official residence of the Chief Secretary. My wife had already left for Yangsan with some of our belongings. The realization that it was my final night at the Blue House filled me with a bittersweet melancholy

Country Life

I settled in Yangsan, but the house was in the worst condition. We couldn't live in the main building because we moved in when it wasn't entirely prepared for residence. We stayed in a small room in a separate building next to the valley for almost a month and a half. It was still winter; we survived by burning wood in a fireplace. There were no washrooms or toilets, so I washed my face in the valley and used the outdoors as a bathroom. It seemed just like the life of an exile. My neighbors gave me rice in an electric rice bowl and gave me a side dish. My wife took bread and pork to the town hall and shared.

After a few months, I made the transition back to my previous profession as an attorney. Although it is different from the preferential treatment* given to high-ranking officials in the courts or prosecution, I still believed it was inappropriate for someone who had served as the Minister of Civil Affairs and Secretary Chief to open a law practice immediately. I spent a few months at home, caring for the yard and making a small-sized garden. After repairing the house for about a month, I was able to

When the event was over, we went to Seoul Station.
The president and I were to take the KTX (Korean Train Express).
Many people gathered at Seoul Station for our farewell.

live in the main house.

Our household now includes three dogs, two cats, and eight chickens. When they wake up in the morning, I feed them and clean after them. The dogs have been loyal companions since our time in Busan, and the cats were a delightful addition to our family, a gift from my daughter who could no longer care for them after finding employment.

The chickens would easily enter our rooms as if they were their territory. It was worthwhile to get organic eggs, and sometimes, it was fun to see chicks hatch. Sometimes, a snake was in the yard, so I bought an industrial-size bag of white powder and sprinkled it around the yard. We also grew vegetables on our little farm. It was so tiny but gave us more than enough to feed two people.

During summer, there was a lot of grass in our yard. If we procrastinated just for a weekend or two, lots of work accumulated. When someone asked what exercises I do, I replied that I don't exercise but farm. With no tips or tricks, it took much longer to grow vegetables. But it was the life I had dreamed of. Sometimes, I dream about making a living by working as a full-time farmer.

* **Preferential Treatment** A high-ranking official above the ministerial level, taking advantage of privileges associated with the position, even after retirement.

Farmer Roh Moo-hyun

The president was thriving in Bongha, finding solace in his farming endeavors. I would often make the journey from Yangsan to visit him. The president emphasized the importance of maintaining formality during state visits, a duty he took seriously. I would accompany him to these official functions, ensuring he didn't lose face.

It was good every time I went. Day by day, more and more visitors visited the village. They would scream and ask the president to come outside and cheer, and they enjoyed taking pictures with him. The president was called out of his house several times a day. Greeting the visitors was exhausting, but he enjoyed it very much.

While he enjoyed greeting people, he preferred engaging in conversations with them even more. Once immersed in a discussion, he lost track of time. Sometimes, he spoke with visitors for over an hour. Occasionally, he would deliver lengthy talks on complex topics as if he were giving a university lecture. Had he still been alive, he might have lived modestly, farming, having informal chats with ordinary citizens, and giving special lectures at undergraduate and graduate universities.

His face would light up with enthusiasm when discussing topics such as eco-friendly agriculture, forestry, and the revitalization of the Hwapocheon Stream. He was driven by a deep-seated desire to transform Bongha Village into a thriving model of a prosperous and livable rural community.

As a simple citizen and former president, the president envisioned many ways to contribute to the country. First, he set up a site called Democracy 2.0. He wanted to contribute to society by creating a space for discussing high-level democratic ethics and progressive discourses. However, it failed. Although many posts were uploaded, there was no high level of discourse formation, and the debate culture didn't improve a notch. There were comments criticizing Lee Myung-bak's administration, and various opinions were not tolerated. It did go as the president expected. The president told them to stop and wrote, "If you are going to criticize, have evidence and base it on truth," but it was no use. Eventually, he closed the site.

He worked hard in the Hwapocheon Stream cleanup movement, eco-friendly farming, and duck farming. It was something that the president truly enjoyed doing. It might seem that he returned home; however, it was an uncomfortable life for the president and his family in many ways. Whenever the media exploited bad press, it was difficult for them to leave the house. Though in his various inconveniences, he found happiness in such jobs as eco-friendly agriculture and the revival of the

Hwapocheon Stream. Above all, the people liked this image of the retired president.

Happiness didn't last long in Bongha. The plans he had set in motion began to fizzle out, the overwhelming influx of visitors to Bongha, and the rise of President Roh's popularity after retirement were all politically interpreted by the Lee Myung-bak administration. It was a sign of unfortunate events to begin later. But until then, we didn't know anything.

It was good every time I went. Day by day, more and more visitors visited the village. They would scream and ask the president to come outside and cheer, and they enjoyed taking pictures with him.
The president was called out of his house several times a day.
Greeting the visitors was exhausting, but he enjoyed it very much.

Political Retaliation

Candlelight demonstrations took place in Seoul and all over the country due to imports of U.S. beef. At that time, President Roh was very cautious and modest. President Lee Myung-bak and his officials continuously made remarks about the responsibility of the Participatory Government; though the president might have been disheartened, he showed respect to the incumbent president. He publicly criticized the "resignation of president" slogans and chants from the candlelight vigil, saying it wasn't the right way to deal with the problem. He also expressed concern that the movement toward the Blue House after the candlelight vigil was not desirable.

Neither the president nor we could have imagined that the subsequent response to the candlelight protests would be political retaliation, with the brunt of it directed at us. It was only much later that we learned that the Lee Myung-bak administration's hatred and hostility towards President Roh and the Participatory Government began from that time. It was also much later that we learned they suspected us of being behind the candlelight protests. This was truly a display of astonishing imagination and a sense of victimization.

The beginning of political retaliation was a shameless background check of the people of the Participatory Government. They summoned and investigated former Prime Minister Lee Hae-chan and former Prime Minister Han Myeong-sook. Furthermore, friends and families of the former Education Deputy, Kim-Byung-jun, and former Chief Secretary, Lee Byung-wan, were investigated to find charges against them. That was not the end. The Lee administration was trying to find faults of some secretaries from the 386 generation. If there was not a good enough case, they probed around the families and friends of the target.

The president was aware of all the hardships of those who had supported him. He didn't say anything other than telling them not to visit him in Bongha. He feared that his people would suffer more if others saw them visiting the president in Bongha. Later, I learned how painful it was for him, as it was also written in his will: "The suffering endured by many people due to my action is too profound."

The blade began to subtly point towards the president. The humiliation began with the presidential records. It became a comedy to pain the president, who had left and transferred the most records in history, as a 'shameless person who embezzled records.'

There was a legal disadvantage due to the absence of a system, as well as an institutional loophole in which the former president does not have easy access to view the records of his term. People continued to spread lies. The former Secretary of Administration, Jung Sang-mun, and I attempted to clarify facts by calling Yu Wook-ik, the Chief of Staff at the time, and Kim Baek-jun, the Secretary of Administration. At the time, they seemed to be generally understanding but turned their back so quickly and cruelly.

The problem could have been solved simply by finding a measure that allows the former president to view records of his presidency. They chose not to do that but to make a case. They made it appear like a serious crime.

The purpose of the Presidential Records Management Law is to let the state manage the presidential records by handing them over to the Presidential Archives within the National Archives. Anyone who violates the law is to be penalized. If we had taken all the materials that we were supposed to hand over to the Archives, we would be violating the law. However, we just made a copy and handed over the original documents. The only reason we made copies was because it was difficult to access the documents due to the inadequate system; we did not infringe upon the state's control over Roh's record.

It does not count as a violation from the lawmaking perspective, either. Realistically speaking, how can a former president write or give a lecture if he cannot access records from his tenure?

The president and I were going to argue over right and wrong because, legally, it was so clear. However, the president eventually gave in, in a humiliating way, because he could not bear the fact that all his people from the Participatory Government were being summoned for investigation. The president publicly stated, "It is I who made them do what they did. It's all my fault," to protect people.

It felt like our efforts in transferring every record went in vain. Our staff stayed up so many nights to do that. We didn't realize that our good deeds of archiving records for the next government and handing them over to the Archives would backfire on us as a means of political retaliation.

In the past, presidents either discarded records or took them home after the end of their terms. President Roh Moo-hyun established the law because he thought that unless those documents were accessible to former presidents, they would be taken away. It is regrettable that we did not follow up by establishing necessary policies and systems to make them more readily available; still, I could not help but feel bitter and betrayed.

Moreover, all the copies were in President Roh's possession and were never leaked. President Roh himself had not opened them at the time. Even if it was a violation, they did not have to condemn the president like that.

There was a rumor that some were concerned that the records would be used to criticize and attack the Lee administration. I suppose that there was a body designed to consider, handle, and respond to all possible problems from the perspective of political science.

After the archive case was over, the president was discredited for the rice subsidy. The Lee administration made it appear as if they were cleaning after the mess created by the Participatory Government. It was then that it became apparent that the new government was creating political antagonism against President Roh and the town of Bongha. It was more than blaming the former government; it clearly had malicious intentions behind all the offenses. It did not take long before my speculation proved to be true.

Beginning of a Tragedy

As the investigation unfolded, it became clear that individuals and businesses with close ties to the president were being targeted. The presidents of Wooridul Hospital, Lee Sang-ho and Kim Soo-kyung, were under tax investigations, and the president of Chang-shin Fiber, Kang Gum-won, was under prosecution investigation. The gravity of the situation escalated when President Kang Gum-won was arrested. In July 2008, Taekwang Ind Co., Ltd was also under a tax investigation. The situation took a turn when the corruption at Sejong Securities came to light, with President Roh's older brother Roh Gun-pyung at the center of it all. It was later revealed that his older brother was the catalyst for these events.

In fact, his older brother's problem was paid close attention to even when President Roh was in the Blue House. The issue with Sejong Securities and Park Yeon-cha also did not feel right. When I was in the Blue House, I heard disgraceful stories. The Special Inspection Group within the Senior Presidential Secretary for Civil Affairs office obtained relevant intelligence. I instructed them to get thorough information. Many people in business strongly denied the investigation of the Special Inspection Group. They fervently denied that no such thing would happen. We also checked out his older brother. He said the same thing, that he never did it. It was later realized that his older brother and the people in business were not telling the truth. There was no way to have caught them at once then. Since the Blue House did not have the authority to investigate, it was challenging to probe any further. If there were any clues or if his brother had told the truth, President Roh would not have ignored it and covered it up. We would have filed the case ourselves.

When imprisonment was imminent and the prosecution filed for a warrant, his brother was so deeply involved with the incident that it was already difficult for us to deal with. It would have been less regrettable if it had happened without us knowing about it, but it was unfortunate because we could not probe into the probability after we obtained intelligence.

In addition to his brother, Secretary of Administration Chung Sanmoon was also arrested for being tangled up in dishonorable business. He was linked with President Park Yeon-cha. To deal with the incident, I often went to Bongha. Secretary of Civil Affairs Chun Hae-chil, Attorney Chun Jae-sung, and I were in charge of taking legal action.

Our biggest mistake concerning the president was that the First Lady could not look at us. When we were inevitably in a position to discuss the case, she would sit with us, but if that wasn't the case, she avoided being in the same room as the president. Even when she was with us, she would slip away quietly if the president entered.

At that time, the president acted a bit strange. He didn't know the exact facts, but many times, he would find out by watching us ask the First Lady questions and hearing her stories. He would normally have gotten angry and scolded us, but not once did he display it. In the end, he never raised his voice in front of us. I thought it was strange. It was because he was taking a philosophical view of the case when it was utterly difficult to do so.

He firmly stated, "Ultimately, it all falls on me. I've been financially inept for a long time and couldn't instill any confidence in the future for my wife and Secretary of Administration Chung San-moon. Isn't that why they did it? It's all my fault. I've grown accustomed to it since I've been in politics for a long time, but I couldn't with my family."

The president, not only towards his wife but also Secretary of Administration Chung San-moon, was willing to embrace it even though it happened without his acknowledgment. He told Secretary of Administration Chung San-moon to testify that he made him do it, but he didn't listen to the president. He confessed, revealing that he did it. After a while, he wrote again, saying, "You have to throw me away."

What he said was true. The president was embarrassed to look at us and lost face. I personally expressed my feelings. I knew very well how brutal it was for him to accept the situation. Though it was heartbreaking and I worried, I had no choice but to hold on to the conviction that he would eventually be found innocent.

The prosecution and the media became a popular topic, and the public trial and witch-hunt were intolerable. They started to treat the president as a heinous criminal. In the prosecution, Investigation Planning Officer Hong Man-pyo held official briefings in the morning and evening. Prosecutors under the department head level leaked all the investigation details to the media. Even the prosecution participants had a richer story.

There was a poem about him throwing a watch worth around one hundred million won (US $88,000.00) into a ridge between rice paddies because it was bribery, called "Rice Paddy Watch." Due to the lack of a judicial process, he seemed to be being ridiculed through the media and pressured to surrender. The media was willing to be the accomplice.

What was even more painful was the progress of the media. News articles were not much different from the conservative press, but the columns and editorials were vicious as if piercing human flesh. When Venerable Beopjeong* passed away, he left a will saying not to have his sweet writings that could comfort people published because of karma. I never saw people who wrote hurtful things as if using a sharp object to cause others pain reflected in their writing and not refrain from inflicting suffering.

Compared to him, we had no means of correspondence with people. It was not like we had a separate press secretary at Bongha. I had no choice but to take on the media response. I responded to all the press calls that I received while going to and from the law firm and Bongha. During that time, the majority of my answers reported in the press were done while I was driving.

There were many times when I would have to answer on the spot questions like "The briefing of the prosecution said this, and how do you feel?" or "A certain media reported such and such, what are your thoughts?" without being briefed by the prosecution or watching the press reports. If we were doing something else and wasn't able to receive the call, they would not even write about our situation and move on. So, we had to be grateful that they were asking us.

I am not quick in thinking or speaking. In addition, public opinion and media coverage were extremely difficult. When journalists asked, I had to quickly judge what expressions needed to be used to convince them and be helpful. Though I answered under great anxiety, seeing how the incident played out there was regretful.

At that time, since the president was subjected to various facets of unfairness in various sections, I contemplated whether to take political or legal action. I examined methods of how to directly politically respond to what is and is not valid. It was primarily the public relations advisors who made such assertions. Although it was ultimately not sent, a document like "A Letter to President Lee Myung-bak" was prepared. Eventually, the president chose for a thorough legal response. This was because it was judged that public opinion would not be receptive, and it was anticipated that this would lead to even harsher criticism.

The president and we responded with immense patience at that time. Reflecting on that period, I deeply regret whether our response was appropriate. I wonder if we were too cautious, or if we failed to fully express what the president really wanted to say...Perhaps we should have confronted the issue head-on, declaring it a 'despicable political investigation targeting the former president!' And at times, we should have considered outright refusing the investigation or responding more aggressively.'

Of course, if we had done it, we would not have known if it would have been much better and if the president would have felt more relieved and regained his strength. Regardless, the thought that 'had we known that's how you felt, we should have at least struggled on our part' remains indelible.

* **Venerable Beopjeong** most respected Buddhist priest in Korea.

Day of Humiliation

On the morning of April 30, 2009, the president had to appear at the Supreme Prosecutors' Office in Seoul for an investigation. It was a humiliating day. Despite the president's request for people not to come, many gathered. The First Lady silently held back her tears while the president remained composed. Those who came to support the president ended up bursting into tears instead of offering comfort. The president, in turn, tried to lighten the mood by cracking light-hearted jokes to ease their minds.

The president left his residence. The tears that the First Lady had held back for such a long time poured down her cheeks when she looked at the president's back. He stopped in his tracks and walked back to comfort her.

A news helicopter continued to fly over the bus the president was in, and many news vehicles followed behind. There was heavy silence flowing in the bus. While many were heavy-hearted, the president was composed throughout.

We arrived at the prosecutors. Lee In-kyu, head of the department, greeted the president and offered a cup of tea. He was very arrogant. Though his speech was polite, his attitude was filled with arrogance and pride. The first chief started the investigation. The president tried his best to answer calmly and clearly. His discipline was remarkable. While observing the prosecution's interrogations, it was repeatedly apparent that there wasn't any evidence other than President Park Yeon-cha's testimony. The words of the president and President Park differed, and there was no evidence to support that President Park was telling the truth. There was not even a call record. If there was no call record, then there wasn't any truth that there was a call.

Once the president's investigation was over, meeting President Park was even more surprising. First, the prosecution's idea of President Park's confrontation was upholding any respect for the former president. If the words differed from both sides, the prosecutor must keep a close eye on who was right through different objective means. To create a confrontation was great disrespect. In the end, due to the attorneys' objection, there wasn't a confrontation, but we were asked to meet with him, who had been waiting for a long time to confront him. The president warmly greeted him and comforted him in that situation.

The president's empathy towards President Park was evident. He never held a grudge or spoke ill of him, even until his death. The president understood that President Park had endured a difficult situation, and he believed that when President Park was freer, he would be able to reveal the whole truth.

President Park's daughters were also investigated. It was said they were charged with violating the Foreign Exchange Law. In addition, they were investigated regarding the Taekwang Ind Co., Ltd.'s facility fund loan. If your family and business were placed on top of your palm and you froze, it would be difficult for you to bear. Those types of stories were heard.

After the prosecutor's investigation, there was a heavy silence on the returning bus. We were also exhausted from the lengthy interrogation. Above all, his feelings must have been complicated. It was not the mood to tell him a light story to make him feel better.

Maybe because that day's course was difficult to endure, I was confident once the prosecution had been indicted, we would be able to defeat it in court. No matter how much the prosecution and the media said, "public trial" or "political trial," the law was the law. It was impossible to cover the insufficiencies of the investigative report. Due to the power of "fact," unreasonable investigation or manipulation was limited. That was how it was with that case. We could win. Even in that situation, the president believed in "the power of truth" and the "power of clear facts."

The investigation of the president's summons was the last procedure. Then, it was normal to immediately request custody or prosecution without detention or to dismiss clear of suspicion. But we could not do that. Even after the prosecutor's investigation was over, he was dragged without anything being settled. The reason was simple.

The prosecution would have judged whether or not it would remain

On the morning of April 30, 2009, the president had to appear at the Supreme Prosecutors' Office in Seoul for an investigation. It was a humiliating day. Despite the president's request for people not to come, many gathered. The First Lady silently held back her tears while the president remained composed. Those who came to support the president ended up bursting into tears instead of offering comfort.

in the public prosecution. It was, of course, difficult to claim a warrant in that state. If the warrant had been dismissed, all the investigations that the prosecution had gone through at the time would have been destroyed. Even if the prosecution proceeded without detention, they believed it would not be easy for a public prosecution. Inevitably, nothing was settled, and it continued to drag on. Except for the insults and pressure through the media, nothing could be done.

After bringing the president back to his residence, I returned home very late at night. I was disheartened. All kinds of thoughts were weighing down on my mind. It had been a terrible day, and I was suddenly tired due to the tension I had endured all day. However, I still was not able to sleep.

How did the president put himself in such a predicament? I could understand the president. He was poor. Poverty forced him to rely on studying, leading him to the path of a human rights attorney. If he was not poor, he might not have been able to show interest in those who suffered like he did. His humble beginning in aiming to help the poor and oppressed was to become a human rights attorney and democratic movement. Politics was an extension. His sincerity towards politics was what made him a president.

Still, he wasn't able to free himself from poverty. When he first became an attorney, he was barely able to escape from poverty, but as he started to help others who were oppressed and poor, he fell into their lives and he became poor again. Though Bongha village is remote and the price of land is extremely low, he had to take out a loan from the bank because he did not have enough money to build his residence. He even borrowed money from President Park Yeon-cha. The president told me, "I regret that I have only been politically disciplined myself and failed to politically train my family." However, ultimately, this happened because no separate measures were prepared for the president after retirement.

After President Roh's passing, when filing the inheritance declaration, it was found that his debts exceeded his assets by about 400 million won (US $3,900.00).

1 My Encounter

2 My Life

3 My Accompaniment

4 My Destiny

Chief Mourner Moon Jae-in

On May 23rd, 2009, the news of President Roh Moo-hyun's death shocked the entire nation. After hearing the news, the Participatory Government officials started to flood into Busan National University Hospital.

People couldn't believe the news and repeatedly asked me if it was true. Many doubted the possibility that he would throw himself off the cliffs. And whenever I explained, the image of his brutal state would linger, unable to be erased from my memories. Only the bodyguard, Secretary Moon Young-wook, and I saw the horrific image of the president before he was cleaned up so the First Lady wouldn't be exposed to a tremendous shock. It was atrocious having to be the one to announce his death and explain the situation to the people. I didn't want to do it and resented that I had to.

After facing the sad news of the president's death, a rush of guilt hovered over me that I couldn't endure. A week before the president passed, I didn't go to Bongha. There was nothing scheduled for me to do, and there weren't any pending issues that needed to be addressed. The president was already finished with the prosecution's investigation, and no official decisions were made.

Initially, I went there often to prepare him if there was an arrest warrant. Even after I was sure a warrant wouldn't be issued, I continued to go to Bongha to discuss the possibility of prosecution without detention. But as the deliberation of the prosecution was delayed, I thought it best that the president rested. Besides, the president was too ashamed to see me. So I thought it was best that he rested alone, even briefly.

The president and his attorneys were convinced that pleading not guilty wouldn't be a problem even if he was prosecuted. No one could fathom the president was contemplating throwing himself off a cliff.

I heard later on that he spent the final weekend alone before he died. He even gave up on writing a book called *The Future of Progressivism*, which he wanted to do for a long time. On the morning of the 19th, he expressed his gratitude to his secretaries, Yoon Tae-young and Yang Jung-chul, for their hard work and discontinued writing. That was the last time he met with other acquaintances. Except for the evening of the 21st, when his friend, Lee Jae-woo, a union representative who lived in the neighborhood, visited, he didn't meet with anyone else from the afternoon of the 19th to early dawn on the 23rd. The day before, he briefly went to drop off some cigarettes for the secretaries at the private residence. As if he was saying his goodbyes, it was reported that he just stood there silently, looked at them, and left without saying a word. Early morning on the 23rd, he left his house and departed for his long journey.

No one, including myself, was with him when he was spending painful solitary time alone making his final decision. After the initial shock of seeing the suicide note had somewhat subsided, what tormented me was the thought of how long he had been harboring the idea of leaving a note.

Since it was not something that he could have left on the computer to be revised, he must have thought about it over and over again in his mind so that no one could possibly anticipate his thoughts.

His first sentence, "I am indebted to so many people," was added after the rest of the text had been entered into the computer. Like the person he always was, after he completed his will, he reread it and made revisions. It was unbearable when I thought about how long the president must have had his intention lingering until the last minute.

When did it all begin? Even when he posted "You must get over me" online, I didn't understand the president's heart. How lonely he must have been...

How could others believe this incident when I couldn't either? Neither the people nor the reporters could believe that the president threw himself off the cliff. I asked Secretary Kim Kyung-soo to go public with the complete will and to also distribute it to the reporters. After it was printed the first original print was shown to the First Lady and I later embosomed it. Even to this day, I keep his will in my journal. There's no specific reason why. I just couldn't throw it away...

Many of us discussed where to hold his mortuary. We decided not to make a temporary mortuary at the hospital but to bring him to Bongha village. I told them to quickly make a temporary mortuary in Bongha. So, Secretary Kim Jung-ho started construction in haste with the help of the villagers.

My wife, with tears overflowing, came to the hospital with my black suit and tie. Now, I became the chief mourner to hold his funeral.

We got a call saying that the temporary mortuary in Bongha was completed. When the sun started to peak over the horizon, the president was returning to Bongha within twelve hours after he had left. But now,... returning as a cold corpse.

There was an enormous crowd of people in Bongha who had already heard about the sad news. However, I didn't have the luxury of being sad with them. We had to prepare for the funeral at the village villa and held meetings to discuss various practical issues till dawn.

That is how that long day of May 23rd passed. It was the longest day of my life. That day, I never regretted being the last chief secretary. From verifying his body, announcing his death, presiding over meetings to sending him off...I was unable to be alone and couldn't cry.

My wife, with tears overflowing,
came to the hospital with my black suit and tie.
Now, I became the chief mourner to hold his funeral.

Sending Him Off

In a meeting the next day, former Prime Minister Lee Hae-chan recommended that former Prime Minister Han Myung-sook be the chief funeral commissioner. Others agreed this recommendation was good, and former Prime Minister Han accepted the position. During the meetings and arrangements, everyone took shifts, presiding as the chief mourner throughout the funeral.

The memorial response was phenomenal. There were crowds of people coming to cherish his memories. Not just on the first day but even afterward, unimaginable crowds were coming to Bongha. They traveled for many hours to express their condolences for a minute or two. Even when they arrived, they had to wait for a long time. The scorching sun and heat in May and the sudden rainfall couldn't disrupt the line. It was like seeing people line up for a solemn religious ceremony. What made them go there?

There was a lot of work to be discussed and decided upon concerning the funeral. Since the First Lady nor the relatives were in any condition to attend the meetings, I was their messenger.

The first problem was whether to make it a national or private funeral. There were many who sided with making it public, but others who wanted it to be a private funeral were making strong arguments. These were the minority, and they weren't going to yield. Even the family and relatives all at first wanted a private funeral, and they were deliberating for a long time.

President Kim Dae-jung, through Chief Secretary Park Ji-won, said it was advisable that a national funeral should be held. In his methodical manner, he reasoned that first, President Roh lived his life supporting human rights and democracy. Secondly, he became the president with the support of the people; and thirdly, even during his presidency, he worked hard for his people, so the people should send off President Roh. Gradually, many started to lean towards holding a national funeral, and in the end, the bereaved family members agreed.

Though the family agreed upon a national funeral, the government didn't allow the organization of a funeral committee. However, the problem was solved by forming a collaborative committee of the government and ourselves and having the current Prime Minister and former Prime Minister Han Myung-sook act as co-chief funeral commissioners. Even after that, the bereaved family did not accept the investigation done by the current Prime Minister of the government, and that, too, took a lot of persuasion.

Next, the location of the funeral ceremony was discussed. At first, I thought that it would be best to hold the ceremony and *nojae** in his hometown of Jinyoung and to erect a small memorial stone in Bongha, where he resided after retirement. If the president's death wasn't such a sad tragedy, I probably would have pushed for this idea.

However, President Roh's death wasn't a political homicide or anything equivalent to it. His values and his frustration were the root. The dream of the people who had sought a political ideology from him collapsed completely.

Of course, many people viewed the former president's atonement for his family and acquaintances as a mistake and the result of our underdeveloped political culture. No matter how his death was viewed, more people took part in the funeral, causing us to contemplate the meaning of his death. I thought that it was necessary that all the people who were expressing pain and sorry should converge together in sending him off.

To achieve this, though the ceremony itself was important, the venue for the funeral procession and nojae so that many people could gather together was more important. Finally, we had Seoul Square in mind for the nojae and held the funeral ceremony in Seoul. The bereaved family members easily agreed. The decision to hold the funeral ceremony in Seoul also helped obtain permission to hold a national funeral.

The family members had a difficult time deciding which cemetery to select for his burial. According to the president's will, bringing him to Bongha was reasonable. However, there were objections regarding what was considered respectful treatment for the former president. Some argued that the president needed to go to Seoul National Cemetery because of his death. There were also many realistic worries about how we would care for his graveyard. In particular, the First Lady had a difficult time making a decision. The will of the president was not just written with emotion but with death in his mind. It was a premeditated idea and plan he made a long time ago to return to his hometown after retirement.

He disliked standardized honorific treatment like the Seoul National Cemetery, and the First Lady and I were well aware of his thoughts. In the end, we decided to follow the president's will.

What was more difficult was where to put his tomb in Bongha. The present location of the tomb didn't fit traditional notions. The bereaved family members suggested the mountain's foothills in the back of the house. However, creating a memorial space where people could come to pay their respects was difficult. The foothills of the mountain across from the tomb were better, but it was difficult to acquire ownership of them.

In the end, we focused on a "national memorial space" and chose the place where it is located now. From the beginning, it was also a decision to erect a foundation stone for national participation. The First Lady didn't like the idea that the Bueongi Rock, where the tragic accident happened, could be seen. And I felt the same way. However, there wasn't a better alternative. After the completion of the current location, the bereaved family was satisfied.

Whenever I look down at the grave from the Lion Rock at Bonghwa Mountain, I think it was the fated place originally planned as the president's graveyard.

Since the ground is triangular, the head of the topography of Bonghwa Mountain flows into the Bongha village, exquisitely connecting the apex with the places where people live. The lotus pond on the other side of the street was created by hand by the president when he came home, bringing lotuses from everywhere and planting them there. Now, the pond enriches the vicinity of the cemetery. Was it preplanned? Who could have known the fate of these consoling flowers...?

Once the big guidelines were in tow, the government's illiberal attitude made things difficult for us. First, the government was against the nojae being held at Seoul Square because they feared a mass demonstration could spread due to the citizens' intensifying emotions. The decision couldn't be made until the dawn of that day. We convinced them with the logic that "Even though you don't allow the nojae, the funeral procession will pass Seoul Square. Then, surely, many people will block the procession. There is a high possibility that an improvisatory nojae will be held where we'll be in a situation where we can't move. It's not desirable and will be more difficult for the government. Rather, I think it's best that you control us in an orderly manner and provide us a designated time when we can hold the nojae." With this reasoning, the government changed its mind.

Next, the elegy* was the problem. They said it was likely that the elegy flagpole could be used as a demonstration tool. One couldn't help but observe their uneasiness over the excitement of public sentiment due

The head of the topography of Bonghwa Mountain flows into the Bongha village, exquisitely connecting the apex and the places where people live.

to the president's death. So, the elegy flagpole was changed from wood to PVC. I indicated that the elegies were only allowed to be held by the people whose identifications were checked out and that once the nojae was completed, the IDs would be collected immediately. But the government didn't trust us, so they said we could also use public officials. Once we agreed, they permitted us to proceed. At the dawn of the day, everything was to be done, and all the problems were resolved.

It seemed like they were calculating and weighing everything. But we strictly wanted to hold dignity and have order for the funeral ceremony. We noticed that no anti-government demonstrations were held at the funeral ceremony or at the nojae, and that no one used the situation politically in any form. I thought it wouldn't fit the pure commemoration of the people, nor was it a way to send the president off appropriately. We even asked for special cooperation from the Civil Society Organizations. They had the same idea as we did. They were aware that, at least on that day, there shouldn't be any actions that could harass the president.

Perhaps the government didn't like the fact that many people were gathered for the president's nojae. That was the attitude towards the memorial altar in front of Daehan Gate.

Since the government had agreed on a national funeral venue, they could not impose the memorial on the people. It was their duty to provide commemoration venues and create an atmosphere where many people could come to pay their respects. Isn't it?

It was rather sad to see the government's attitude toward trying to prevent memorialization. And it wasn't as if we didn't have that kind of attitude on our side. When the Grand National Party Representative Park Hye-tae and former Chairwoman Park Geun-hye, Chairman of the National Assembly Kim Hyung-Oh, and the ruling party politicians, Prime Minister Han Seung-soo and other governmental officials came to Bongha to give their condolences, people blocked them. It wasn't necessary, but we couldn't dissuade their engagement. We were informed that President Lee Myung-bak also wanted to come to Bongha to pay his respects, but we dissuaded him from doing so because it wouldn't be a pretty picture. However, we ensured that President Lee's floral condolences were recognized.

The one thing the government didn't allow us to proceed with was President Kim Dae-jung's funeral service for President Roh. I suggested it, and everyone agreed. Though his health was in bad condition, and we worried if he would be able to do it, I decided to ask him for this favor anyway. And he gladly accepted.

However, the government unexpectedly denied it. The reason was utterly destitute: no precedent had previously been established, and no comparable situations had ever existed with other former presidents.

Does it make sense that the former president isn't allowed to have a memorial service for his successor's funeral? It was the same for the then-current president in office. The only thing that the current president could do at the former president's national funeral was to burn incense or offer flowers. I had seen an article once that the American president, President Obama, attended Senator Edward Kennedy's funeral and held a commemorating speech for him. However, in Korea, though the current president attends a funeral, they are encouraged not to participate in commemorative speeches. Even if the political party or affiliations differ, isn't it normal for the current president to give a commemorating speech at the former president's national funeral? The same is true for other funerals that need to be honored by the people.

When President Kim Dae-jung wasn't allowed to give his speech due to the government's refusal, the day before the funeral ceremony, he took his uncomfortable body in a wheelchair to the memorial altar located in Seoul Station and gave his commemorating speech then. That wasn't all. When *Oh My News* CEO Oh Yoon-hee wrote a book titled *Roh Moo-hyun's Last Interview*, he wrote a testimonial of the things he couldn't say from the heart at the funeral ceremony in his commemorating speech. His fervent eulogy began with "Roh Moo-hyun, even in death, do not die" and concluded with "As long as we remain awake, though former President Roh Moo-hyun has passed, he will never die." I cannot begin to express my gratitude twards the now deceased President Kim Dae-jung.

* **Nojae** memorial service done on the streets.

* **Elegy** a poem written in a sad or mournful state for the dead. Sometimes the poem will be written on silk or a paper to make a flag. The flag is carried behind the pallbearers when the body is brought to its grave.

Sea of Tears

During the funeral ceremony, tears were flowing down my face. Looking back, I didn't have time to let it all out and grieve. Though I teared up when people came to show their respects at Bongha, bringing their condolences, I quickly composed myself.

Former Prime Minister Han Myeong-sook's heartbreaking commemorating speech triggered my tears. I couldn't stop my tears from flowing when he said, "President! Dear President, where are you now?"

During President Lee Myung-bak's floral tribute, a small problem occurred. Congressman Baek Won-woo, who couldn't contain his rage, jumped up and yelled at President Lee, "Apologize for your political retaliation!" I understood where he was coming from. However, as a mourner, he had to apologize. So, when the funeral ceremony was over, as the head of operations for the national funeral committee, I apologized to President Lee Myung-bak and said, "It was a show a poor display of manners. It wasn't polite to do that to someone who had come to pay their respects" and bowed my head. Former Prime Minister Han, the chief funeral commissioner, also agreed with me, and we apologized together. President Lee said, "It's okay. I understand. Pay no attention to it." Later, the prosecution charged Baek Won-woo with obstruction of funeral services, but he was found innocent.

I was sitting right behind him, and I remember it well when President Kim Dae-jung went to comfort the First Lady after placing his flowers on the funeral site. The country's greatest former politician couldn't overcome the sadness and woe and fell apart on the spot. His face was distorted, and he was weeping as if incessantly wailing. My heart ached even more because I had asked him to give a speech at the funeral, but due to the government's refusal, it didn't occur. That wasn't the only thing. After President Roh's death, the image he displayed as the nation's adult and top official was truly admirable. Soon afterward, the death of President Kim ripped at my heart again. His health wasn't in the best condition, and due to President Roh's death, his physical and emotional condition worsened. Visiting the memorial altar at Seoul Station and then continuing for long hours at the funeral ceremony was detrimental to his health. I was indeed sorry for his passing.

The four greatest denominational leaders oversaw the religious ceremonies at the funeral ceremony. At that time, Bongeunsa Temple's chief Buddhist priest, Monk Myung-jin, the manager of The National Council of Churches of Korea, Pastor Kwon Oh-sung, Father Song Ki-in from the Catholic Church, and Seoul University's parish priest Lee Sun-jong of Won Buddhism, held their own ceremonies. I was grateful to all but was

When the funeral ceremony was over and the funeral procession headed for "Seoul Square", there were hordes of people. There were so many people gathered in the center of the city that it was difficult to go through.

especially sorry for Monk Myung-jin. The monk was in prayer for 1,000 days at the Bongeunsa Temple. Only a couple more days remained in the 1,000-day prayer ritual, which he didn't complete to serve at President Roh's observance, causing me to feel extremely sorry. Later, I was even more disturbed because he was subjected to political persecution.

When the funeral ceremony was over, and the funeral procession headed for Seoul Square, there were hordes of people. So many gathered in the city's center that it was difficult to go through. They even fortified us when we were following behind the funeral car. The huge crowd and the funereal car slowly moved towards Seoul Square. There were especially a lot of common people and young women as well. There was also a noticeable amount of people with disabilities. You could feel how much the general public really loved the president. Many people wanted to touch the funeral car as the funeral procession started to slow down.

More than half a million-people gathered together for the nojae. Everyone focused on the stage and sang together, shouted together and cried together. I was so busy crying that I didn't know what was happening on stage. I was just able to feel the atmosphere around me.

I saw iridescent clouds* in the sky during nojae. It was amazing. It was the third time in my life that I had witnessed such a mysterious phenomenon.

The first time I saw it, it had been so long ago that I couldn't remember the exact time, but it was when hundreds of thousands of Catholics gathered at Yeouido Square for some type of religious rally. I don't remember if it was when Pope John Paul II visited Korea or another time. My mother wanted to go, so I took her there, and I could clearly see the shape of a large cross in the sky on the opposite side. It was the topic of discussion for a while as a miracle in Catholicism.

The second time was in 2005, during a funeral ceremony for Monk Fazang, the director of managers of the Jogye Order. It was held at Jogyesa Temple. I attended as one of the representatives of the Blue House. When I was chief of Civil Affairs and Civil Society, I often dealt with Buddhism to act as a liaison. When the Participatory Government faced difficulties due to the problems of the Sapae Mountain Tunnel and Chunsung Mountain Tunnel, they helped us greatly by playing an arbitral role regarding the dispute. Unlike the Buddhist ritual that cremates the body of the deceased monk, they participated in the Sharing Life Movement and left a great impression on the people by making a body donation.

Moreover, the written text, *I have a knapsack that doesn't have an opening or a bottom. No matter what I put in, it doesn't overflow*, and *no matter how much I give, it doesn't become empty'* moved people even more and was often discussed. A solar halo that was difficult to see during the funeral ceremony was clearly observed. It was a perfectly rounded ring around the sun. Everyone was amazed. Maybe when many sincere people with earnest minds gather, the stage for such a spiritual phenomenon is set.

When the nojae was finished, and the funeral procession took place, many people held onto the funeral car. We weren't sure until when they would follow, but the roads became more crowded with endless numbers of people. Their hearts were so saddened that we couldn't speed up the car. It was only after passing Seoul Station that we separated from the crowd. Once the funeral procession could leave them, I greeted the people as a representative. " Thank you so very much. You won't be forgotten."

At Suwon's cremation center, leaving the people's sadness and mourning behind, the president became a handful of ashes. The First Lady and their daughter were outside, and the son and I cremated him and put his remains in a cremation urn, completing the final procedure.

The president's cremation urn was finally brought to Bongha village at 2 o'clock in the morning the next day. There was a common saying that it shouldn't pass midnight, but it couldn't be helped because it took a lot of time for the funeral car to leave the memorial crowd in the center of Seoul city. By the time the installation ceremony was over, it was 3 o'clock in the morning. And that is how the national funeral ended.

* **Iridescent Clouds** are multicolored clouds. Light is diffracted into the water droplets or ice crystals that form the clouds, which appear to be finely colored.

Everyone focused on the stage,
sang, shouted, and cried together.

A Small Tombstone

After the funeral, we held a weekly ceremony until the 49th *Jae* and the burial ceremony. In the process, the Buddhist community did not spare any special support. The Buddhist community has shown all forms of sincerity since the president's demise. In addition to the Buddhist Order, the nearby large temples, including Tongdo Temple, Beomeo Temple, and Haein Temple, provided active support. The monks came to Bongha alternately to pray for the ceremony. During the 49th *Jae* period, all the temples in the Busan and Gyeongnam area held the 49th *Jae* ceremony and Jeongtowon.

The 49th *Jae* is a ritual that combines ideas from Buddhism and Confucianism. It has been said that the Confucian idea of ancestral worship and Buddhism's reincarnation have been compromised.

In Buddhism, every time a person dies, a *Jae* (ritual) is given by reciting the Buddhist scriptures every seven days. This is for the dead to realize the wrongful activities of the past and to be born in a better place in their next life. In Confucianism, if the descendants of the deceased hold a *Jae* for forty-nine days with all sincerity, their already deceased parents or ancestors will be reborn as human beings in a better place, and the ancestral spirits will bless their descendants.

Whatever the meaning, religion, or ceremony, it didn't matter. The hearts of the people facing the sudden death of their beloved president will always be one of remorse. What else was there left to hope for except the desire for the president's relief from all his agony and heavy burdens of the times and just to enjoy his rest and freedom? I'm Catholic, but I attended all seven *Jaes* and prayed earnestly.

After the funeral ceremony, we had little time left until the burial. In that short period, we had to finish the minimal boundaries of the cemetery. We couldn't do it with our strengths. Our arts and cultural experts, with great talent, reputation, and passion, formed a dream team called the "Very Small Monument Committee," which took charge.

The former Director of the Cultural Heritage Administration, Yoo Hong-joon, named the committee based on the president's will. Although it must have been a burden, Yoo gladly volunteered and brought together experts from all walks of life.

Professor Yoo Hong-joon, historian Ahn Byung-wook, architects Jung Gi-yong and Seung Hyo-sang, artists Im Ok-sang and Ahn Kyu-cheol, landscape architect Jung Young-sun and poet Hwang Ji-woo gathered together. I, too, was a member of the committee. Thanks to the experts, the work was made easy, and the cemetery of today was so beautifully crafted and decorated.

It wasn't easy to comply with the spirit of the *one very small monument* that the president requested in his will. Everybody had different ideas of what it meant. If the words of the president's will were taken literally, we were supposed to scatter his ashes and not build a mausoleum. A small memorial headstone near his house would be enough.

But the president's will was reflected in a humble letter as he parted this world, so more people agreed that even if the president said so, we should serve him properly. It may seem more meaningful to have followed the president's will as time passed. But what about the hearts of the people, expressed in the 5-6 million mourning memorial crowd?

The *very little monument* had to provide a memorial area where people could convey their heartfelt tributes of honor and appreciation, so we decided to create a mausoleum by burying the ashes and laying broad and flat rocks in dolmen style instead of burrows. Without erecting a tombstone, we engraved the inscription onto the rock, and the rock became the headstone.

It was the idea of former director Yoo Hong-Joon. Poet Hwang Ji-woo said that if we received the messages of the people on the bottom of the pavement, there would be no better inscription than that. So, we decided to engrave only President Roh Moo-hyun's name without any additional inscriptions.

The president's burial ceremony took place on July 10, 2009. Tens of thousands of guests joined. Heavy rain poured in Bongha until the day before the burial and then stopped at the dawn of the burial. The president's ashes were buried in white porcelain pottery inside a lotus flower stone case.

I put two items in the stone case. One was a memorial video that filmed the memorial crowd after the president's death. Another was a five-part documentary DVD titled *Five Years of Participatory Government.* The memorial film contained the warming thoughts of people's memories and tears of separation. I put it there as a memento that the people did not abandon him.

The documentary was a collection of the five-year history, recounting all the possible accomplishments throughout his presidential term. He was called a failed president and a failed government as he left the Blue House. He heard criticisms from the progressive camp as if he was the one who had ruined the progress. But we believed that history would justify our efforts. The five-year record would be the basis for evaluation. The president left, carrying all these burdens by himself. He rejected the Court of Humanity and chose the Court of History. A record of those five years is needed for the court of history. They were the words that the president himself always emphasized. With that perspective in mind, I put the two items by his side.

The final farewell ceremony wasn't long. The president's funeral ended with covering the ashes with broad, flat rocks. Until then, the graveyard was not organized, so his site seemed desolate and shabby. My heart ached. What remained was to cultivate and improve the graveyard.

I put two items in the stone case. One was a memorial video that filmed the memorial crowd after the president's death. Another was a five-part documentary DVD titled Five Years of Participatory Government.

A Memorial Stone by the People

I poured my heart and strength into constructing the graveyard for ten months after his burial ceremony. Around 18,000 people wrote memorial inscriptions on arch stones and laid them around the grave. Architect Seung Hyo-sang conceptualized and designed the graveyard, and artist Lim Yok-sang designed the arrangements of the arch stones.

When arch stones recruitment started, there were instantly many hopeful applicants, so it was quickly closed. Later, due to the increase in complaints from those who couldn't apply, the design had to be changed to increase the stones. The memorial inscriptions that each person carved were impressive and emotional, line by line. As poet Hwang Ji-woo would say, which poet can think of better epitaphs? Nowadays, many people come with their families to the graveyard and look at their and others' memorial inscriptions. I think it was rewarding to encourage public participation at the graveyard site.

My wife and I also applied for a stone. "Rest well" was all I wrote. That was the only thing I could say to him. There were many who had written about their sorrow concerning his death, and I didn't think it was necessary for me to write that as well. It was just really regretful that he had a really difficult time from the start to the end of his presidency. At that time, and even now, the only thing that I desired was that he rested well. I was relieved when the arch-stones were finally laid down, and the graveyard was complete.

After the funeral service, I saw a vast, barren field with only a large flat rock and a *gokjang**, which was embarrassingly desolate. I felt sorry for its pitiful state. My mind was finally at ease when the burial site took shape on the first anniversary. With the paving stones laid and the site adequately formed as a grave, I felt relieved.

Nevertheless, I still didn't feel peaceful. Instead, it felt cold and dry. Maybe it was because there wasn't enough landscaping. Once the trees are properly planted and a forest is formed, it will create a more relaxed atmosphere. This was our remaining task.

* **Gokjang(曲墻)** A low fence wall encircling behind royal tombs and graves.

My wife and I also
applied for a stone.
"Rest well" was all I wrote.
That was the only thing
I could say to him.

The Place He Left Behind

After the funeral was completed, the Bongha Foundation was established in Bongha, and the Roh Moo-hyun Foundation was established nationwide to continue the commemoration memorial business. I was the auditor for the Bongha Foundation and the executive director for the Roh Moo-hyun Foundation. I naturally thought that it was something I had to do until things were settled.

I had to make time to work there nearly twice a week. Though I felt sorry for the law firm's office, everyone understood. Although it was difficult to go to Seoul once a week from Busan, it was rewarding to see the commemoration memorial business start to settle and obtain satisfactory results.

After the first anniversary of the president's death, there were great results in the regional elections from those who wanted to continue to advance the president's values. Among them were Kim Doo-kwan, Ahn Hee-jung, and Lee Gwang-jae, whose rapid progress was especially impressive. It was great happiness to see Ahn Hee-Jung recovering his honor. It was something that President Roh would have been happy to see from heaven.

Many people talk about Roh Moo-hyun's mind and values nowadays, and I'm very grateful. But no matter how much meaning we give to his death, he isn't alive.

During the first anniversary memorial service, actor Myung Gae-nam cried out in sorrow, "You should have just lived." *Yes...* I thought the same thing. It wasn't that the president couldn't endure his failures, but it was unbearable to see the process and the reformation camp abolished. It also disturbed him to think about all the people who might experience pain and suffering due to his decisions.

But if pursued, the truth would have been revealed. It would have been legally investigated, and I thought he needed to endure. If he hadn't, there were so many things that he could have done if he had been still by our side.

I met him sometimes in my dreams. Once, there were a lot of worries about what needed to be done concerning the graveyard, and we discussed various opinions about what the use of the arch-stones was and the construction of the graveyard. In one of my dreams, there was a materials warehouse on site. The president and I went to the warehouse, and he was pleased to see the preparations. Even though it was a dream, I interpreted it as *the president not seeming to dislike the idea we had planned for construction.* So I was relieved.

There were times that I would return to the times I spent at the Blue

House. It was a dream where, while verifying personnel affairs, I took the president somewhere to investigate a probing problem. It was the night before the Supreme Court election for Governor Lee Gwang-jae. It was a very pleasant dream. Some of us and the president were gathered around looking at work that was translated by someone from Chinese characters to Korean. A section of the translation was done so poorly that the president made a unique and pleasant joke that made the whole assembly laugh. It was just a pleasant dream that even after I had woken up, the pleasant energy lingered. I wondered if something good was going to happen today and realized that it was the day of the Supreme Court election. I expected good results, but the situation was quite the opposite. Though they were only dreams, it was nice to meet with him once in a while.

Whenever I had a drink, I would reminisce about the old days and ask myself, "What was Roh Moo-hyun in my life?" I wasn't sure. However, he stimulated my life a lot. If I hadn't met him, my life would have been completely different. It was fate in that respect. If I was asked if it was good, I don't think I'd be able to easily answer because there were many painful and difficult moments.

But what can be said? Even though my encounter with him, our long companionship, and his parting weren't something that I planned, they weren't something that could have been avoided. It's the same now. If there was an assignment he left behind, who could be free from the duties?

I was more like that. You should be willing to live your life. It is the same reason why I lingered as the foundational chairman of the board of

"What was Roh Moo-hyun in my life?"
I wasn't sure. However, he stimulated my life a lot.
If I hadn't met him, my life would have been completely different.
It was fate in that respect. If I were asked if it was good,
I don't think I'd be able to easily answer.

President Roh Moo-hyun's memorial business. It's not something that should cease in our generation. I want to construct a foundation that will continue to develop. I think it was inevitable to look back, evaluate, and reflect on the five years of the Participatory Government.

Returning to Law

I lived as an attorney my entire life. If one could be a little bit more abundant in money, being an attorney would be a great occupation because you can help those in need. It's also good to consider investing one's abilities for the party or common good. With such an attitude, it allows you to have self-respect and great self-worth.

I tried to practice with that mindset. Fortunately, I succeeded as an attorney. As I was earning money, my reputation as a human rights attorney was good. Though I kept a good distance from practices that I didn't like, such as receiving commission for case introductions, entertaining judges and prosecutors, giving parting gifts, etc., I was able to maintain the office well and received a good reputation from the judicial officers. My luck was good, too.

I lived thinking of being an attorney as a vocation. When I was an attorney, I had the experience of being the attorney in charge of maintenance for a public prosecution, a special prosecutor, to put it simply. It was before I was the special prosecutor for the Bucheon Police Station sexual torture case. It was an incident about a customs official's torture case that occurred at Busan Customs. Even though it was punishment for torture that I hated, it wasn't easy for me to demand a severe sentence from the court. I felt sorry for the person who served as a public official for twenty years, who not only received punishment and exclusion but was also in a situation where he wouldn't receive his retirement pension. While working on the case as a special prosecutor, "reason for defense" caught my eye. I thought it was inevitable for me to be an attorney.

As an attorney, I accepted countless cases. In particular, I don't think there was any other attorney who took as many labor and state of affairs cases as I did. It wasn't because I was special but because of the position I was in. I couldn't help but take the big labor cases of Ulsan and Changwon, which were the center of the large-scale eruption of the labor movement, at first with Attorney Roh and later by myself. Though Seoul definitely had a lot more state of affairs cases, there was an abundance of human rights attorneys, so the cases were easily divided. However, it wasn't like that in Busan, so we were in charge of a lot more cases.

To be honest, the term "human rights attorney" is not a suitable term because all attorneys' basic mission is to protect human rights. That is how it is elucidated in the Attorneys at Law Act. However, it isn't easy during the horrible reality of dictatorial power. Unavoidably, a few attorneys were in charge of that job, giving them a special title, namely "Human Rights Attorney."

A world without the need for special titles is a desirable world. Regardless of titles, I felt useful when defending labor and state of affairs cases. It was because I was able to help underserved people who needed the assistance of an attorney. Also, at that time, human rights advocacy was a movement that resisted dictatorship and was a democratic movement that could be done by attorneys. I would tell my young lawyers, "That's what attorneys do."

Once one hears that they are a human rights attorney, they will naturally receive cases from many people. This is not only about cases of collective layoffs but also disputes amongst apartment residents, disputes over the right to work, and collective damages. Since people were put in the worst situation simultaneously, the happiness and joy felt from success amid hardship were incomparable. Those are the moments when I felt becoming an attorney was most rewarding.

Leaving my legal lifestyle and entering the Blue House was a "deviation" from my former lifestyle. I was uncomfortable throughout my tenure there. It seemed like I was wearing clothes that didn't fit, in a place that wasn't suited for me. I spent my days thinking *I want to go back to being an attorney*. However, I couldn't be an attorney when I left the Blue House halfway through. No one told me not to do it. Nevertheless, one of the good things about being an attorney is that you can immediately enter a law firm.

After all, I thought that I shouldn't have been an attorney during the Participatory Government period anyway. It wasn't required. I just thought that I shouldn't have been an attorney or make additional income given the role I needed to carry out in the Participatory Government. That was the reason why I left for trekking in Nepal. During the Participatory Government, I took only one case: the impending *Impeachment of President Roh.*

When the Participatory Government ended, I shouted, "I'm finally free!" I was able to return to being an attorney. But I thought it wasn't appropriate to open a practice immediately. Though it wasn't the same as when judges or prosecutors are granted the privileges of their former post once they complete a term of office, I just thought it wasn't an appropriate action that should be done.

After the Participatory Government ended, I had a seven to eight-month career break before returning as an attorney. It was to the original law firm where I started. Once I returned, I laughed at myself for worrying about being granted the privileges of my former post. My experience as a high-ranking member of the Participatory Government didn't help legal business during Lee Myung-bak's administration. The problem had nothing to do with privileges but rather the inhospitable treatment of the predecessor.

Anyway, I finally returned to my original post. Of course, it wasn't like the olden days. Many years had passed, and the leave of absence was not short. In the legal profession, I might have become the "passing water." Back then, many people were comfortable with me as their adviser. However, it didn't seem like that. Still, my heart was comfortable. Working as an attorney and working with the Roh Moo-hyun Foundation has changed since the olden days because I was able to work together with the Roh Moo-hyun Foundation. I think I was lucky that I was an attorney.

Looking Back

President Roh Moo-hyun's death and Lee Myung-bak's administration's serious regression became the new subject of conversation for the public. Many worried about the country's future. Even I had a serious sense of crisis and concern. I thought there was a need for diversified, serious discussions on which road to take. But there was also a sense of regret.

President Roh Moo-hyun worked hard throughout his term. Though some skills might have been lacking or some objectives might have been unachieved, he always tried his best and did not have ulterior motives.

That was the same with me. In the beginning, I was inexperienced in government administration and didn't know what the duties of the Civil Affairs Administration Office were. But I thought handling the situation with diligence and unselfishness was best. All those who were part of the Participatory Government had the same attitude.

However, President Roh and I left the Blue House with many fingers pointing at us for an unsuccessful presidency and government. We were criticized as if we were the individuals who brought down the entire progressive camp. At one point, due to contrition, I thought, *What did we put all our efforts into when everything's in vain?*

What was the problem? What were we lacking? We needed to calmly reflect and review and find a new lesson that could come out of it. Putting our emotions aside, we needed to learn the lessons of success and failure with an objective mind. Otherwise, ten years of democratic government, including the five years of the Participatory Government, would become a "lost decade." It couldn't happen that way.

So, I concentrated on reviewing the five-year reign of the Participatory Government. The reviews weren't only for those operating the regime. Still, I thought the whole country, the civil society group, the labor movement camp, and the progressive-reformation camps all needed to do it together. Through such work, we needed to overcome President Roh Moo-hyun's successes and failures as well as the Participatory Government's successes and failures. Unfortunately, I think that our society seems to have forgotten that process.

Towards the end of the Participatory Government, there was a tendency to direct all the blame with statements like "because of the Participatory Government" or "because of Roh Moo-hyun." As a result, there was no room for any analytical reflection. After President Roh's death, the mood reversed and got better, causing people to feel there was no need for reflection.

Our next step was to think about hope and the methodology needed to seize power. However, I was worried. Before we could discuss seizing

Putting our emotions aside, we need to learn lessons of success and failure with an objective mind. Otherwise, ten years of democratic government, including five years of Participatory Government, will become the "lost decade." It can't happen.

power, I questioned how differently the progressive- reformation camp might have changed. How much our progressive-reformation camps' competency and capability to seize power had improved compared to the start of the 2003 Participatory Government ... How much their sagacity improved in utilizing the entire camp's resources and capabilities.

I don't think that even the election of President Roh in the 2002 presidential campaigning was achieved alone but was made possible through the capacity and competency of our camp. Although everyone's efforts were valuable, the greater factor was that President Roh brought the hope and support he received from the public, inspiring the staff to participate. The dramatic events of the times and coincidental factors, as if moved by fate, were significant contributors. If you evaluate President Roh's election as successfully achieved based on the capacity of the progressive-reformation camp alone, I believe that only half of that judgment is accurate.

To address the issue of hope for the 2012 presidential election, we needed to observe where we stood at that moment. We had to start by reflecting on our capabilities and limitations in the successes and frustrations of the five years of the Participatory Government and, furthermore, the past decade of the democratic government.

Of course, as the ones operating the administration, we should stand at the forefront of the reflection. There must be a sharp reflection and deep introspection on whether we did the best we could. So, when the people entrust the government's authority, there must be a clear plan for the overall administration of the state. Everyone working in the government should have the utmost level of morality and qualifications. If one asks whether that was the case in the Participatory Government, I can only reflect in humility. I, too, was inexperienced then. As the president's advisors and staff, we all had the best of will and intentions, but we could have served him better in terms of ability and capability. There is no way to deny or evade the fact that we were inexperienced and unfamiliar, and there were disagreements between the ideal and reality.

Then the question arises, could the "reformation" and "national welfare" be elevated to the level demanded by the progressive and reformation camps be achieved only through the power of the government? I didn't believe that it could be easily achieved given the then current political topography of our society. I think this is what the Participatory Government has demonstrated, and left as lessons for the future.

President Roh and the Participatory Government were like "isolated islands" in the ever-strong conservative forces that drove the conservative climate and kept public opinion flowing on the grounds of our society. Reform was hindered and blocked by conservative forces and those with vested interests, left, right, and center.

The conservative ideology that "a small government is always good and a big government is always evil" was rooted as a firm reality, and we were faced with a wall that we were not able to overcome in implementing our welfare policies. Even the progressive-reformation camps, which didn't exceed the minority, failed to gather their strength and ended up splitting in the hegemonic battle.

The Participatory Government was attacked from both left and right. Normally, if you were attacked by the conservative camp, you were encouraged or supported by the progressive camp, but that was not the case for us. The progressive camp turned their backs on us and joined the attack. Did this "resistance" and "wall" disappear, or was it significantly lowered regarding the new administration? There may have been such an illusion initially, but eventually, the Lee Myung-bak administration was performing so poorly and lost support. However, at the moment of the change of government, the "resistance" and the "wall" became clearer and higher again. What I want to emphasize is that if we failed to gather the strength of the entire progressive and reformation camps, any democratic reformist government that wins the election would eventually follow the same path as the Participatory Government.

We can take the example of the National Security Law abolition, which failed in the Participatory Government. The president, the ruling party, and civil society all agreed on the agenda and pushed for its abolition, but it failed. The president, enduring heavy criticism from the conservative camp, stressed that the "National Security Law should be sent to the museum."

The Uri Party made the abolition of the National Security Law as the first task of the four major reform legislations. The Civil Society also formed the National Solidarity for the Abolition of the National Security Law and poured all efforts, including signing petitions and protesting. Moreover, the Uri Party was the majority party at the time, and even after losing a few seats later on, we were still the majority when the Democratic Labor Party joined us. But we still failed to abolish the law. What was the problem?

There was a grave mistake in negotiating the constitution of the National Assembly, at a time when legislation reform was so crucial. Also, our conscience, not being able to call for ex officio proposal, played a part. If it was difficult to abolish the law in such a situation, we should have looked for ways to modify and revise clauses that were being abused. But again, the fundamentalism of our camp didn't tolerate such a compromise.

More fundamentally, even if we had combined the power of all the progressive and reformation camps, we would not have been able to abolish the National Security Law. It was a cold, crude reality. Although the Uri Party was the majority, many members of the party opposed the abolishment of the National Security Law or were very passive. I believe we should have started by accepting this reality as our objective in the current position at that time.

If the camp's power was not solidified, the government's ability to bring about reform alone, no matter how much effort was invested, would be limited.

Now, the reform of the Public Prosecution was rising as the mission of the times. Over-prominent prosecution power, overly politicized prosecution power, and uncontrollable omnipotent prosecution power were serious problems.

As all other countries were doing, it seemed that many agreed that handing over the investigative authority to the police would be a fundamental reform plan. The Participatory Government had made failed attempts at this plan, and it was questionable whether its method was the best way to implement the plan.

Personally, I regretted not being able to include the issue of "Prosecution-Police Investigatory Authority Adjustment*" into the judicial reform framework and to implement it along with judicial reformation. However, when the Participatory Government pursued the reform, there was little interest from civil societies such as Minbyun and the "People's Solidarity for Participatory Democracy." Perhaps it was because of the deeply rooted distrust of the police. With the disinterest and indifference of civil society, the government pushed through the agenda but couldn't complete it.

The same was true of the High Ranking Official Corruption Investigation Office. It could be a measure to keep public prosecution in check, but it couldn't be legislated because the National Assembly blocked it. Even in the civil society camps, only some were favorable, and most were not interested and didn't support legislation.

The Participatory Government guaranteed the political neutrality and independence of the prosecutors as much as possible. Although the prosecution was not entirely willing, the president and the Participatory Government did so with self-determination and self-control. Of course, it was also a reform task required by civil society. However, as soon as the

Lee Myung-bak administration came in, it quickly returned to what it was before the Participatory Government.

Our society was not able to protect the political neutrality and independence of the prosecution, which the Participatory Government had worked tremendously hard to guarantee. However, the progressive and reformation camps argued that the Participatory Government had failed to reform the prosecution. More fundamental reforms of the prosecution should indeed have been implemented during the Participatory Government, but is it really a reasonable evaluation to simply stipulate it as the responsibility of the Participatory Government?

The first occasion for the progressive camp to turn its back on the Participatory Government would have been the dispatch of troops to Iraq. I think it was only natural that the civil society camp opposed sending troops to Iraq. However, for the government, there was no choice but to dispatch them, even at a minimal level, for the peaceful and diplomatic resolution of the North Korean nuclear crisis.

In fact, the decision to send troops was a great help in leading the North Korean nuclear issue to a diplomatic solution through the Six-Party Talks. If the September 19th agreement of the Six-Party Talks was implemented, it would be possible for North and South Korea to pursue a peaceful resolution regarding all factors that threatened peace, including the complete disarmament of the North Korean nuclear program, denuclearization of North Korea, normalization of NK-U.S.A and NK-Japan diplomacy, and ultimately leading to the signing of the South-

foot from the beginning due to the conflict surrounding the NEIS (National Education Information System). As a result, more than a year after the initial phase of the reforms was spent on the NEIS issue, the reformist Minister of Education lost his position.

NEIS was an important issue because it could invade students' private information and human rights. But more serious and fundamental reform challenges were lined up ahead. In addition, the NEIS could have been implemented and improved if problems arose.

Every time I met the teachers from KTU, I got their attention and persuaded them. "How many more important reform challenges were ahead of us? If you shake us with this single issue of the NEIS, the minister will lose strength and will not be able to advance the coming reforms. If you push the minister out of the way, it will be difficult for us to have reformist ministers in the future, and we will end up choosing more and more conservative ministers. The educational reform will be long gone then." Everyone agreed with me. Many teachers were worried about the stubbornness of the union executives, but that was all. When they returned to the union, they couldn't be separated from the union's logic.

I do not mean to blame the KTU executives at the time. They would have pushed the government's educational reform with great anticipation. In fact, during the 2002 presidential election, the KTU teachers greatly contributed to the election. It was hoped that the Participatory Government would reform education greatly. It's such a shame that they didn't have a more strategic approach to lobby for the reforms they desired.

The area of labor is also very regretful. As soon as the Participatory Government was launched, the labor groups caused a series of massive strikes, such as railway, cargo union, and Chohung Bank strikes. In addition to the challenges, the requests for the railway and cargo strikes were largely accommodated by the government at the time of the first strike, even though the government faced criticism from public opinion. However, they soon started a second strike, which nullified the achievements of the first strike altogether.

Also, when the government pushed through to implement the 40-hour (5-day working week) system and to legalize the unionization of public servants, in spite of opposition from corporations and the finance sector, the labor groups were more vigorous in campaigning, shouting for the administration's resignation, even though they would be on the receiving end of the benefits. The reason was that the government bill was inadequate.

It was probably to aim high and push more to achieve higher goals while the labor-friendly Participatory Government was in power. However, such impatience on the part of the labor groups weakened the Participatory Government's position as a result, and the unreasonable demands of the labor unions instead prevented the reforms.

The reform of the labor sector in the Participatory Government was discussed in the "Tripartite Commission*." However, the KTU didn't participate in the tripartite committee. They would have had their reasons, but there were a lot of reforms that we couldn't carry out because of their absence.

There were many disappointments in the response to the Participatory Government regarding polarization and the issue of temporary employees. Although the Temporary Employee Protection Law was established, it couldn't prevent in advance the movement of corporations that used methods such as outsourcing to be exempted from its application. I believe we should have prioritized the policy's top priority in polarization and measures for temporary workers. However, the Participatory Government and the labor community could not discuss these important issues with each other. This was an additional limitation of the Participatory Government.

Recently, the *Progressive Governance Plan* written by Seoul National University professor Cho Kuk was a hot topic of conversation at that time. I think it was a very well-written book. It explained what kind of a society we should strive for in a way that was easy for people to understand. A popular SNU law professor talking about progressiveness and the state's welfare is highly effective in enlightening readers about the concepts of "progress" and "welfare." Yet, as I read Cho's book, I couldn't help but worry about other dimensions.

When the next democratic and reformist government returned to power, how many reforms presented in the book would be possible? It was easy to think that everything was possible if the government was willing, but there was only so much the government could do during its five-year term. What would happen then? The conservative camp would attack the reforms and welfare, and the progressive reformation camp would attack the government's mistakes, resulting in crossfire from both sides. Wouldn't the government end up walking the same path that the Participatory Government did?

Like the *Progressive Governance Plan*, people were only discussing what the progressive and reformed government should do, but there seemed to be a lack of discussion about how to realize and implement those challenges. What's more important to us now is not "what" we should do but "how" to do it.

Questions should have been asked, such as: How will we overcome resistance and opposition from those with vested interests in the conservative political landscape, and how will we draw public support and consent? How will the government push forward, and how will the civil society camps support the government? How will we set priorities among them, reform agendas, and set the scope and time frame for those reforms?

The follow-up should have been: We should now discuss this agenda to form a common consensus and make it the basis of solidarity. That way, we would not and could not break up even after a change of government.

At the time the Participatory Government was inaugurated, Professor Park Se-il of Seoul National University published a book entitled *The Successful Conditions of a President*. It dealt with how to reorganize the Office of the Presidential Secretariat to make the Blue House efficient, democratic, and non-authoritative. It was originally a book to prepare for the conservative government, but we were the ones who actually made reference to the book. I do not think that the reorganization of the office with reference to the book was necessarily successful. The creation of a new Human Resources advisor was good, but many aspects weren't as effective.

When the Participatory Government was inaugurated, Professor Park Se-il of Seoul National University published a book entitled *The Successful Conditions of a President*. It dealt with reorganizing the Office of the Presidential Secretariat to make the Blue House efficient, democratic, and non-authoritative. It was originally a book to prepare for the conservative government, but we were the ones who actually referred to the book. I do not think that the reorganization of the office with reference to the book was necessarily successful. The creation of a new Human Resources advisor was good, but many aspects weren't as effective.

Particularly, the removal of the respective Blue House Chief overseeing each ministry's department was intended to eliminate the negative effects of preexisting chiefs' reigning over the departments, but it was doubtful whether it was desirable when strong reforms needed to be led by the Blue House. I want to emphasize that the conservative camp prepared for their government that way.

During the Transition Commission of the Participatory Government, I received one document from a university senior who later served as a senior official at the Lee Myung-bak administration. It was an enormous amount of information, enough to make several books. It contained the state administration program, planned from the day of the election to the president's retirement, had candidate Lee Hoi-chang won the election.

They had arranged their national reform agenda for each year, quarter, and month and divided it into weekly and daily plans. Major reform periods were selected considering the upcoming election schedules, including a tailored public relations plan. It even contained concrete advice, such as conducting the election ceremony as a meeting with the neighborhood's residents instead of the old-fashioned ceremony in the party head office and visiting the regional university students each week until the inauguration.

It was written for candidate Lee Hoi-chang's election, but since it became useless, he had given it to us to refer to. The direction and scope of the reform of the state were very different from ours and couldn't be utilized. However, knowing how to manage the president's schedule was helpful. I don't know if they would have been able to execute the program as planned if they were in power, but it was astonishing that they had planned the administration of the state so precisely in advance.

Frankly, the Participatory Government took on the regime without it. The president had studied hard and prepared himself, but there was no such preparation anywhere in this camp, whether it was the political party or a research institute. That was our shortcoming and limitation.

Integration or solidarity of the progressive and reformation camp was being discussed for the next government. The past April 27th by-election showed the power of unification of the candidates of the opposition party and, at the same time, demonstrated the limits of the unification method that had been used so far. Unification through the competition between the political parties is always difficult, and often, even after the unification of candidates, the desired synergistic effect won't activate properly.

Considering this shortcoming, I believe integration is a desirable method. Of course, in that case, the significant power gap between the Democratic Party and other parties should be fully considered. In other words, we need to devise a way for the different political parties to feel that it is not an absorption into the larger Democratic Party or extinction of their party.

Integration is more desirable, even after the government is in power. Unification alone makes it difficult to prevent division after a change of government. Unification can be possible with a common goal to prevent the GNP from taking power or with a minimum set of codes. But it's challenging to continue collective assistance after the change of power. In order to maintain the driving power of reform, we need a higher level of solidarity.

It is desirable to run a coalition government between the political parties within the framework of the integrated political party, at least until the progressive tendency in our society's social-political terrain increases and hegemonic battles within the progressive-reformation camp don't affect general trends.

During the Participatory Government, President Roh Moo-hyun wanted personnel recommended by the Democratic Labor Party (DLP) to join the Cabinet as the Minister of Labor. If it was a recommendation by the DLP, it was okay for him to keep his register as a member of the

DLP and enter the Cabinet personally. It was thought that the Participatory Government's labor policies would be able to receive stable support from the labor groups, and the DLP would have a more responsible attitude together with the experience of the national government.

It was from the 17th General Election that the Uri Party became a majority by the headwind of the impeachment movement, and the Democratic Labor Party started advancing quite strongly. The president mentioned this idea to me a few times, and there was a shuffling of the Cabinet every time. But I couldn't say a word. There was no possibility that the DLP would be accepted in our political culture at the time. First, DLP members wouldn't tolerate it. Even if the party leadership accepted it positively, the idea would have received tremendous criticism from the party members. We would also be accused of collusion or political manipulation.

It could be similar in the future. I believe it's necessary to envision the integration and coalition government from the beginning in order to overcome such a strong wall in our society.

* **Prosecution-Police Investigatory Authority** Adjustment A policy of distributing the authority excessively concentrated in the prosecution by granting the police the right to investigate (that is currently exclusive to the prosecution), abolishing the police investigation right of command of the prosecutor, and deleting the police's duty of submission to the prosecution.

* **The Tripartite Commission** A social consensus body created in 1998 to discuss labor policies and related matters by workers, users and the government during the 1997 financial crisis. The current name is Economic and Social Development and Tripartite Commission.

It's Destiny

Eventually, like fate, I became the chief director of Roh Moo-hyun's Foundation. I became the chief director because former Prime Minister Han Myeong-sook, who was the first chief director, resigned while running for mayor of Seoul. He was often told that there was no need for his resignation and that it would be better to run for office with the position of chief director. However, due to his mysophobia and the possibility that he might burden the foundation, he decided to resign. I had no choice but to take over the role. The position I was to take part in didn't matter because it felt like fate that I should be part of the Roh Moo-hyun Foundation.

Roh Moo-hyun Foundation wasn't only for the commemoration and memorial project but also aimed at developing success or motivation through his spirit and values.

It was the duty of those he had left behind. It wasn't only because he was liked or of the long relationships. The succession and development of his spirit and values are now in accordance with the spirit of our society.

Eventually, like fate, I became the chief director of Roh Moo-hyun's Foundation. It didn't matter what position I was to take part in because it felt like I was fated to be part of the Roh Moo-Hyun Foundation.

Roh Moo-hyun's spirit and values are summed up in the words "Making the world a better place," which he has used throughout his political career. "Making the world a better place" was an election slogan he used while running for the 13th General Elections in 1988. Since then, he would always say, "Making the world a better place," whenever and wherever he went. Even when he signed his signature, he wrote, "Making the world a better place." Even during his presidency and after retirement. Perhaps even when he was president, he felt that the circumstances were still far from "making the world a better place," so he thought the slogan was needed.

Once, for a short period, he signed with "Like a river." No matter how tortuous, he expressed his willingness to walk along his path like a river that never gave up, becoming one with the ocean.

"Making the world a better place" can be described as "the dream of national welfare" nowadays. Of course, there's even a deeper meaning. Beyond economic welfare, it means a world where everyone is equally dignified, with no separation, regardless of wealth. The welfare states can be referred to as the bases. After retirement, President Roh dedicated the remainder of his life to researching "progressive democracy" and ultimately aiming for democracy toward a national welfare state.

The original intentions that he brought with him when he entered politics didn't change when he became the president until he left office.

Thus, one can say the Roh Moo-hyun Foundation's purpose can be called national welfare. The goal of the Roh Moo-hyun Foundation is to cultivate the soil in which a progressive democracy pursuing a welfare state is accepted by the people and developed into the universal values of our society.

Whenever I think of the word "welfare," there's a stirring of my childhood memories, especially a scene I could never forget.

During the summer of my freshman year in junior high school, my mother woke me early one Sunday morning. She asked me to go with her to Busan station. I didn't know the reason why, but I just followed her. It was early dawn, even before the buses ran, and we walked to the station in darkness. It was a long walk at a young age. It was probably 6-7 km or 7-8 km. As we were walking, my mother started to talk. On Sunday, the limited express train tickets were very valuable (at that time, "express" meant the best). She heard from others that if you buy tickets and sell them at premium prices to those who could buy it, you would make some profit.

Basically, it was scalping tickets. When we arrived at Busan station, they weren't selling tickets yet, so we had to wait. However, once the tickets were being sold, my mother looked for a long time, didn't buy tickets, and said, "Let's go."

While walking back home, I was famished because it was long past breakfast. We arrived at a store near our house that was run by people we knew. That's when we bought a couple of tomatoes and ate some to appease the hunger. I don't understand why my mother just came back home. And after that, she never tried to scalp tickets again.

No one else in the family knew—only my mother and me. Even between us, we never discussed it. Later, I asked my mother why she had just come back while I was writing this book. She answered that "it was completely different from what I expected." I didn't ask anymore. Back then, if it was rumored that one would be able to earn a living, many people would either gather for it or get busted for doing it, making it different from what was first heard. Or... maybe she was unwilling to do it together with her young son.

Even now, when I see people in need, I remember that memory. Of course, when I wrote this book, we were not in a difficult situation. Even my relatives who evacuated with us and suffered a lot are now generally doing well. Success was due to the parents' relentless zeal for educating their children and making them study.

However, even now, there are many people who are in need like we were back then. We received a lot of help in enduring the difficult times we had in the past. There were the relief supplies distributed by the church and the school lunch. My siblings and I also received help from scholarships, some from benefactors and some from Hamyungnamdo and Heungnam Citizens' Association. My sister also received a scholarship once.

If you think about it, it was welfare. Since the country at that time was poor and welfare wasn't functioning well, people stepped up and helped those in dire need. Anyone can have a difficult time in life. Ours were due to evacuation, but there are many causes, such as unemployment, illness, accident, childcare, old age, etc. It is a welfare state that can do things properly.

Memories of poverty during my childhood became life lessons as I lived. I didn't want to be poor anymore, but I didn't want to live well by myself. Like the help we received in our difficult times, I wanted to live by helping those in need. It wasn't irrelevant that I participated in student movements and became a human rights attorney.

They were the bends and bumps of life. Looking back, I think it was God's providence or fate that brought me to where I am now.

And amidst all that, there was the encounter with Attorney Roh Moo-hyun. He was in a worse condition than I was growing up and wasn't able to attend college. His passion in helping those in need was a lot more fervent than mine and he was a lot more committed to helping.

If I hadn't met him, I might have lived reasonably well and would have lived helping others moderately. His passion kept me enlightened all the time.

Even his death pulled me back on his road. The president said, "It is destiny" in his will. And I thought to myself.... I, for one, was destined.

Though you might have been freed from your fate, I remain here, unable to move from the assignment you left behind.

The government of Moon Jae-in, born out of the Candlelight Revolution, continues the legacy of the June Struggle, the People's Government, and the Participatory Government. Dreaming of a country where truth triumphs over falsehood, a country that can't be shaken.

Moon Jae-in's Destiny

Publication of the first issue : May 30th, 2024

Author : Moon Jae-in
Translator : Hannah Shin
Publisher : Jang Young-jae
Publishing : Co. : Thehuman
Phone : Number 02)3141-4421
Fax : 0505-333-4428
Registration : No.313-2012-81(16 March, 2012)
Address : 12, 32gil Seongmisan-ro Mapo-gu, Seoul (Zip code: 03983)
E-mail : sanhonjinju@naver.com
Website : cafe.naver.com/mirbookcompany
Instagram : www.instagram.com/mirbooks

* Damaged books can be exchanged at the bookstore where you purchased them.
* The price of the book is on the back cover.